Volatile Social Movements and the Origins of Terrorism

Volatile Social Movements and the Origins of Terrorism

The Radicalization of Change

Christine Sixta Rinehart

LEXINGTON BOOKS
Lanham • Boulder • New York • Toronto • Plymouth, UK

Published by Lexington Books
An imprint of The Rowman & Littlefield Publishing Group, Inc.
4501 Forbes Boulevard, Suite 200, Lanham, Maryland 20706
www.rowman.com

16 Carlisle Street, London W1D 3BT, United Kingdom

British Library Cataloguing in Publication Information Available

Library of Congress Cataloging-in-Publication Data
The hardback edition of this book was previously cataloged by the Library of Congress as folbws:

Rinehart, Christine Sixta, 1980-
Volatile social movements and the origins of terrorism : the radicalization of change / Christine Sixta
Rinehart.
p. cm.
1. Terrorism. 2. Radicalism. 3. Social movements--Political aspects. 4. Political violence. I. Title.
HV6431.R56 2013
363.325'11--dc23
2012038437

ISBN 978-0-7391-7770-9 (cloth : alk. paper)
ISBN 978-0-7391-9732-5 (pbk : alk. paper)
ISBN 978-0-7391-7771-6 (electronic)

Printed in the United States of America

Contents

Acknowledgments

I would like to thank my husband, Todd, for his endless love, patience, and support while I worked on this manuscript and chased my dreams. I am so grateful that I have you in my life. I would also like to thank Dr. Kevin Lasher for his friendship and irreplaceable leadership in the Department of Political Science and Geography at Francis Marion University. In addition, thank you for the great class schedules, conference funding, and endless pep talks so I could finish the manuscript. I would also like to thank my dear friend and mentor, Dr. Laura Woliver, for everything she has ever done for me. You are absolutely fabulous! And of course, Dr. Donald Puchala, Dr. Roger Coate, Dr. Mathieu Deflem, and Dr. Peter Sederberg—thank you for all your help with the original dissertation and then some.

Introduction

The Radicalization of Social Movements and Political Parties

Neither terrorists nor terrorist groups appear out of thin air. Many terrorist groups spring from ineffective and unpopular social movements. Extremists inclined to use terrorism for various reasons will often hijack a social movement that has been unable to accomplish its objectives and will transform the social movement into a terrorist organization. This transformation takes time, in fact, several years for the case studies that have been included within this book. Such terrorist groups are created by frustrated individuals prone to violence within the social movement.

Throughout the history of scholarship concerning terrorism, one theory has prevailed. Scholars have blamed the external environment for the terrorist group's violent, radical ideology. Research that focuses on the external environment as the reason for the emergence and development of terrorist organizations is underdeveloped and vague at best. For instance, the group dynamics within mass movements have been ignored. Scholars have rarely studied terrorism from the aspect of its initial origins in social movements. Many of the contemporary terrorist organizations were initially social movements in that they formed for a specific purpose using nonviolent tactics to accomplish their agendas. Eventually terrorist tactics became the method of choice for these once peaceful movements.

This book focuses on why this transition occurred. Why did a peaceful social movement transition to a terrorist organization? This research concentrates on the individual characteristics, group dynamics, and external forces that cause social movements to adopt terrorist tactics. In each case study, it is ascertained who made the decision to use terrorism and why and how that

1

person or group of people ascended to a leadership position within the social movement. After the (person) people, time, and place are found pertaining to the first decision to use terrorism, the chapters closely examine why terrorism became an attractive option. The book argues that there are other ways to incite change besides the use of terrorist tactics and makes clear what spark ignited these movements to turn to terror.

The contribution of this book to existing terrorism scholarship is as follows: It is found that 1) charismatic leadership as defined by Max Weber is pertinent to the radicalization of social movements because the charismatic leader makes the decision to use terrorism and his supporters follow. In addition, according to Dollard's frustration-aggression theory, frustration leads to aggression. 2) It is found that frustration occurs because the political goals of social movements are not accomplished for various reasons and this leads to violence or terrorism. 3) Lastly, the ascendances of violent personalities to leadership positions within the organizations are also responsible for the radicalization of social movements and the use of terrorism.

BACKGROUND AND CASE STUDIES

This book began as my dissertation and quickly morphed into the idea for a book. My interest in studying terrorism came about somewhat late in graduate school, which was unfortunate because I spent a lot of time pursuing things that were not as interesting to me. Once I got started on the topic, I could not stop reading or thinking about it. This interest first began when I published an article looking at the motivations behind female terrorism in a women's studies class. However, because of a lack of source material on female terrorists, my interest in why social movements transform into terrorist organizations became a much more feasible project for a dissertation. As time progressed, I wanted to examine more terrorist organizations. Consequently, two of the case studies included in the book were initially political parties as opposed to social movements. However, I would advocate that these parties took on somewhat of a social movement persona before they became terrorist organizations.

The case studies for this book were chosen because these groups were powerful or still are powerful terrorist organizations. In addition, these groups provide a good international sample as they are from four different regions throughout the world: the Middle East, Europe, Latin America, and Asia. The first case, the Muslim Brotherhood, has spread throughout the world and has also become a strong (although at times, banned) political party. Currently, the Muslim Brotherhood is in position to control Egypt after its recent Arab Spring Revolution. The Muslim Brotherhood also provided the prototype for other Islamic terrorist organizations such as Al Qaida or

Hamas. The former groups were influenced by the writings of Hasan al-Banna, the founder of the Muslim Brotherhood. The Euskadi ta Askatasuna (ETA), although less active, still exists and was at one time quite powerful, although it became so violent that it was rejected by its own people. The Fuerzas Armadas Revolucionarias de Colombia (FARC), although it has been somewhat destroyed by succeeding Colombian presidents, is likely to reemerge once powerful leaders are found that can replace Marulanda and Arenas within the organization. It is doubtful that the FARC will disband. Lastly, the Liberation Tigers of Tamil Eelam (LTTE) in Sri Lanka has also been decimated since the death of Prabhakaran but will most likely experience a resurgence because many problems still plague the Tamil minority that have not been resolved. The chapters on the FARC and LTTE were written before the organizations had experienced decimating attacks from their respective governments.

In addition, both the ETA and the FARC offered several sources that I could translate from Spanish. I ran into several difficulties with the Muslim Brotherhood, although much of the information had already been translated by scholars that have studied the Brotherhood. The LTTE presented few difficulties since scholars have spent much time researching this organization and very few people read or speak Tamil.

WHAT DOES THE LITERATURE SAY?

The literature that is relevant to the transformation of social movements into terrorist organizations is somewhat scattered across several different areas of scholarship. Although presented in a disjointed fashion, the following paragraphs describe existing literature that is relevant to the origins of terrorist tactics in social movements. The literature has been organized according to levels of analysis. Individual and state levels of analysis are presented.

THE INDIVIDUAL LEVEL OF ANALYSIS

Individuals and Radicalization

Individual-level explanations of terrorism have tried to explain why people participating in social movements turn to violence. Many early terrorism scholars in the 1970s and 1980s concluded that terrorism requires a certain type of personality. Certain personality types are susceptible to engaging in terrorism and are likely to join a terrorist group. In my own research, I have found that moderates in social movements are often expelled or otherwise eliminated by those participants who have certain personalities susceptible to terrorism. When the extremists take over, the social movement can become a terrorist organization.

Although dated, Eric Hoffer's book *The True Believer* is one of the most comprehensive political psychology books on social movements and violence.[1] Although he does not really address terrorism, Hoffer's book can be applied to why individuals become violent within social movements. Hoffer states that the frustration with oneself can make a true believer regardless of outside influences. Effective techniques of conversion to a mass movement consist of harnessing responses and proclivities inherent to the frustrated mind. "The discarded and rejected are often the raw material of a nation's future."[2] In other words, those who are dissatisfied with their personal lives find redemption in joining a mass movement.

Extreme paranoia has often been identified as one of the components of a terrorist personality.[3] In an in-depth analysis of nine terrorists, Pearlstein[4] found that terrorists were egocentric and only attacked to provide ego reinforcement. Another study by Post[5] looks at several psychological analyses of terrorists. Post found that individuals are drawn to terrorism so that they can commit violence. Terrorists are action-oriented, aggressive people who seek excitement and stimulation. They are narcissistic and have borderline personality disturbances. Terrorists tend to come from broken homes and have hostile relationships with their fathers and juvenile criminal records. Post finds that terrorists have often failed in their personal, vocational, and educational lives.[6]

Many scholars have also noted that terrorists commit violence just for the sake of committing violence.[7] Violence becomes an end in itself, which is why terrorist groups tend not to disband even after they have accomplished some of their goals; instead, some groups have become political parties. Weinberg and Pedahzur[8] state that the transformation of terrorist organizations is not an irreversible process; depending on the goals of the leadership, a terrorist group and political party may frequently switch roles. Alonso[9] adds that people make logical and rational decisions to join terrorist groups because violence can actually accomplish their goals. However, the socio-structural proximity to the movement and the other group members may cause an individual to join that group; in other words, Alonso states that people assume the identity of the people they socialize with on a regular basis. Violence may not be the original goal for people who join terrorist groups, but it eventually becomes a consuming goal for terrorist organizations.

According to Richardson,[10] terrorists are motivated by revenge, renownment, and reaction. Terrorists identify with others who are perceived to be suffering and see themselves as defenders of these victims. Therefore, terrorists react to protect the masses and avenge the perceived harm that has been done to them. Terrorists also commit attacks to be renowned or notorious figures who will be remembered throughout all of history. Terrorists seek fame. Gupta[11] adds to this stating that terrorists are selfish altruists in that they seek to avenge wrongs that they perceive have been committed against the masses. The terrorists' actions are outcomes of self-interest in that terrorists find their personal value in allegedly helping their society and perpetuating the beliefs of their particular group.

Leadership and Radicalization

Leadership within a social movement has also been attributed as a cause of radicalization. Weber finds that there are three kinds of leadership: traditional, legal-rational, and charismatic. Traditional leadership is defined as the populace believing in the legitimacy of leadership because it has always been this way such as in a monarchy. Legal-rational leadership is based upon the idea that individuals are given authority because it is based on the affirmation of a legal system. An example of this would be in a democracy where someone has been given authority because he/she won an election according to its specification within the constitution. For the purpose of this book, we are concerned with Weber's theory of charismatic leadership. Max Weber states in *The Sociology of Religion* that the prophet is the "purely individual bearer of charisma, who by virtue of his mission proclaims a religious doctrine or divine commandment."[12] Charisma is a gift that is given to him by the creator, or he is naturally endowed with charisma. This charismat then imposes his demands on the rest of society, which is then compelled by duty to follow his commands. One who is endowed with charisma, according to Weber, is also a natural born leader and is "larger than life."

Leaders endowed with charisma may also be a factor in a social movement's decision to use terrorism. Leaders by definition have charisma, although perhaps not to the extent that Weber describes. Donatella della Porta and Mario Diani emphasize that leadership in social movements "is charismatic in the Weberian sense, dependent above all on the ability of leaders to embody the movement as a whole, contributing to the creation of a collective identity."[13] Hoffer states that leaders of mass movements are "men of words." These "fanatics" come in after the prevailing order has been discredited. "The preliminary work of undermining existing institutions, of familiarizing the masses with the idea of change, and of creating a receptivity to a new faith, can be done only by men who are, first and foremost, talkers or writers and are recognized as such by all."[14] These leaders or "men of words" can then be responsible for militant action perpetrated by the masses.

Louise Richardson[15] states that terrorist group leaders tend to be from higher educational and socioeconomic backgrounds. Leaders are responsible for arranging training, providing ideology, identifying the enemy, and articulating a strategy. Leaders tend to be older than group members and may personally represent the group or its mission. The leader who is prone to militant action embodies the social movement.

Dawson states that charismatic modes of leadership are more volatile because certain problems are rooted in the inherent legitimacy of a charismatic leader. These problems are the need to maintain the personality of the charismat, moderating the effects of psychological identification of followers with the leader, negotiating the routinization of charisma, and achieving new successes.[16] The charismat must constantly maintain his or her authority so that stability will continue to define a group. Six strategies can be used by the charismat to preserve his or her authority: 1) shifting doctrines and policies, 2) escalating demands for service and commitment from followers, 3) playing on a group's fear of persecution by creating new and more powerful enemies, 4) dissent may be quieted through the public ridicule of rising leaders within the group, 5) testing loyalty by separating members from each other, and lastly, 6) changing the physical environment of the group. In addition to apocalyptic worldviews and a totalitarian organization, Robbins agrees that charismatic leadership is a key cause of religious terrorism.[17] It appears from the literature that charismatic leadership is more instrumental in radicalizing a movement than other types of leadership such as Weber's, traditional or legal-rational types of leadership.

Frustration-Aggression Theory and Relative Deprivation

The frustration-aggression theory also may help to explain why social movements use terrorist tactics. In 1939, five psychologists published the book *Frustration and Aggression*. Dollard and his cohorts argue that human frustration always leads to aggression.[18] However, aggression is broadly defined. Dollard specifically explains that aggression may be so much as a critical remark, a defensive posture, an angry thought, or pouting. Aggression is not always displayed by human physical violence, although it can be.

Berkowitz[19] later redeveloped Dollard and his cohorts' theory. Berkowitz argues that frustration-aggression is a more general model of the relationship between unpleasant stimuli and negative effect. Negative effect is unpleasant feelings such as anger, sadness, pain, or resentment. This negative effect can make an actor produce either "fight or flight," as well as other reactions related to these negative experiences. People's responses to this frustration depends on how they view and assess the negative effect and the control they have over their emotions. Either way, a person makes the choice as to whether his/her frustration leads to aggression, and this choice reflects the uniqueness of the individual. Like individuals, social movements may become so frustrated because they cannot accomplish their goals that they may turn to violence.

Ted Robert Gurr's work *Why Men Rebel*, published in 1970, later developed frustration-aggression theory even further into what Gurr called "relative deprivation theory." Gurr coined the term "relative deprivation" to explain the tension that develops between what man thinks he ought to have and what he actually has. When people do not receive the things that they think they are rightfully entitled to, they rebel and seek to remedy the situation by getting the things they want or need. Of course, violence becomes one vehicle to remedy this disparity. Gurr's theory is essentially an economic explanation stating that people turn to terrorism because of poverty or because they are not particularly satisfied with their economic situation.[20]

Most of the previous scholarship that has been presented here concludes that there are certain personality traits commonly found in terrorist personalities. These scholars state that terrorists are violence-seeking, paranoid, and arrogant social rejects. Terrorists are the weird misfits in society. If the terrorists are not responsible for violence, then their leaders must be; either way, scholars are asserting that there is a "terrorist personality." On the contrary, other scholars, such as Merari[21], Silke[22], and McCauley and Segal[23] state that terrorists are essentially normal and that research stating that terrorists have a certain type of personality is not based on solid science. Silke systematically refutes several works of scholarship regarding a "terrorist personality." There is no consensus regarding a "terrorist personality" and it is obvious that more research needs to be done.

However, leadership is extremely important in this equation and the radicalization of leadership needs to be examined in greater depth. The radicalization of a militant cannot be attributed to brainwashing by the leadership; if so, one loses the projection of the terrorist as a rational entity. These conclusions are problematic because scholars often find that these people function well within society before they become terrorists. I have found that terrorists are not typically poor nor are they uneducated. If anything, many of them are educated and middle class; there are students, doctors, lawyers, and teachers. They certainly do not appear "crazy." Vertigans, in his book on Islamic militancy, summarizes the work of Tilly, Stern, and Crenshaw, in addition to other scholars.[24] "There is no single set of cause-effect propositions that can explain terrorism as a whole." "This overemphasis upon single causal analysis remains prominent, particularly within accounts that examine the relationship between militancy and materialism."[25] Every terrorist is different, so therefore every path to radicalization is different.

In addition, explanations such as relative deprivation theory are also problematic. As relative deprivation increases, or as I become more dissatisfied with my present situation, my propensity to commit violence does not always come to fruition. For example, I may in fact withdraw from the public arena instead of committing violence or I may publicly protest the regime in power. The inability of my expectations to reflect my current situation does not always lead to violence. In fact, most of the time people are less volatile as their life situations worsen. Perhaps as one's economic situation in life declines, so does the optimism concerning the change in their destitute situation. In addition, terrorist groups have a political purpose that is not always defined by their economic needs. Terrorism is a political tactic. However, Dollard and his coauthors are helpful in explaining why people turn to violence: frustration leads to aggression. The question is, how much or what type of frustration leads to violence in reference to social movements?

THE STATE LEVEL OF ANALYSIS

Literature Pertaining to the Formation of Terrorist Groups

The most progressive studies on the origins of terrorism have come from studying the environment where terrorist organizations are created within the state. If the state is ineffective or is inadequately performing its duties, then scholars have ascertained that the state has caused the formation of terrorist organizations. There are many similarities between environments where terrorist groups form and where terrorist attacks transpire. Martha Crenshaw[26] states that preconditions or permissive causes set the stage over the long run for terrorism. There are also precipitants, which immediately precede terrorist attacks. Crenshaw identifies modernization, urbanization, and the government's inability to prevent or fight terrorism as possible preconditions for terrorism. According to Crenshaw, precipitants such as the existence of grievances among a subgroup of people, lack of opportunity for political participation, and elite dissatisfaction may be direct causes of terrorism.

Weinberg[27] and Weinberg and Pedahzur[28] ascertain why political parties turn to terrorism. In their research, they come up with somewhat of a rational choice explanation. Political parties use terrorist tactics because they have grandiose goals to achieve and because they view the current government as illegitimate. Circumstances that may lead political parties to become terrorist organizations are recent national integration, recent national disintegration, coup d'états and military interventions, a crisis of political legitimacy, elections, and polarized multiparty systems.[29] Terrorism is used when the protest movement is still nonexistent to the public and terrorism brings the political party to life.

Related scholars have pointed to the political system as a cause of terrorism. Lutz and Lutz[30] have identified democracies as facilitators of terrorism because democracies are prone to institutional weakness. Turk[31] explains why terrorist attacks are more likely to occur in democracies: Terrorist groups are more likely to appear in totalitarian structures but acts of terror are frequent in democratic structures. Terrorist attacks occur in democracies because totalitarian regimes force terrorists to leave, thus abdicating to democracies. Li[32] states, "We may just have to acknowledge and accept the fact that aspects of democratic polity are associated with more terrorist incidents" and finds that institutional constraints are a cause for these attacks. Gurr[33] adds the caveat that terrorism occurs in democracies because there are underlying large social problems within democracies. Chenoweth[34] finds through multiple regression analysis that politically unstable regimes in general are more likely to provide ripe environments for the development of terrorist groups because the inability of the government to control its people provides opportunities for terrorists groups to develop. Robert Pape[35] states in *Dying to Win* that suicide bombers are trying to get rid of a democratic occupier and dying to get the enemy out of their country.

As is evident, there is no consensus on what types of political systems terrorist groups emerge in or attack; in fact, some of the theories are polar opposites. Are terrorists groups more likely to form in democracies or totalitarian regimes? Are terrorist groups more likely to attack democratic or totalitarian states? It is evident that more research needs to be completed to ascertain some type of definitive conclusion. Most assuredly, political institutions are very important in the formation of terrorist groups.

What is pointedly missing in this literature review is the group or societal level of analysis. Early case studies focusing on one or two groups provide somewhat of a foundation for understanding a social movement's radicalization. Beach[36] found that the People's Democracy in Northern Ireland radicalized for eight reasons: physical repression by the authorities, change in the orientation of a movement's constituency, societal cleavages, a low probability of co-optation with the government, weak leadership that does not punish radical members, radical leadership, a public codification of demands, and collaboration with similar ideological groups. McCauley and Segal[37] point out that terrorism is a "phenomenon of group dynamics."

It is clear that individual levels of analysis concerning the terrorist personality are inconclusive. There is no one explicit reason as to why individuals turn to terrorism; the motivation for terrorism is as different as the individuals explored. State levels of analyses point to large transformations within society occurring at the national level or political systems also occurring at the national level. The state is not doing its job. This literature is also inconclusive. There are differing results. It is true that there are certainly fewer terrorist organizations in democracies than in autocracies; however, how does one explain the IRA or the FARC? Democracies, although illiberal, still allow individuals to participate in the political process to some extent. In addition, the state is always blamed for the radicalization of a social movement; however, in many instances, the state does not address or is indifferent to the terrorist organization until it starts to kill citizens or destroy property. Although underlying processes are certainly at work within the state, such as modernization or globalization, it is a fact that the state cannot singularly explain why a social movement turns to terrorism. It is clear that there may be a societal or group explanation for the radicalization of movements. The purpose of this book is to examine the role that group dynamics play in the radicalization of a social movement.

DEFINITION OF CONCEPTS AND CLARIFICATION OF TERMS

One Man's Terrorist is NOT another Man's Freedom Fighter

First, it is important to define what is meant by the word "terrorism" within this book. Vastly different definitions of terrorism have been constructed because it is a politically charged and complicated phenomenon to explain. It is important to establish that those who have power define terrorism. A Western-state-based definition of terrorism will differ greatly from a definition of terrorism that may come from a terrorist group such as the Revolutionary Armed Forces of Colombia (FARC) or the Tamil Tigers (LTTE). The FARC or LTTE would not call themselves terrorists but revolutionaries, a much more positive word. Western states label non-Western violent groups as terrorist groups while the non-Western terrorist groups call themselves revolutionaries in their quest to end Western domination.

Ronald Reagan popularized the cliché "One man's terrorist is another man's freedom fighter" in a press conference. Directly afterward, in the same press conference, Reagan stated that the previous quote was nonsense and that terrorists were, "people who deliberately chose as a target to murder and maim innocent people who have no influence upon the things that they think of as their political goals" (May 1986).

Zulaika and Douglass state, "From this perspective, what is noteworthy about terrorism as a contemporary phenomenon is that, while manipulating the referential circularity between media stories and violent actions, it has succeeded in imposing an apocalyptic frame in which suspension of disbelief appears to be the rational course and no comment as to its discursive configuration seems relevant."[38] Scholars have tried relentlessly to distinguish revolutionaries and terrorists or to make the two terms synonymous. However, the problem really lies within the subjectivity of the researcher, not the so-called ambiguity of the term and/or tactic of terrorism.

Several scholars have fallen prey to the problem of association within their research. After spending time with one's object of research, a researcher might be persuaded to view the problem in an entirely different way based on his or her emotions. This is especially exemplified in scholar's studies of the Euzkadi ta Askatasuna (ETA) in Spain. Many scholars who study the Basque terrorists are Basques themselves or hail from the Basque area of Spain or France. If one is inclined to feel sympathy or empathize with the terrorist or revolutionary, depending again on the position of the researcher, then one is most likely to refer to terrorism as a revolutionary tactic. Perhaps the old cliché "Where you stand depends on where you sit" is the most illustrative description of the problem of research objectivity. For we as researchers know, complete objectivity is not attainable in research.

In my previous research, I have distinguished between the two terms: "terrorist" and "revolutionary." My own working definition of terrorism, which I differentiate from revolution, is as follows:[39] Terrorist groups are nongovernmental[40] entities who intentionally attack civilian populations who are noncombatants within their own struggle for power. Specifically, noncombatants refer to people who are not involved in any way with the terrorists' struggle and cannot really change the outcome of the terrorist organization's situation. For example, the president of a country may be a legitimate revolutionary target, but a postal worker or bridge builder is not. Purposefully attacking people who hold political and military power is an act of war, not an act of terrorism. These people who hold political and military power would include off-duty soldiers or reserve soldiers. Revolutionaries who use terrorist tactics (like the White Terror in the French Revolution where thousands were killed) become terrorists. One who uses terrorist tactics is a terrorist. Terrorists may subscribe to revolutionary ideology, but the killing or terrorizing of noncombatants is what defines a terrorist as a terrorist, and differentiates the terrorist from a revolutionary. As a side note, this definition of terrorism does not include state-sponsored terrorism, which I believe is an entirely separate topic and somewhat of a misnomer. I think that state-sponsored terrorism should be categorized under human rights abuses, and should not be confused with nonstate entities that commit terrorist acts as it just muddies the field and confuses anyone who is not familiar with terrorism.

Social Movements

Many terrorist organizations begin as social movements and eventually transform into terrorist organizations such as the ETA, the Muslim Brotherhood, the FARC, and the LTTE. The work of Dieter Rucht (1996) will be used to present the reader with a definition of social movements. Rucht writes that social movements consist of two components: "(1) networks of groups and organizations prepared to mobilize for protest actions to promote (or resist) social change (which is the ultimate goal of social movements); and (2) individuals who attend protest activities or contribute resources without necessarily being attached to movement groups or organizations."[41] Therefore, using Rucht's definition, social movements are groups of people that come together to agitate for social change. Individuals that participate in social movements may or may not be intrinsically connected to the movement but participate in the movement to fight a greater common adversary. The actual individuals within the social movement are responsible for the changes they create.

In many instances, forming a social movement is one of the initial steps toward becoming a terrorist organization. This is not to say that every social movement becomes a terrorist organization, but that every terrorist organization was likely once a social movement. Social movements are important to this research because in many cases they are crucial to understanding the emergence and development of terrorist groups. To my knowledge, no scholar has comprehensively studied terrorist organizations in the context of their original purpose as social movements.

Initially, the social movement Ekin, which later became the terrorist group ETA, wanted to foment social change; in Ekin's case, the Basque dissidents wanted to protect and further the notion of Basque independence. Hasan al-Banna, the founder of the Muslim Brotherhood, wanted to establish an Islamic government and bring the Egyptian people back to a lifestyle committed to Islamic principles. Manuel Marulanda from the FARC, who was originally part of the Communist Party, was also once interested in participating in Communist Party politics to help change the lives of the working peasants, although this party morphed into a social movement. Velluppillai Prabhakaran was also part of a Tamil social movement that wanted to create more rights in the Sinhalese-dominated government. The interesting question and the focus of my research is when, why, and how these social movements morphed into terrorist organizations.

As a side note, all of the terrorist organizations that are analyzed within this book were part of a larger social movement at one point, whether before or after their creations. Since my analysis is based on the formation of the terrorist groups, I am not concerned with examining these larger social movements composed of several organizations. The scope of this book is to examine only the initial origins of the terrorist organizations.

Charismatic Leadership

Charismatic leadership is one of the key components in this study as it will be used to explain how charismatic leaders were able to transform social movements into terrorist organizations. In *The Sociology of Religion*, Max Weber states that the Muslim prophet is the "purely individual bearer of charisma, who by virtue of his mission proclaims a religious doctrine or divine commandment."[42] Charisma is a gift that is given to him by the creator, or he is naturally endowed with charisma; therefore, this prophet or charismat has authority because he has been given that authority by a higher spiritual entity. This charismat then imposes his demands on the rest of society, which is then compelled by duty to follow his commands. One who is endowed with charisma, according to Weber, is also a natural-born leader and is "larger than life." The charismat inspires people to follow and obey him.

When scholars later interpreted Weber's idea of a charismat, the idea of charismatic leadership evolved. Weber had applied the term "charisma" to a prophet-type person like Jesus Christ or Muhammed, but scholars have gone beyond the confines of Weber's definition to describe any inspiring leader. Weber's idea of charisma was a positive one in that Weber thought that the charismat helped humanity. Weber never addressed whether he viewed the charismat as legitimate.

I am using Weber's idea of a charismat to describe how one acts on his or her divine authority and knowledge which they feel has been given to them by god. Charismats feel they must use this gift to command and help others. However, perhaps the difference in Weber's and my own concept of charismatic leadership is that I doubt the legitimacy of the charismat, whereas Weber did not give his opinion. Weber determined that legitimacy in the eyes of the masses came from this charismat's divine authority. I doubt the legitimacy of these self-proclaimed charismats, but I do believe that the followers and leader believed in the divine authority of the leader.

The leader of the Muslim Brotherhood was a charismatic leader. The Muslim Brotherhood leader, Hasan al-Banna, relied on religion to establish his legitimacy in the eyes of the public and within his own social movement. The Muslim Brotherhood believed that Allah had chosen them to bring the people back to the fold of Islam. When I use Weber's notion of the charismat or charismatic leadership, I am using it to imply how a terrorist leader, terrorist group, and supporters view the leader himself. Of course, looking at whether the followers support the leader regardless of the repercussions they may face can test this proposition. The people who are prone to violence will follow the charismatic leader to the path of violence and will establish a hicrarchical terrorist organization. Thus, the nonviolent followers will diverge from the group to avoid joining a terrorist organization.

THE ARRANGEMENT OF THE BOOK

The introduction to the book provides the research question that is pursued throughout the continuing chapters, in addition to other scholarship that has been completed concerning this topic. The contribution of the book to existing scholarship is also included. Chapter 1 looks at the radicalization of the Muslim Brotherhood in Egypt from a social movement to a terrorist organization. The leadership and radicalization of Hasan al-Banna is deeply examined. Chapter 2 looks particularly at the radicalization of Ekin in Spain from a social movement to a terrorist organization, the ETA. The takeover of the ETA by violent extremists is also explored. Chapter 3 pays attention to the

radicalization of the Communist Party and the leadership of Manuel Marulanda over the FARC in Colombia. Chapter 4 looks at the radicalization of
the Tamil leader S. J. V. Chelvanayagam and his Federal Party (FP) in Sri
Lanka. In addition, the charismatic leadership of Prabhakaran is explored in
chapter 4. Finally, the concluding chapter summarizes the differences and
similarities between the case studies, in addition to exploring other avenues
of research that this project presents. The concluding chapter also seeks to
establish some preliminary theory on the radicalization of social movements
into terrorist organizations.

NOTES

1. Eric Hoffer, *The True Believer* (New York: Harper and Row Publishers, 1951).
2. Hoffer, *The True Believer*, 24.
3. Konrad Kellen, "Terrorists: What Are They Like? How Some Terrorists Describe Their
World and Actions," A Rand Note prepared for the Sandia Laboratories (November 1979). Joe
Navarro, *Hunting Terrorists, A Look at the Psychopathology of Terror* (Springfield, IL:
Charles C. Thomas, 2005). Robert S. Robins and Jerrold M. Post, *Political Paranoia, The
Psychopolitics of Hatred* (New Haven: Yale University Press, 1997). Leighton C. Whitaker,
Understanding and Preventing Violence, The Psychology of Human Destructiveness (Boca
Raton, FL: CRC Press, 2000). David Whittaker (ed.), *The Terrorism Reader*, 2nd ed. (New
York: Routledge, 2001).
4. Richard M. Pearlstein, *The Mind of the Political Terrorist* (Wilmington, DE: SR Books,
1991).
5. Jerrold M. Post, "Terrorist Psycho-logic: Terrorist Behavior as a Product of Psychological Forces," in Walter Reich, ed., *Origins of Terrorism, Psychologies, Ideologies, Theologies,
and States of Mind* (Washington, DC: Woodrow Wilson Center Press, 1998), 25–40.
6. Jerrold M. Post, "Terrorist Psycho-logic: Terrorist Behavior as a Product of Psychological Forces," in Walter Reich, ed., *Origins of Terrorism, Psychologies, Ideologies, Theologies,
and States of Mind* (Washington, DC: Woodrow Wilson Center Press, 1998), 25–40.
7. Martha Crenshaw, "The Causes of Terrorism," *Comparative Politics* 13 (4) (July 1981),
370–399. Martha Crenshaw, "The Logic of Terrorism: Terrorist Behavior as a Product of
Strategic Choice" in Walter Reich, ed., *Origins of Terrorism, Psychologies, Ideologies, Theologies, and States of Mind* (Washington, DC: Woodrow Wilson Center Press, 1998), 7–24.
Martha Crenshaw, "The Causes of Terrorism, Past and Present" in Charles W. Kegley, ed., *The
New Global Terrorism* (Upper Saddle River, NJ: Pearson Education, Inc, 2003), 92–105.
Martha M. Crenshaw, "Theories of Terrorism: Instrumental and Organizational Approaches,"
in David C. Rapoport, ed., *Inside Terrorist Organizations* (Portland, OR: Frank Cass Publishers, 2001), 13–31. Anatol Rapoport, *The Origins of Violence: Approaches to the Study of
Conflict* (New Brunswick: Transaction Publishers, 2005). Chris Hedges, *War Is a Force That
Gives Us Meaning* (New York: Anchor Books, 2002).
8. See works written by Leonard Weinberg and Ami Pedahzur.
9. Rogelio Alonso, *The IRA and the Armed Struggle* (New York: Routledge, 2007).
10. Louise Richardson, *What Terrorists Want, Understanding the Enemy, Containing the
Threat* (New York: Random House, 2006).
11. Dipak K. Gupta, *Understanding Terrorism and Political Violence* (New York: Routledge, 2008).
12. Max Weber, *Religionssoziologie* [The Sociology of Religion (4th ed.)] (Ephraim Fischoff, trans.) (Boston: Beacon Press, 1963) (original work published 1922), 46.
13. Donatella della Porta and Mario Diani, *Social Movements, An Introduction* (Oxford,
UK: Blackwell Publishers, Ltd, 1999), 142.
14. Hoffer, *The True Believer*, 129.

15. Richardson, *What Terrorists Want, Understanding the Enemy, Containing the Threat.*

16. Lorne L. Dawson, "Crises of Charismatic Legitimacy and Violent Behavior in New Religious Movements," in David G. Bromley and J. Gordon Melton eds., *Cults, Religion, and Violence* (Cambridge, UK: Cambridge University Press, 2002), 80–101, 81.

17. Thomas Robbins, "Sources of Volatility in Religious Movements," in David G. Bromley and J. Gordon Melton, eds., *Cults, Religions, and Violence* (Cambridge, UK: Cambridge University Press, 2002), 57–79.

18. John Dollard, Neal E. Miller, Leonard W. Doob, O. H. Mowrer, and Robert R. Sears, *Frustration and Aggression* (New Haven, CT: Yale University Press, 1939), 1.

19. Leonard Berkowitz, *Roots of Aggression, A Re-examination of Frustration-Aggression Hypothesis* (New York: Atherton Press, 1969).

20. Ted Robert Gurr, *Why Men Rebel* (Princeton: Princeton University Press, 1970).

21. Ariel Merari, "Social, Organizational, and Psychological Factors in Suicide Terrorism," in Tore Bjørgo, ed., *Root Causes of Terrorism* (New York: Routledge, 2005), 70–86.

22. Andrew Silke, "Cheshire-cat logic: The recurring theme of terrorist abnormality in psychological research," *Psychology, Crime, and Law*, 4 (1) (1998), 51–69.

23. Clark R. McCauley and Mary E. Segal, "Social Psychology of Terrorist Groups," in Clyde Hendrick, ed., *Group Processes and Intergroup Relations*, vol. 9 (Newbury Park, CA: Sage Publications, 1987), 231–256.

24. Charles Tilly, "Terror as Strategy and Relational Process," paper presented at the American Sociological Association Conference, August 14–17, 2004. Jessica Stern, *Terror in the Name of God* (New York: Ecco, 2003). Crenshaw, "The Logic of Terrorism: Terrorist Behavior as a Product of Strategic Choice," 7–24.

25. Stephen Vertigans, *Militant Islam, A Sociology of Characteristics, Causes, and Consequences* (New York: Routledge, 2009), 21.

26. Crenshaw, "The Causes of Terrorism," 92–105, 370–399. Crenshaw, "The Logic of Terrorism: Terrorist Behavior as a Product of Strategic Choice," 7–24. Martha M. Crenshaw, "Theories of Terrorism: Instrumental and Organizational Approaches," in David C. Rapoport, ed., *Inside Terrorist Organizations* (Portland, OR: Frank Cass Publishers, 2001), 13–31.

27. Leonard Weinberg, "Turning to Terror: The Conditions Under Which Political Parties Turn to Terrorist Activities," *Comparative Politics* 23 (4) (July 1991), 423–438.

28. Leonard Weinberg and Ami Pedahzur, *Political Parties and Terrorist Groups* (New York: Routledge, 2003).

29. Weinberg and Pedahzur, *Political Parties and Terrorist Groups,* 17.

30. James M. Lutz and Brenda J. Lutz, *Terrorism: Origins and Evolution* (New York: Palgrave MacMillan, 2005).

31. Austin T. Turk, "Social Dynamics of Terrorism," *Annals of the American Academy of Political Science, International Terrorism*, (September 1982), 463.

32. Quan Li, "Does Democracy Promote or Reduce Transnational Terrorist Incidents?" *Journal of Conflict Resolution* 49 (2005), 278–297, 294.

33. Ted Robert Gurr, "Terrorism in Democracies: Its Social and Political Bases," in Walter Reich, ed., *Origins of Terrorism, Psychologies, Ideologies, Theologies, and States of Mind* (Washington, DC: Woodrow Wilson Center Press, 1998), 86–102.

34. Erica Chenoweth, "Terrorism and Instability: A Structural Study of the Origins of Terror," paper presented at the meeting of the International Studies Association, Honolulu, Hawaii (March 2005).

35. Robert A. Pape, *Dying to Win, The Strategic Logic of Suicide Terrorism* (New York: Random House, 2005).

36. Steven W. Beach, "Social Movement Radicalization: The Case of the People's Democracy in Northern Ireland," *The Sociological Quarterly* 18 (3) (Summer 1977), 305–318.

37. Clark R. McCauley and Mary E. Segal, "Social Psychology of Terrorist Groups," in Clyde Hendrick, ed., *Group Processes and Intergroup Relations*, vol. 9 (Newbury Park, CA: Sage Publications, 1987), 231–256.

38. Joseba Zulaika and William A. Douglass, *Terror and Taboo, The Follies, Fables, and Faces of Terrorism* (New York City: Routledge, 1996), 30.

39. This definition is part of an article I wrote that was published in 2008 in *The Journal of Women, Politics, and Policy*. The title of the article is "The Illusive Third Wave: Are Female Terrorists the New 'New Women' in Developing Societies?"

40. State-sponsored terrorism is terrorism that is paid for by a government. Payment may come in many forms such as weaponry, money, or political protection. Saddam Hussein sponsored terrorism in Israel through Palestinian fighters. Although different countries may sponsor terrorist groups in this paper, they are violent for their own purposes regardless of where their money comes from. I am not concerned with state-sponsored terrorism in this book. My definition applies only to the terrorist organizations I have chosen to study. State-sponsored terrorism is an extremely complicated issue that deserves separate scholarship apart from nongovernmental terrorism.

41. Dieter Rucht, "The Impact of National Contexts on Social Movement Structures: A Cross-Movement and Cross-National Comparison," in Doug McAdam, John D. McCarthy, and Mayer N. Zald, eds., *Comparative Perspectives on Social Movements* (Cambridge, UK: Cambridge University Press, 1996), 185–204, 186.

42. Max Weber, *Religionssoziologie* [The Sociology of Religion (4th ed.)], 46.

Chapter One

Revolutionizing Terrorism

The Radicalization of Hasan al-Banna and the Egyptian Muslim Brotherhood

When you consider the history of the Muslim Brotherhood, it started with a pretty brilliant strategy: Create terrorist groups that use violence to advance your goals, distance yourself from those groups, present yourself as the "reasonable" alternative, and enjoy the accolades of the very people you are trying to destroy.[1]

In 1928, an infamous social movement was born that not only transformed into a terrorist organization but also eventually spawned some of the most violent terrorist organizations throughout the world. The Muslim Brotherhood became the prototype for the Muslim fundamentalist terrorist organization and some of its members later created organizations such as Hamas and Al Qaeda. This chapter focuses on why this transition occurred; why did a peaceful social movement such as the Muslim Brotherhood transition to a terrorist organization? What spark ignited the Egyptian Muslim Brotherhood to turn to terror? I will show that the Egyptian Muslim Brotherhood's transition to terrorism was caused by the 1) charismatic leadership and 2) radicalization of Hasan al-Banna, the founder of the Muslim Brotherhood, and 3) frustration within the Muslim Brotherhood.

THE HISTORY OF THE MUSLIM BROTHERHOOD AND ITS RELATIONSHIP WITH THE EGYPTIAN GOVERNMENT

As a direct consequence of the Revolution of 1919, Britain declared Egypt an independent constitutional monarchy in 1922. However, after independence,

Britain continued to control Egypt in areas such as defense, the communications system, and the Capitulations system, which was the legal code. Britain largely controlled the Egyptian political system after independence. In the Anglo-Egyptian Treaty of 1936, Egypt gained an independent army, the abolition of Capitulations, and an independent membership in the League of Nations. Britain managed to secure some legal occupation of Egypt because it was allowed to keep its army in Egypt. Egypt saw the Anglo-Egyptian Treaty as another step toward independence, while Britain saw the treaty as a means to solidify its presence in Egypt.[2]

The Muslim Brotherhood was created in 1928 to bring Egyptian society back to an Islamic lifestyle. The Brotherhood wrote a letter to King Fuad in 1933, which was ignored. The Brotherhood did not attract the attention of the Egyptian government until 1936 when al-Banna wrote a letter to King Farouk, al-Nahhas Pasha, and the royalty of the Islamic telling them to follow the path of Islam and to reject everything Western. He placed a program before them containing fifty provisions for complete Islamic reform, which he believed they should institute.[3] These letters were ignored.

King Farouk had only recently ascended to the throne in July 1937 after his father, Fuad, had passed away in April 1936. In between this period, a regency council ruled Egypt. It was obvious that Farouk was a young king and really had no political skills since he was pushed onto the throne after his father's demise. He preferred to hide from the uncertain political arena in his palace.[4]

In the beginning of his reign, the Egyptian press jumped to make King Farouk appear as the Islamic sovereign crusading to return Egypt to an Islamic theocracy. Farouk must have felt as though he were like King Arthur bringing the kingdom back to long lost times of Islamic rule. However, Farouk quickly fell short of his expected Islamic high ground and the Brotherhood jumped to condemn his faults. The Brotherhood criticized palace debauchery quite frequently in their writings and society meetings. The parties at the palace for a newly married Farouk had belly dancers that performed all night and alcohol was served. The Brotherhood strongly condemned the mixing of sexes at these parties.

To make matters worse for the young king, Sir Miles Lampson, the British ambassador to Egypt, was not fond of Farouk. To Lampson, Egypt was a veiled protectorate of England that needed a high-handed ambassador. In fact, Lampson was constantly paranoid that the Egyptians were planning an uprising or uniting themselves with the Axis powers. The British viewed the Egyptians as racial equals but regarded them as British subjects.

In addition, the Wafdists (the nationalist liberal political party) controlled the cabinet at the end of King Fuad's reign, and after Fuad died, the country waited in suspense to see whether the Wafdists or the king would acquire the support of the Egyptian nationalists. Ali Mahir Pasha controlled the Palace opposition to the Wafdists. Mustafa al-Nahhas Pasha was King Farouk's prime minister. During 1937 when conflict arose between the Wafdists and the Palace, the Brotherhood chose to stay out of the conflict and to separate themselves from both sides. After constant arguments between the Wafdist cabinet and the Palace, King Farouk had had enough and he dismissed the Wafdist cabinet. After the Wafdist government was dismissed, al-Banna openly stated that he had little confidence in the Palace government being a better solution for Egypt than the Wafdist government. On March 3, 1938, the Brotherhood later condemned the current Wafdist campaign against the government when it appeared the Palace would provide financial and political support for the Muslim Brotherhood.[5]

The Palace then publicly embraced the Brotherhood, hoping to gain popular support from the Egyptian people. The Rover Scouts who were al-Banna's little army marched into Alexandria lead by al-Banna where Ali Mahir Pasha introduced them to King Farouk. Ali Mahir Pasha also made sure that Palace funds were given to the Brotherhood. This was the beginning of a strong relationship between Ali Mahir Pasha and the Muslim Brotherhood. Hesitant to appear under the Palace's control, al-Banna wrote in his autobiography that he still had the ability to criticize the Palace if it was needed.

Nevertheless, the Brotherhood did pay lip service to King Farouk to ensure good treatment from the King. The Rover Scouts made sure to greet the king in Cairo after he had harrowingly escaped an accident. The Brothers also sent a telegram to the Palace to wish the King a happy birthday, but immediately after a thank-you telegram was received from the King, the Brotherhood criticized the monarchy during their meeting.

In late 1938 and early 1939, the Palace cut funds to the Brotherhood because it was suspicious of their activities. General Aziz al-Misri tried to force the Brotherhood to combine with the Young Egypt Party to form a political party, but al-Banna strongly declined, making it difficult to build a better relationship with the Palace. In October 1939, the government, still suspicious, closed two of the Brotherhood's publications: *al-Manar* (the Lighthouse) and *al-Nadhir* (the Harbinger).[6]

In August 1939, Muhammad Mahmud Pasha resigned because of ill health and Ali Mahir Pasha was instructed by King Farouk to build a new cabinet. After Ali Mahir Pasha lost his ministry on June 24, 1940, Anglophile Prime Minister Hassan Sabri replaced him on June 27, 1940. However, after his resignation, Mahir still managed to get a job as the head of the Special Branch of Egyptian Police.

With Ali Mahir Pasha's support, al-Banna felt more confident politically trying to get the British out of Egypt. In January 1941, the Society held its Sixth Conference in Cairo and the Brothers openly advocated the nationalization of the Suez Canal. However, al-Banna's support from Ali Mahir Pasha was not solid. In 1941, the government shut down all Brotherhood publications, including *Majallat al-Ta'aruf, al-Nidal*, and *al-Shu'a'*.[7]

World War II began and the Brothers supported the neutrality of King Farouk and the government that refused to declare war on the Axis powers. King Farouk felt that Anglo-Egyptian Treaty did not require him to enter a war that the British appeared to be badly losing.

The British finally ordered that al-Banna be sent to teach at a school in Qena to think about his actions. Although many Brothers were disturbed by this order, al-Banna left for Qena aware of the military orders that would be issued if he did not comply. In Qena, al-Banna continued to build branches for the Brotherhood. Four months later after his transfer, al-Banna was ordered back to Cairo. However, shortly before al-Banna returned in June of 1941, Ahmad al-Sukkari, al-Banna's second in command, was arrested in Cairo. Al-Sukkari had had a relationship with General Aziz al-Mishri, who was violently anti-British and had commanded the Egyptian army until the British forcibly retired him. During al-Sukkari's arrest, al-Banna had sent warnings to members to remain completely quiet and threatened expulsion if anything happened. In June 6, 1941, the General was arrested and al-Sukkari was immediately released.[8]

Meanwhile, in Cairo, Ali Mahir Pasha had managed to conceal the anti-British rhetoric of the Brotherhood and ordered that the Brothers be left alone. However, the rumors persisted that the Brotherhood was planning to attack the British. The British were concerned and on October 17, 1941, al-Banna and al-Sukkari were again arrested. The Society's press was closed down and the newspapers were forbidden to mention the Brotherhood. In response, the Brotherhood gathered 11,000 signatures supporting the release of al-Banna and al-Sukkari and gave them to the Royal Councilor and the Prime Minister.[9]

At this point, the radicals in the Brotherhood could no longer remain quiet. Two hundred Brothers organized a demonstration that led to a conflict with the police and over thirty Brothers were arrested. Fearing a religious revolution, the new Prime Minister Husayn Sirri Pasha, who came to power in November 1940, released al-Banna, al-Sukkari, and another prominent Brother who had been arrested against British orders. In al-Banna's absence, someone had released pamphlets accusing al-Banna of running the Brotherhood as he pleased according to his greed. The Brothers dismissed these pamphlets as British propaganda even though it was highly unlikely that the British wrote the pamphlets.[10]

By the end of January 1942, Egypt was experiencing several food shortages. Ali Mahir Pasha was trying to portray himself as the strongman of Egyptian politics. Prime Minister Husayn Sirri Pasha resigned on February 1, 1942. The British intervened to calm intense protests and force the palace to accept a Wafdist government headed by Prime Minister al-Nahhas Pasha.

King Farouk was in his Abdin Palace when Sir Miles Lampson burst in on February 4, 1942, backed by an entire regiment with thousands of troops in the general vicinity. Sir Miles Lampson forced the King by threatening him with military action to accept the Wafdist government headed by al-Nahhas and force Mahir to resign.[11]

During the next few months, Ali Mahir Pasha and all his allies were interred. Although the British would have liked to imprison al-Banna, the new Prime Minister Mustafa al-Nahhas thought it was best to leave the Brotherhood alone. He would rather control the Brotherhood, using it as means of social welfare distribution instead of imprisoning its leader, thus possibly causing a religious uprising.

The Brotherhood decided to put forth seventeen candidates for the upcoming elections. In the middle of March 1942, Prime Minister al-Nahhas ordered al-Banna to withdraw his candidates and cancel any Brotherhood involvement in the upcoming elections. He also forced al-Banna to publicly declare his loyalty to the 1936 Anglo-Egyptian Treaty and to the Egyptian government. If he did not comply, al-Banna and his associates would be imprisoned again. The MIA, or General Guidance Council, did not want al-Banna to comply. However, al-Banna published a letter in *al-Ahram* doing as the Prime Minister asked. Many of the Brothers viewed this acquiescence as betrayal, although in return, al-Banna made the government promise to let the Brotherhood continue its activities without government interference.[12]

In 1944, King Farouk expelled the al-Nahhas government and took back control of Egypt in a royal coup d'état. At this point, the British were too concerned with problems at home to worry about Egypt and they did not challenge Farouk. Farouk also called for the closing of party ranks and a national multiparty government excluding the Wafd party. After much squabbling, the multiple parties managed to form a government headed by Ahmad Mahir Pasha, a member of the Sa'dist Party.[13]

Ahmad Mahir apparently treated the Brothers harshly. In 1945, when al-Banna ran for parliament, the election was allegedly rigged and the Brotherhood lost their seat in Ismailiya. After al-Banna's defeat, the Muslim Brotherhood assassinated Ahmad Mahir Pasha. Mahir had recently read his decision to join the Allies in World War II and to declare war on the Axis powers.[14]

Mahmud Fahmi al-Nuqrashi then took over on February 25, 1945, and accused the Brotherhood of assassinating Ahmad Mahir. He then imprisoned al-Banna and several other Brothers. The Attorney General later released al-Banna and the Brothers. In fear, al-Nuqrashi had the Brothers under surveillance and restricted their ability to meet, although he later revoked this order and then quickly reinstated it. World War II ended in 1945 and the Brotherhood formally headed toward a path of violence. Al-Banna stated,

In the time when you will have—Oh ye Moslem Brethren—three hundred phalanxes, each one of them equipped spiritually with faith and principle, mentally with science and culture, and physically with training and exercise; at that time ask me to plunge with you into the depth of the seas, to rend the skies with you, and to attack with you every stubborn tyrant; then God-willing I will do it.[15]

Al-Banna also stated that the Brotherhood was directing all its actions toward the Islamic government which should have implemented the Brotherhood's reforms.

During one of their armistices, al-Banna spoke with al-Nuqrashi. Al-Banna urged the Prime Minister to quicken the independence and unity of the Nile Valley. Otherwise, al-Banna warned he would call for jihad and lead it himself. Al-Nuqrashi sent this request to the British government, but to no avail. The Brotherhood took to the streets in demonstration and protest.[16]

At this point, the Brotherhood was trying to stir things up and calling people to arms. Al-Nuqrashi resigned, February 14, 1946. Isma'il Sidqi then became prime minister. Al-Banna repeatedly sent messages to the Prime Minister, telling him to declare the country's complete independence. When he was not appeased, al-Banna accused the cabinet of being false Egyptians and favoring British foreign companies. Al-Banna even sent a letter to King Farouk telling him to dismiss the cabinet. Al-Banna was also fervently calling for jihad at this time.[17] There was a distinct change in al-Banna's rhetoric from a cooperative Islamic scholar to a radical Muslim.

When al-Banna left for Mecca on October 27, 1946, al-Sidqi Pasha arrested several Brothers, confiscated their newspaper, and put the Society-General in jail. When the Brothers began a counterattack against Sidqi Pasha, he deported Brothers and dispersed them. Sidqi blamed the Brothers for attacks in Cairo and Alexandria.

On December 10, 1946, al-Sidqi resigned and al-Nuqrashi took his place. On that day, al-Banna published a letter telling the new government to end negotiations, respect the will of Egypt, and to take up jihad. Al-Banna, complaining of how the government had imprisoned Brothers and harassed them, published many more letters. A civil war between the Brotherhood and al-Nuqrashi began shortly afterward.[18]

On May 6, 1948, al-Banna held a meeting with the founding committee. They made an important decision "to declare jihad against the Jews and to adopt all measures which would guarantee the deliverance of Palestine." In reference to Egypt they demanded "the cessation of discussions and negotiations and the declaration of a newspaper war until the country's status is made clear, inasmuch as the constitution makes Islam the official religion."[19]

The Arab-Israeli War began on May 15, 1948. The Muslim Brothers fought under the Arab League. It was during the war that the Brotherhood learned how valuable their training had been and gained combat experience. Egypt paid the highest price in men, supplies, and other war costs. The loss was a tremendous blow to Egyptian pride.

When al-Nuqrashi found out that the Brotherhood had been participating in combat units and hiding bombs in the countryside, he issued a military order on December 8, 1948. Al-Nuqrashi banned the Brotherhood and all of their publications. He also ordered all their documents seized. Al-Nuqrashi was then assassinated on December 28, 1948, by the Brotherhood.[20]

Al-Nuqrashi's successor Ibrahim 'Abd al-Hadi Pasha attacked the Muslim Brotherhood. He put several members in jail or concentration camps. Al-Husaini states that al-Hadi attacked the Brothers' property and families. On February 12, 1949, al-Banna was assassinated while sitting in his car in front of the Young Men's Muslim Association. King Farouk had lost Egypt's pride in the Arab-Israeli War and he eventually lost his throne on July 26, 1952. General Abd el Nasser started a military coup, overthrowing King Farouk of Egypt.[21]

Unlike the Muslim Brotherhood sects located in other Middle Eastern countries such as Jordan, the Muslim Brotherhood has had a tumultuous past in Egypt.[22] Larson states that a somewhat repressive institutional political system facilitated violent revolutionary action by the Muslim Brotherhood in Egypt.[23] However, the Brotherhood had been creating militant sectors within the Brotherhood since 1931. This predates Egyptian government repression of the Brotherhood by several years. The Brotherhood had also been using terrorist tactics since 1945. In addition, al-Banna had expressed his support of jihad since the time of the movement's inception. It is understandable why the government would want to repress a movement that had approximately 75,000 militant members by the late 1940s and obviously had a violent purpose. The Muslim Brotherhood had developed an army that infiltrated the Egyptian army and was poised to overthrow the Egyptian government. The Brotherhood also verbally threatened the government several times.

It is true that the government violently repressed the Muslim Brotherhood later in 1954. However, Nasser had a good reason to oppress the Brotherhood. On October 26, 1954, one Brother tried to assassinate President Nasser as he delivered a speech in Alexandria. After the failed assassination attempt, several hundred Brothers were arrested and many were tortured. The property of the Brothers was burned by mobs. Nasser had cracked down on the Brotherhood and tried to eradicate it. However, he was unsuccessful because the Brotherhood was too deeply imbedded in Egyptian society and would eventually reemerge.[24]

In conclusion, Vatikiotis summarizes the government's position toward the Muslim Brotherhood in the most comprehensible manner before 1954:

What also helped the Brethren was not merely their own vitality, but the fact that succeeding governments encouraged them in their chosen course and range of activities. Nor did any government ever proceed to apply strict police measures against their leaders, commercial ventures or social programmes. It was therefore impossible, once the government decided to proscribe and dissolve them, to actually do so, for in twenty years they had "extended their tentacles everywhere, and joined their interests with those of the people."[25]

The Brotherhood had grown tremendously powerful since its inception and the Egyptian government ignored the Brotherhood until it became a threat to the sovereignty of Egypt.

When the Egyptian government finally dealt seriously with the Brotherhood, the Brotherhood had already performed several terrorist attacks and assassinations. This is the most telling reason why the Egyptian government was not responsible for the radicalization of the Muslim Brotherhood to a terrorist organization. The Brotherhood had been plotting against the government several years before the Egyptian government confronted the Brotherhood. Although the Muslim Brotherhood was frustrated with the Egyptian government's lack of reform, this cannot excuse or singularly explain the Brotherhood's use of terrorism.

This next part of the chapter will focus on the research that has been completed in an effort to answer why the Egyptian Muslim Brotherhood radicalized if the Egyptian government was not responsible for its radicalization. I will begin with a discussion of the charismatic leadership of Hasan al-Banna and then explain how Hasan al-Banna was radicalized. Lastly, I will explain why frustration led to the use of terrorist tactics within the Muslim Brotherhood.

THE CHARISMATIC LEADERSHIP OF HASAN AL-BANNA

Scholars have often used the word "charismatic" to describe the leadership of the founder of the Muslim Brotherhood, Hasan al-Banna[26] and many of these scholars have merely used the word in passing without examination. Few academics have seriously applied Weber's components of charismatic leadership to Hasan al-Banna in a scholarly fashion.

Those few scholars who did look at Weber's work to validate the leadership style of Hasan al-Banna have left inconclusive and conflicting results. Goldberg states that al-Banna was a "truly charismatic figure."[27] Studying charismatic leadership from the Brothers' points of view, Goldberg asserts that al-Banna was magnificent at reaching out toward his followers and making them comply with his demands. However, Goldberg does not strictly apply Weber's criteria to Hasan al-Banna; he makes a sweeping generalization about al-Banna's charismatic qualities.

Brynjar Lia provides a partial appraisal of al-Banna's leadership according to Weber's criteria of charismatic leadership. Brynjar Lia states that charismatic leadership "only applies to certain aspects of Hasan al-Banna's leadership."[28] The Society was based on communal relationships and leaders within the society were chosen for their charismatic personalities. However, unlike Weber's criteria for charismatic leadership, Lia believes that al-Banna's authority was always stable and his mission did not depend on divine instruction. Followers were also able to air their grievances in front of a council, which Lia believes is contrary to Weber's concept of charismatic leadership. Lia also believes that Weber's idea of charismatic leadership fails to provide a comprehensive model for explaining the strength of the Muslim Brotherhood within society and can only truly be applied to messianic movements within hierarchical structures.

I argue that al-Banna truly was a charismatic leader within the Muslim Brotherhood and that the crucial role that al-Banna's charismatic leadership played in the development and use of terrorist tactics in the Muslim Brotherhood cannot be underestimated.

HASAN AL-BANNA'S CHARISMATIC LEADERSHIP WITHIN THE MUSLIM BROTHERHOOD

Hasan al-Banna's life effectively prepared him to assume the leadership of the Muslim Brotherhood. The following table identifies Weber's criteria for charismatic leadership and whether al-Banna satisfied those criteria. All of Weber's criteria will be discussed in the same order as the chart in the following pages.

Hasan al-Banna states in his memoirs that the founding of the Muslim Brotherhood occurred in March 1928 when seven friends of Hasan al-Banna came to see him: Hafiz Abdul Hamid, Ahmad Al Hasri, Fowad Ibrahim, Abdur Rehman, Hasabullah, Ismail Izz, and Zaki Al Maghribi. Impressed with al-Banna's speeches, they said:

> We have heard your speech, pondered over it with heart and soul and felt extraordinarily impressed. But we do not know what to do practically. We are disgusted with the present way of life. This is the life of captivity and disgrace. You say that the Arabs and Muslims have no respectable place within this country. They are just the most obedient servants of the foreigners. And we have hot blood running in our veins. We possess the vitality of faith (Iman) and sense of honor. We have brought these Dirhams after curtailing the expenses of our families. You know better than we do how best to serve Islam, the Muslim Ummah and the country. We have come to you to present to you whatever we possess so that we can feel relieved of our duties towards Allah. It is for you to guide us. The group which determines to serve the cause of Islam and Muslims does it simply to earn the pleasure of Allah and nothing

Table 1.1.   Weber's Assessment of Hasan al-Banna's Charismatic Leadership

Max Weber's Criteria for Charismatic Leadership	Characteristic of Hasan al-Banna?
Authority of Higher Being for Mission?	Yes
Complete Obedience of Followers?	Yes
Brings Followers Material and Social Rewards?	Yes
Charismatic Leader Directs and Organizes Organization?	Yes
Delegates Power to Followers?	Yes
Seeks to Defray Costs from His Own Pocket?	Yes
Develops an Army Trained and Equipped by Leader?	Yes
Rejects Personal Profit from Organization and Has No Rational Economic Behavior?	Yes
Followers Do Not Elect Him?	Yes
Leadership Is Not Stable?	Yes
Charismatic Leader Selects His Successor?	Yes

else. Such a group deserves success, however small it may be and its resources. [29]

Al-Banna was deeply impressed by their request and all seven men took an
oath of allegiance to what then became known as Al Ikhwanul Muslemoon
(The Muslim Brotherhood). They promised to "work for the glory of Islam
and launch Jihad against it." [30]

There is no doubt that several of the Brothers viewed al-Banna as a
spiritual messiah and that God had given al-Banna a divine mission. One
Brother stated, "Is he not the man God has chosen to bring renewal of
religion to the people? Is he not the man to steady this stumbling people and
restore its greatness and glory?" [31]

Zainab al-Ghazali was the first director of the women's part of the Muslim Brotherhood, The Muslim Sisters. She stated in 1948, after the recent
temporary dissolution of the Muslim Brotherhood, "He [al-Banna] was the
Imam that all Muslims must pledge allegiance to, in order that they struggle
for the return of Muslims to their positions of responsibility and true existence, and can implement Allah's commands." [32] Later when she assumed the
position of Director of the Muslim Sisters, al-Ghazali stated, "I pledge alle-

giance to you for the establishment of the Islamic State. The least I can give for this is shedding my blood and merging the Muslim Ladies' Group with the ikhwan."[33] Al-Banna accepted the pledge.

Al-Banna acquired a reputation as an imam, a position he did not discourage but encouraged when his followers referred to him as so. He bolstered his image as an imam by recounting stories when Allah had miraculously saved him from his tribulations.[34] According to Sufi principles, al-Banna demanded that he be called a murshid, which denotes a teacher of spirituality. Al-Banna could justify an oath of obedience from his followers because of his position as a murshid. Members had to swear an oath to the Muslim Brotherhood. Originally, in the 1930s, the oath, also known as Article 6, was as follows:

> Do you pledge to uphold the principles of the Society and work for the realization of its aims and adhere firmly to the moral of Islam and preserve the dignity of the Society, so let God be my witness? [Requiring the response, "I do."] Then I accept you on behalf of myself and the Muslim Brothers as one of our Brothers in God and I enjoin on you patience and truthfulness and may God forgive me and you. [The response being, "I do. I have accepted this and will be your brother."] [35]

However, later the Brotherhood changed this oath and the degree of obedience depended on the rank of the Brother in particular. Most of the lesser "associates" greatly revered al-Banna as it was, and so these "associates" had to pledge a rather subtle oath similar to the one above. However, "activists" and "workers" had to take an oath of complete obedience to Hasan al-Banna, the General Guide, and to do the biding of the MIA, or General Guidance Council, at any time or place. As a member worked his way up in the meritocracy of the Muslim Brotherhood, he was forced to give more and more obedience to al-Banna. In 1935, at the Third Conference, it was required that the members "swore complete confidence and absolute obedience to the General Guide in what one likes or dislikes to do."[36] From 1935 onward, a pamphlet titled "Duty of Obedience" and including the previous oath was circulated along with the repercussions for breaking the rules.

Article 10 read from the Third Conference identified al-Banna's position within the society:

> The MIA is the general executive body of the Muslim Brothers. It consists of the General Guide who is the head of all organizational bodies of the Society. He also represents its ideas and ideology. Additionally, the MIA consists of a number of members whom the General Guide selects to assist him. The MIA's headquarters is where the General Guide is.[37]

Al-Banna already controlled the MIA, or General Guidance Council, since he had picked its members. He had complete obedience from these members. The MIA could also supervise special training to whomever it chose and could grant honorary titles to any member it chose.

Al-Banna's position as General Guide was to last for the duration of his life—he could not resign from the position.[38] However, as a necessary caveat in Article 15, al-Banna could be dismissed if he put the Society on a course that did not follow the tenets of Islam or the ideals of the Brotherhood. Since al-Banna embodied the Muslim Brotherhood, it was highly unlikely that al-Banna could stray from the ideals of the Muslim Brotherhood.

Hasan al-Banna not only demanded obedience from his followers but also inspired them to follow him. "His mastery over his followers was a complete, total mastery approaching wizardry. For each person, he had a special story, a special manner and a special logic."[39] In addition, al-Banna was gifted with words; he was an excellent conversationalist, speaker, and writer. One Brother, Ahmad Anwar al-Jundi, stated:

> He [al-Banna] is one of the ablest writers, the most capable of revealing what is in his soul and one of the most eloquent of expression, making the deepest impression on men's souls with noble words and clear, concise meaning. When he speaks, the old and the young, the highly cultured, the literate, and the ignorant understand him . . . in his voice there is a deep resonance and from his tongue comes magic. When he speaks, he plays upon hearts.[40]

Another writer, Ahmad Hasan al-Hajjaji, stated:

> He is an illustrious writer, faultless and irreproachable. Through the eloquence of his words, the ordered continuity of his thought, and the beauty and ease of his style, he has attained the rank of great, outstanding writers and eminent men of letters . . . in writing memoirs, articles, pamphlets, and letters. . . . In his eloquence, the clarity of his argument, the impressiveness of his speech, and the appropriateness of his words, he is an excellent orator without peer. No voice could approach his heights and none of his contemporaries could challenge him in his field. He gripped the minds of his listeners and shook their emotions. He has a special air about him of self-assurance, intentiveness, and originality. He did not imitate nor follow the lead of anyone, predecessor or follower . . . in this (his eloquence as a speaker) he was aided by his abundant knowledge and his ability to tie up the loose ends of any subject no matter how raveled they were. He would gather it up and carry it to the mind of his listener without abridgement, without confusion, with breadth and profusion. He is an encyclopedia, extensive and complete, talking on any subject extemporaneously. He chooses an easy style in his lectures and uses expressions appropriate to his listeners.[41]

Others unaffiliated with the Muslim Brotherhood also complained of the fanaticism of the Muslim Brothers and the authoritarian personality of Hasan al-Banna, specifically during the Palestinian Uprising in which the Brothers infiltrated the Egyptian Army. Al-Misri warned the young Egyptian officers against Hasan al-Banna and his hidden agenda. "Their personal admiration of him was matched only by their suspicions of his motives. They had a problem with his personality: his answers were never clear and he demanded obedience."[42] Although al-Banna could find his way into anyone's admiration, others who were not his Brothers found his personality somewhat oppressive.

Members of the Muslim Brotherhood could expect some material and/or social rewards for their participation in the Muslim Brotherhood. By 1936, the Muslim Brotherhood had over three hundred branches throughout Egypt and was a highly respected organization. Members, especially those from the lower classes, would receive social respect for their participation in the Muslim Brotherhood. All members received an Islamic education, and a member killed in jihad would earn martyrdom, giving the family social prestige and admiration for their sacrifice. The Muslim Brotherhood also provided material rewards such as hospitals, pharmacies, literacy campaigns, gymnasiums, labor unions, employment agencies, and schools to its members. The Brotherhood also operated industries such as textile mills and farms, which would not only support the organization but also provide jobs for the Brothers in need of employment.[43]

As one may have noticed from the previous quotes regarding Brotherhood publications, al-Banna organized the Brotherhood as the General Guide. When looking at figure 1.1, one will notice that Hasan al-Banna had complete control over the Brotherhood and that he was the highest ranked member within the Muslim Brotherhood. Al-Banna also delegated power to his subordinates and the other committees below the General Guide.

The Muslim Brotherhood was not financed by the Egyptian state or any philanthropic organization. Members financed the Brotherhood from their own income and were proud that they owned their own organization. Supporters within Saudi Arabia also funded the Muslim Brotherhood.[44] Al-Banna also supplied his own income to help defray the costs of the organization throughout the life of the organization. When the first internal crisis occurred in 1931–1932, al-Banna paid the Brotherhood's debts from the building of a mosque by taking a loan out in his own name. He stated, "And as far as my debt is concerned, I have made such an arrangement that I shall be able to repay the whole amount in easy installment."[45] As soon as they could, the Brothers rounded up money to pay for al-Banna's loan from the mosque.

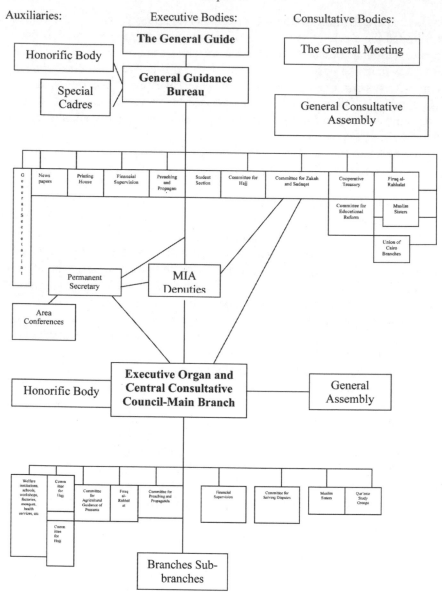

Auxiliaries: Executive Bodies: Consultative Bodies:

**Figure 1.1.   The Hierarchy of the Muslim Brotherhood in 1935. Most branch or-
ganizations had only some of these groups or committee. The sub-groups and
committees depended on the particular branch. This is a general suggestion of
the Muslim Brotherhood.** [46]

As Weber states, a charismatic leader creates an army that he trains and
equips, and that is answerable to the leader. Al-Banna personally oversaw
and attended all of the training all of the militant groups he created, including
the Rover Scouts, the Battalions, and the Special Apparatus. Al-Banna also

began buying weapons for the Brotherhood and stockpiling them in the early 1940s, according to Nasser. The Special Apparatus was a secret militant unit and only the General Guide and the MIA could command them.

Al-Banna also rejected personal profit from the Muslim Brotherhood. There were some accusations that al-Banna may have misappropriated funds at other branches of the Muslim Brotherhood, but these accusations were never proved. When people tried to pay al-Banna, he would refuse the money or give the money to the Muslim Brotherhood. One journalist, a supporter of the Muslim Brotherhood, stated:

> What distinguished this man [Hasan al-Banna] most of all is the fact that he has kept a particular bearing throughout all his life. This quality surpasses his dignity, greatness, manliness, honour, spiritual purity and noble character. This particular bearing is his simple austere lifestyle, devoid of all kinds of luxury, snobbery, haughtiness, wealth and personal glory.[47]

Al-Banna did not allow democracy within the Muslim Brotherhood. He once stated, "We have been greatly affected by some loose systems of life that are presented to us in the name of democracy and freedom of the individual. Disruption in society can never be tolerated in the name of democracy and individual freedom."[48] Similar to the preconditions described by Max Weber for charismatic leadership, al-Banna did not want anyone to challenge his authority and democracy could provide that opportunity.

Al-Banna's charismatic leadership was not always stable. One internal leadership crisis occurred when other Brothers were vying to be al-Banna's successor in 1931–1932. After this crisis, al-Banna was forced to reestablish his position as the charismatic leader when his position was contested within the higher echelons of the Muslim Brotherhood. In fact, al-Banna took even greater precautions to secure his leadership position and strengthen his qualities as a charismatic leader.

Al-Banna chose his successor, Shaikh Ali Al Jadavi, to fill his leadership position should he be transferred or killed. Al-Banna stated:

> The Ikwhan [Brothers] feared that I might be transferred from Ishmailiya and they wish to see some one appointed as my successor. . . . Finally I suggested the name of Shaikh Ali Al Jadavi who was the best among us from the religious as well as the moral point of view.[49]

Al-Banna appeared to his followers as the infallible leader of the Muslim Brotherhood. Al-Banna worked tirelessly for the Muslim Brotherhood. He would tour Egypt accompanied by several of his closest Brothers trying to spread the message of the Brotherhood. The Rover Units dressed in immaculate uniforms would greet him at the railroad station singing the Muslim Brotherhood's official hymn, "O God's Prophet." As soon as he entered a town, he would go to the mosque to pray and would defer authority to the local religious leader (imam). Al-Banna would usually arrive on a Friday and spend the rest of the time making speeches, ensuring patronage from local elites, or speaking with the locals. [50]

He would get very little rest in the process, often inspiring more devotion from his men. Al-Banna would often sleep only when he traveled on the train and the Brothers would see him go to bed late at night and rise very early in the morning. He was the "wise and great leader." "He embodies the highest example [of a virtuous life] that I have prescribed for myself," stated a young follower. [51] Some Brothers stated:

> We ride in the car between Mecca and Medina and are car sick while he is not; we eat some food and have stomachache but not he; we come into the hot air of Mecca after our damp air and into the damp air of Medina after the hot air of Mecca and we all catch colds and start coughing, but not so he; walking up to and climbing the Ghar Hira' tires us out, but he does not tire. [52]

Al-Banna possessed a strength that seemed to his followers to have emanated from God.

Al-Banna's qualities as a leader fulfill Weber's criteria for charismatic leadership. Al-Banna believed that he had been told by Allah to bring Egyptian Muslims back to an Islamic life. Al-Banna had the complete obedience of his followers after his leadership crisis, and his followers received material and social benefits for their participation in the Muslim Brotherhood. Al-Banna directed and led the Muslim Brotherhood, delegating power to those he saw fit to lead. Several militant groups affiliated with the Muslim Brotherhood, such as the Secret Apparatus, were trained and personally commanded by al-Banna. Al-Banna did not personally profit from his position as General Guide within the Muslim Brotherhood; he refused to personally accept payment for his work in the Brotherhood. The Muslim Brotherhood was not a democracy. Al-Banna was followed because he inspired people. The charismatic leadership of Hasan al-Banna was not stable; leadership crises and disagreements over tactics occurred during al-Banna's tenure as the General Guide. Lastly, al-Banna chose his successors. The Muslim Brotherhood movement would probably never have been created or grown without its founder and charismatic leader, Hasan al-Banna.

The charismatic leadership of Hasan al-Banna was crucial to the radicalization of the Muslim Brotherhood because al-Banna established complete control over the Brotherhood and commanded obedient Brothers to use terrorism when he deemed it was necessary. As an example, in August 1947, the newspaper *Rose Al Yusuf,* originally a pro-government magazine, printed a story concerning the violent mobilization of the Muslim Brotherhood. On August 20 at 1:00 a.m., the Brotherhood telephoned its branches throughout

Egypt telling them that the time for jihad was here. Two words, "General Jihad," were whispered and twenty minutes later, men were seen coming out of their villages with axes. It was said that "death radiated from their hard eyes." They received their orders from "the Knight of Nights," or Hasan al-Banna, and they obeyed without question.[53]

In another instance, Abdilmajid Hasan, a Muslim Brother, shot al-Nuqra-shi, the Prime Minister in the Department of the Interior. Hasan testified that he was a member of the Brotherhood's paramilitary organization. Hasan indicated that he acted under the impression that al-Banna controlled the paramilitary organization and had an influence over all branches of the Society in the world. "Al-Banna," Hasan stated, "directed the paramilitary organization and often came to our branch and lectured us."[54]

The Brothers admired al-Banna and would have done anything for him. Al-Banna had the complete loyalty and obedience of his followers. This is not only important because al-Banna sanctioned the use of terrorist tactics or violence but it is also important because the Brothers did what al-Banna told them to do. When al-Banna told members of the militant sects of the Brotherhood to use terrorism, those Brothers complied without question. As another testament to his charismatic leadership, the Brotherhood went through severe internal conflict after al-Banna was assassinated because the Brotherhood found it nearly impossible to replace him.

THE RADICALIZATION OF HASAN AL-BANNA

The radicalization of the charismatic leader Hasan al-Banna was by no means a quick process. Instead, it took several years for al-Banna to reach a point wherein he considered terrorism a legitimate alternative for accomplishing his goals. In the beginning, in 1928, al-Banna conceived the Muslim Brotherhood with the idea of generosity and brotherly love. His purpose was to reform Egypt and spread Islam among Egyptians using Islamic fellowship and charity.[55]

One way to trace the radicalization of Hasan al-Banna is to look at the many books and pamphlets he wrote concerning the mission of the Muslim Brotherhood. Around the time of World War I, al-Banna wrote his first pamphlet entitled, *Between Yesterday and Today*. The translator of al-Banna's memoirs, M. N. Shaikh, believes that al-Banna wrote this pamphlet in approximately 1914, when al-Banna was still a boy. Al-Banna was incredibly intelligent so it is likely that he was writing the pamphlet for one of the Muslim organizations he was involved in.[56] Since this pamphlet was written before the Muslim Brotherhood existed, it is likely that al-Banna was referring to all Muslim men as his Muslim Brothers. In this pamphlet, al-Banna states that the mission of the Muslim Brothers is one of reawakening and deliverance. He states that the goals of the Brothers are to free the Islamic fatherland from foreign domination, to establish an Islamic state of Egypt, to reform education, to fight poverty, ignorance, disease, and crime, and lastly, to create an exemplary society that will deserve to be associated with the Islamic Sacred Law.[57]

Then under General Means of Procedure, al-Banna stipulates how the Brothers will arrive at these goals:

> Speeches, pronouncements, letters, lessons, lectures, diagnosis of the ailment and prescription of the medicine- all these by themselves are useless and will never realize a single aim, nor will they advance a single agent of out mission to any one of his goals. Nevertheless, missions do have certain means of procedure which they must adopt and according to which they must operate. The general procedural means used by all missions are invariable and unchanging, and they are limited to the three following matters:
>
> 1. deep faith.
> 2. precise organization
> 3. uninterrupted work.
>
> These are your general procedural measures, Brethren, so believe in your ideology, form your ranks about it, work on its behalf and stand unwaveringly by it.[58]

Deep faith, precise organization, and uninterrupted work were the procedural means needed for Muslim men to accomplish their goals of reforming society and freeing Egypt from foreign domination.

Al-Banna then specifically asks:

> How will you obtain your rights without the use of force? Know, Brethren, that Satan slips his whispered suggestions into the aspirations of every reformer, but that God cancels out what Satan whispers; then God decrees His miracles, for God is Knowing, Wise.[59]

In this first pamphlet, *Between Yesterday and Today*, it is obvious that al-Banna does not intend to use violence to accomplish his agenda of Islamic reform. In fact, al-Banna believes that Satan influences reformers that use violence. Satan is in fact whispering in the ear of those who use violence to reform society. Only through the efforts of prayer and faith would Muslims be successful in reforming society. Terrorism at this point in approximately 1914 is not an option for Hasan al-Banna.

In the early 1930s, a few years after the creation of the Muslim Brotherhood, al-Banna created the Oath of Allegiance which required members to memorize ten principles the Muslim Brotherhood must follow. One of these principles was jihad. Specifically, at this point, jihad was not an important part of the Brotherhood's agenda and al-Banna does not necessarily consider it a violent act. Al Banna writes of jihad:

> And its lowest degree is heartfelt hatred for the wrong and the highest degree is sacrifice of life and placing of oneself at the disposal of Allah. Then between the two, there are different ranks of the struggle, for example; the struggle of the mouth, struggle of the pen, the struggle of the hand, and the struggle of speaking the truth before the tyrant. [60]

A pamphlet that was written later by Hasan al-Banna entitled, *The Concept of Allah in the Islamic Creed* is mostly dedicated to explaining why Muslims must pursue jihad. A majority of the chapters are based on jihad. This pamphlet, according to M. N. Shaikh, the translator of al-Banna's memoirs, was written in approximately 1937 during the Brotherhood's participation in the war in Palestine against the British and the Jews. [61] In 1938, Hasan al-Banna publicly called the Brotherhood to war against the Egyptian state.

Al-Banna states:

> Allah has made *Jehad* (fighting in the way of Allah) an obligatory duty for every Muslim, there being neither any way of escape nor any argument to turn away from it. Allah has persuaded the believers to fight in this way with gusto, and the reward of the Mujahids and the martyrs has been enhanced very much and no other good act can equal it in the manner of reward, except in case every individual takes part in Jehad and emulating the Mujahids in every field, follows them in the field of strife in the way of Allah. Allah had endued the Mujahids and the martyrs with a distinction exclusive to them. He paid the price of their blood in full in the form of His help and decisive victory from Himself in the world and in the next promised them prosperity unsurpassed. Those running away from jehad have been warned and promised the worst punishment and an evil end. They have been regarded as the worst of creation. They have been severely scolded for their cowardice and impotence and called the embodiment of frailty and wretchedness. They have been given to the ill-tidings of a great loss in this world. And nothing can avert that mishap save by making amends and taking part in jehad. And in the life Hereafter they are doomed to torments of hell from which there is no escape, even if they had gold equal in weight equal to the mount Uhad and paid it as ransom for their redemption. They keep away from jehad and to sit at home is regarded the greatest sin by Allah and falls under the category of severe deadly sins with punishment of an abiding nature. [62]

Al-Banna also states:

> See the Quran and it would be found, how Allah has encouraged the believers to always remain alert and in accordance with the occasion has invited them to fight either in the shape of armies or groups or even alone. It would also be noticed how He reprimands the *Ahadis*, useless persons, cowards and selfseek-

ers; how he goads their conscience for the defence of the oppressed and the
support of the weak, and how he mingles prayers and fasts with jehad and
brings forth the reality that jehad is also a pillar of the mansion of Islam. Then
how He treats the patients of hesitation and uncertainty, removes their doubts;
infuses the spirit of courage and valour in the faint-hearted and create in them
boundless determination to look death in the face, as death has to come and
come it shall. But if they lay down their lives in the way of Allah, they shall
receive compensation for it from Allah. They shall not be deprived of a recom-
pense even for the smallest sacrifice. [63]

These three pamphlets illustrate the progressive radicalization of Hasan
al-Banna. When al-Banna was approximately eight years old, he wanted to
reform Egyptian society. Nevertheless, his methods consisted of prayer, service, and love. Later in his life, shortly after the creation of the Muslim
Brotherhood in the early 1930s, we see that al-Banna makes jihad one of the
ten principles that Muslim Brothers must commit to in order to become part
of the social movement of the Muslim Brotherhood. At this point, al-Banna
does not spend much time talking about jihad. Jihad is required of the Muslim Brothers, but al-Banna has not begun to create militant sects in the
Brotherhood, nor has he started emphasizing jihad. Finally, in the late 1930s,
al-Banna's radicalization is complete. Jihad is not only obligatory for every
Muslim but is also required of Muslims who desire to go to heaven. Those
who do not participate in violent jihad and shirk the duties of martyrdom
when they are called by Allah to do so will spend eternity suffering in the
depths of hell. From his childhood to approximately when the Muslim Brotherhood starts becoming violent, participating in the war in Palestine against
the Jews (mid-1930s), we can see the personal radicalization of Hasan al-
Banna. The charismatic leader demands obedience from his followers and
commands that his followers must participate in jihad, and the Muslim
Brotherhood then becomes an organization that uses terrorist tactics in approximately 1945.

In addition, as time progressed the militant groups that al-Banna created
within the Muslim Brotherhood were created for purposes that were more
violent. The Rover Scouts were first formed in 1931 by Hasan al-Banna and
their purpose was do such things as keep order at the Brotherhood's meetings, to march in parades, or to escort Hasan al-Banna in public. The Rover
Scouts were followed by the creation of the Battalions in 1937. The Battalions were literally created to be a personal army of God. Their training was
akin to that of a professional army like the U.S. Army. Lastly, the Secret
Apparatus was created in approximately 1939 or 1940 as a Special Forces
part of the Battalions. It was the Secret Apparatus that performed the terrorist
attacks against the Egyptian government and the civilian population beginning in 1945. All of these groups were foremost loyal to Hasan al-Banna and
were commanded by him. This radicalization of Hasan al-Banna is one of

three factors responsible for the use of terrorist tactics in the Muslim Brotherhood. For without Hasan al-Banna and his formation and command of the militant forces, the Muslim Brotherhood might have never resorted to the use of terrorist tactics.

FRUSTRATION AND AGGRESSION WITHIN THE MUSLIM BROTHERHOOD

In 1939, five psychologists published the book *Frustration and Aggression*.[64] Dollard and his cohorts argued that human frustration always leads to aggression. Although this aggression may manifest itself in different behaviors and may not be immediately apparent, frustration will always cause human aggression. This aggression may manifest in as little as a rude retort or critical statement, or may actually lead to violence. However, according to Dollard, aggression is not always physical violence. The more times a person has become frustrated as a result of a particular incident, the greater his aggression will be—the idea being that minor frustrations add up. When a person is frustrated repeatedly over the same issue, it may lead to violent attacks. According to Dollard et al., this theory is also applicable to groups of people. This theory can be applied to the Muslim Brotherhood and can help to explain why the Egyptian Muslim Brotherhood began to use terrorist tactics.

Frustration within the Muslim Brotherhood accumulated in a series of stages that were defined by Hasan al-Banna himself. These stages overlapped one another and are explained in the following paragraphs. Al-Banna identified his vision of the development of the Egyptian Muslim Brotherhood by stating, "The path of the Muslim Brothers is drawn and well-defined: its stages and future steps are not left to be determined by circumstances or pure coincidences. The stages of this path are three: acquaintance-formation-execution."[65]

The goal of each stage was the same: to bring about reform in the Egyptian people and Egyptian government, and to get the British out of Egypt. The Brotherhood wanted Muslim Egyptians to live a lifestyle dictated by the Q'uran. This means that Egyptians should not smoke, drink, or wear jewelry. A woman should be escorted by a male member of the household and should never be seen by an unrelated male. Egyptians should pray five times a day facing Mecca and should attend services at the local mosque. The Egyptian government should not be beholden to the British government. The Egyptian government should be controlled by an imam, consist of a Muslim theocracy, and should try to set an example for the Egyptian people. Lastly, the Brotherhood wanted the British government to leave Egypt and return the country to its status of a sovereign nation. These three stages of frustration and violence are illustrated below in table 1.2: Stages of Growth of Frustration within the Brotherhood. The stages overlap one another in their progression; what is most important is the inception of a stage.

The Acquaintance Stage: Recruitment and the Disregarded Publications

The Acquaintance Stage began with the creation of the Brotherhood in 1928 when the Brotherhood began recruiting members. Al-Banna would travel to different places in Egypt making speeches and creating new branches of the Brotherhood. In addition, the Brotherhood would try to propagandize Egyptians by providing them with social services. While receiving complementary medical care or using Brotherhood physical facilities, members would be introduced to the message and agenda of the Muslim Brotherhood. The Brotherhood would then try to recruit those people that used their services.

The Brotherhood also produced many publications in the 1930s and 1940s that were instrumental in disseminating its message to the public. The Brotherhood's newspaper, named after the organization, was published daily. The Brotherhood also had a series of newsletters, including *al-Ikhwan al-Muslimun* (The Moslem Brethren) and *al-Manar* (The Lighthouse), which were monthly. The following were published weekly: *al-Ta'aruf* (The Acquaintance), *al-Shu'a'* (The Radiation), *Al-Nadhir* (The Warner), *Al-Shihab* (The Meteor), *al-Mabahith* (The Discourse), *al-Da'wah* (The Mission), and *al-Muslimun* (The Muslims).[66]

In addition to these letters and newsletters, several pamphlets were published containing political and social opinions of the Brotherhood. Most of these pamphlets were written by Hasan al-Banna. A list of these pamphlets

Table 1.2. Stages of Growth of Frustration within the Brotherhood

STAGES	CHARACTERISTICS OF STAGE	DATE STAGE BEGAN
Stage 1: Acquaintance	Creation, Recruitment, Publications, Expansion of Branches, and National Recognition	1928
Stage 2: Formation	Creation of Rover, Scouts, Battalions, Secret Apparatus, Training of Brothers, Ammunition Collection, and Political Involvement (1938)	1931
Stage 3: Execution	Al-Banna Declares War, Secret Apparatus Formed, Use of Terrorist Tactics Soon Followed	1938

includes *al-Minhaj* (The Program), *Man Anta* (Who Are You), *Tatawwurat al-Fikrat al-Islamiyah wa Ahdafuha* (Developments and Aims of the Islamic Idea), *al-Qur'an wa al-Durrah* (The Koran and the Atom), *al-Ta'alim* (Instructions), *Kaifa Nad'u al-Nas* (How We Appeal to the People), *Hal Nanhu Qawm 'Amaliyun* (Are We Practical People), *Nahwa al-Nur* (Towards the Light), *Ahdafuna wa Mabadi'una* (Our Aims and Principles), *Ila Ay Shay' Nad'u al-Nas* (To What Are We Calling the People), *Da'watuna* (Our Movement), *Bayn al-Ams wa al-Yawm* (Between Yesterday and Today), *Risalat al-Jihad* (Mission of Jihad), *Risalat al-Mu'tamar al-Khamis* (Mission of the Fifth Congress), *Ila al-Shabab* (To the Youth), *al-Ikhwan al-Muslimun That Rayat al-Qur'an* (The Muslim Brethren Under the Banner of the Koran), *al-Ma'thurat* (Aphorisms), and a pamphlet that stipulated the duties of Muslim women, a spiritual program, and general regulations. [67]

In addition, al-Banna and other Brothers published several books. [68] These books include *Ma' Ba'that al-Hajj* (With the Pilgrimage Mission), *al-Ikhwan fi Mizan al-Haqq* (The Moslem Brethren in the Scale of Truth), *Qa'id al-Da'wah aw Hasan al-Banna, Hayat Rajul wa Tarikh Madrasah* (The Leader of the Movement or Hasan al-Banna, The Life of a Man or the History of a School), *Qadaya al-Aqtar al-Islamiyah* (Problems of the Islamic Countries), *Filastin wa al-Maghrib* (Palestine and North Africa), *Inhiyar al-Hadarat al-Gharbiyah* (The Fall of Western Civilization), *Al-Islam Yazhaf* (Islam Marches On), *Ruh wa Rayhan* (Repose and Pleasure), *Thawrat al-Dam* (Revolution of Blood), and *Rajal al-Sa'ah* (Man of the Hour). Anwar al-Jundi issued a book on the first of each month, including *Min Khutub Hasan al-Banna* (From the Speeches of Hasan al-Banna), *Rasa'il Hasan al-Banna* (The Letters of Hasan al-Banna), *Majmu'at Hasan al-Banna* (Collected Articles of Hasan al-Banna), and *Mudhakkirat Hasan al-Banna* (Memoirs of Hasan al-Banna).

Al-Banna began to get involved politically in the early 1930s. His goal was to eventually get elected to the Egyptian parliament and work through Egyptian politicians. From then on, the Muslim Brotherhood became a political organization. In 1934, the stipulation that the Brotherhood not be involved in politics was dropped from the Brotherhood's General Law of the Society. The official political agenda of the Muslim Brotherhood was not announced publicly until 1938, which in summary stipulated that the Brotherhood would work with members of parliament and the Egyptian king and would try to form an interest group to get their goals implemented into legislation. The Brotherhood wanted policy changes in the Egyptian government and was not verbally advocating revolution.

Al-Banna began the Brotherhood's political course by forming a committee in July 1932 in Ismailiya to draft a letter to the Minister of Interior suggesting steps that would eliminate legal prostitution in Egypt. He claimed that the government and parliament were responsible for the education and moral downfall of Egypt. Islamic scholars and students were also responsible for the return to Islamic ways of life. The first letter was written in 1936 and was addressed to Muhammad Mahmud Pasha. This letter described the weak political situation of Egypt in the world, its social problems, and the vices of the Egyptian people and its ministers. Turkey had recently abandoned its position as an Islamic republic, and the Brotherhood was deeply concerned that Egypt would follow Turkey's example.

In the late 1930s, the Muslim Brotherhood got more involved in Egyptian politics. In 1938, the Brotherhood sent a letter to King Farouk asking for the dissolution of Egyptian political parties. Later in 1938, the Brotherhood sent a letter Ahmad Khasabah Pasha, the Minister of Justice, demanding that Islamic law be used. The Brotherhood also sent a letter to al-Nahhas in 1938 warning Egypt to be wary of alliances with non-Arab and non-Islamic countries. In 1939, al-Nahhas was addressed again in a letter that criticized the Wafd party for being un-Islamic.

These numerous publications were ignored and the objectives of the Brotherhood were disregarded because neither the Egyptian government nor the Egyptian people changed their course of action and committed themselves to Islamic reform. Nothing different had happened since the inception of the Muslim Brotherhood. Although the Muslim Brotherhood continued to grow steadily in membership, mass reform did not occur within the Egyptian population. The influence of Western immorality was still apparent and Muslims were not living an Islamic lifestyle. The British did not leave Egypt and the Egyptians did not return to a non-secular form of government. Egypt did not become a theocracy. No visual changes could be observed. The Muslim Brotherhood had asked for political change since its inception in 1928.

Frustration over his struggle and lack of accomplishment continued to plague al-Banna.

> He gave lectures and wrote letters to the Government and invited its attention to the reformation of the prevailing conditions. These letters show that he wanted complete change in the educational, economical, social, and political spheres and to bring them in line with the principles of Islam. He continued his struggle from the time of Mahummad Mahmood Pasha until the break of Second World War. Al Ikhwanul Muslimoon became a full-fledged revolutionary movement in 1938.[69]

The Formation Stage: The Rover Scouts

In the early 1930s, the excursion groups were formed in Ismailiya and personally trained by Hasan al-Banna. These scouts were trained according to the concept of jihad. Eventually in the mid-1930s, the term "excursion groups" vanished and the name Rover Scouts (*Jawwala*) replaced it. These Rover Scouts were formed and trained by their local branches. The earliest

Rover Scouts had four clans (*'asha'ir*) that were divided into five subsections (*aqsam*). A complete unit would then have approximately 200 Scouts. However, this system was changed: the clan became the basic unit, consisting of seven to ten scouts and was headed by one man (*rafiq*).

By 1935, the only branches of the Brotherhood that had Rover Scout units were the Ismailiya, Port Said, Suez, Abu Suwayr, and Cairo branches. In 1935, a photograph was taken of Hasan al-Banna with approximately ninety Rover Scouts from Ismailiya. Because of these low numbers, every branch was instructed to form a Rover Scout unit consisting of members ages twenty to thirty. Mukhtar Effendi Isma'il was appointed as the general instructor for the Rover Scouts. These Rover Scouts were supposed to maintain order at meetings and needed to visit other branches to form a communal spirit. The men were supposed to develop a sense of obedience and order and a spirit of masculinity. A sports-like mentality was also essential to the Scouts, and this athleticism helped to recruit several of the young men that joined the Brotherhood. Most of the Rover Scouts were male students from local universities.[70] They were to protect public welfare, meaning they were supposed to uphold the tenets of Islam and provide public service akin to the welfare services the Brotherhood provided. In 1938, the minimum age for a Scout was seventeen, but in 1939, this age was lowered to fifteen.

The zealous spirit of these young Scouts was evident to one of the agents of the Political Police in Egypt. He stated:

> They are all devout young men who make their prayers punctually and who adhere to the tenets of their religion to the point of fanaticism. Some of them deliver speeches in which they urge those present to lament the bygone days of the Arabs and to do their best to chase out imperialists (Cheers of "Down with imperialism"). In the course of these speeches, reference was made to certain Koranic verses and Prophetic sayings dealing with martyrdom and self-sacrifice for the sake of God and Country. . . . I consider that the "Moslem Brethren Society" will in the course of time be in a position to produce a reckless and heedless generation who will not abstain from selling their lives cheap and whose best wish could be to die as martyr for the sake of God and their country. It is a custom of members of this society not to applaud speakers, but to shout in chorus: "God is great! Praise be to God!"[71]

In the late 1930s, al-Banna created a series of summer training camps for the Scouts. One branch was set up outside Alexandria and al-Banna spent two months at this camp providing the Scouts with military and physical training. The first Rover instructors were trained at a similar camp in Cairo. In early 1941, there were approximately 2,000 Rovers. The Rovers rarely participated in violent activities as a group although several of the individuals did participate in violence. In 1945, the Rover Scouts were divided into the Rovers and the Military. The purpose of the Military section of the Rover

Scouts was to provide a reorganization scheme for the Egyptian army should the Brotherhood take over the Egyptian government. This idea of the possibility of taking over the British government began in the early 1940s. [72]

The Battalions

In autumn 1937, the Battalions of Supporters of God (Katibat Ansar Allah), the Battalion of Glory (Katibat al-Majd), or just the Battalions (Katibat), were created to greater fulfill al-Banna's need for a spiritual army of God. The Battalions were closely related to the Rover Scouts and, at times, the two were inseparable. The Battalions were composed of Brothers who would continue the violent struggle for the return to Islamic rule for the Brotherhood. [73]

Members of the Battalions were specifically handpicked from the Brotherhood. The members had to have been attested for by other members of the Brotherhood and needed to have lived according to the Brotherhood's doctrine. Battalions were composed of between ten and forty members between the ages of eighteen and forty. [74] A chief who had been elected by secret ballot with an MIA deputy present headed each Battalion. Each member had his own personal file at headquarters and was required to take an oath of association ("I swear by god to [commit myself to] obedience, action and secrecy"). [75] Those who disobeyed were reprimanded and punished by other members of the Battalions.

The training lasted approximately four weeks and the members were required to be "monks by day and knights by night." Once a week, the Battalion would gather for a night vigil, led by al-Banna. These night vigils included prayer, physical training, and spiritual guidance from al-Banna on topics such as sex and Sufism. In 1938, a pamphlet was distributed to the members of the Battalions specifying their thirty-eight duties. The members of the Battalions received a more in-depth briefing of the views and duties of the Muslim Brotherhood than the general members. Al-Banna would specifically talk to these members about his plans to develop a political party and his political contacts.

By 1939, al-Banna had hoped that the Battalions would grow in membership to 12,000 members split between 400 Battalions, but this dream was never realized. In 1943, the Battalions were divided into Families so that smaller groups could keep individuals free of gambling, alcohol, usury, and adultery. [76]

It is believed that al-Banna formed the Battalions to intimidate the government into adhering to his wishes of reform. The Muslim Brotherhood presented a political challenge to the Egyptian government because it had many supporters and was a strong organization. The formation of an army in an organization that was incredibly popular would most likely secure the cooperation of the Egyptian government.

The Battalions laid the initial groundwork for the Secret Apparatus of the Muslim Brotherhood. When the dream of the Battalions never materialized because of small numbers of militants, al-Banna turned to covert strategies. Frustrated, he formed the Secret Apparatus, which used terrorist tactics and would function as a secret organization without the knowledge of the government. A secret organization that used terrorism did not need to challenge the government with a military force, but instead could attack in secret using only a few men and could cause more damage.

The Execution Stage: The Creation of the Special Apparatus

At the ten-year anniversary of the Muslim Brotherhood at the Fifth Conference in 1938, al-Banna remarked about the history of Egypt and his current response to it. He stated:

> Then there took place a number of incidents and events in Egypt and some other Islamic countries, which fired me to action. The hidden pangs in my heart raised their head. I intensely felt that struggle, efforts and actions were inevitable. After waking the people, and urging them to tread the way of constructions and after teaching and training the people, it is unavoidable to get ready for laying that foundation of work. [77]

In the previous quote, al-Banna talks about his own frustration at the lack of religious reform in Egypt. These actions caused him pain and wrestled him to action. Even after al-Banna stirred the people to reform, he had to lay the foundation for other work. When al-Banna talks about laying the foundation for other work, he is referring to the use of terrorism.

In addition, al-Banna states there are three stages that are inevitable for any invitation. These stages are the same as the frustration stages of the Muslim Brotherhood. In the following quote, al-Banna talks about the procession of these stages and that the final stage has come for terrorism and violence.

1. The invitation should be introduced and publicized to the maximum extent; its good points and expected benefits should be mentioned and it should be made to reach each and every class of the general public. This is the first stage.
2. The invitation should have an organization and shape. Sincere men of sacrifice should be chosen. Armies should be prepared and furnished. Files and rows made and organized. This is the second stage.
3. In the third stage, principles shall be enforced and there shall be practical struggle. Then will the results be gathered.

A team of valiant fighters should be prepared for sacrifice and they should be intensely zealous to fight for the cause of the Invitation and to make the organization very, steady, stable and durable.[78]

It was later in 1938 that the Muslim Brotherhood's frustration grew to monumental proportions and when al-Banna publicly committed the Brotherhood to violence. This was the third stage that al-Banna had spoken about. Since the inception of the Muslim Brotherhood nothing had really changed within Egypt. Egypt had not become an Islamic theocracy; Britain still had political control over Egypt. The Egyptian population was still not living according to Islam in the eyes of the Brotherhood.

In 1938, al-Banna stated that if the authorities did not implement the program of the Brotherhood, "then we are at war with every leader, every party and every organization that does not work for the victory of Islam."[79] Frustrated that the authorities did not follow the program of the Muslim Brotherhood, al-Banna called for war. The Muslim Brotherhood declared war on the Egyptian government and society. He carried out his declaration by creating the terrorist sect of the Muslim Brotherhood, the Secret Apparatus.

In the early 1940s, al-Banna wrote to the entire Brotherhood:

O the members of Al Ikhwan, let me tell you that the majority of you is still not fully ware of the mission of Al Ikhwan. The day you realize and understand its mission you will have to face a lot of opposition and enmity. You will find troubles around you. There will be countless hurdles on your way. When you have overcome these hurdles then you will become the true standard-bearer of Islam. Today you are unknown but you will have to pave the way for the missions of Al Ikhwan. This mission requires tremendous sacrifices. So you will have to be well prepared. The ignorance of the people regarding Islam will also be an obstacle in your way. The official *ulemas* [scholars] will express their surprise over your way of preaching Islam. Your Jihad in the name of Allah will not be appreciated. The rulers, leaders, and the rich will be jealous of you. All governments will oppose you. Every government will try to restrict your activities and sow thorns on your way. The exploiters will use all possible tactics to fail your mission. The weal and the cowards will use the government for this purpose. The men of mean character will always stand in opposition. There will be a group which will express doubt on your mission and put various blames on you. They will present a wrong picture of your mission, and they are the men who have authority, power, wealth, and influence. In these conditions you will in real sense enter the arena of experience and trial. You will be imprisoned, exiled and driven out of your homes. Your property will be confiscated, your houses will be searched, and this period of test, may last long. But it is the promise of Allah that he will help the *Mujahideen* and reward the *Momineen*.[80]

In the previous quote, al-Banna tried to prepare and explain to the Muslim Brothers their missions. He mentions the frustration that the Brothers will feel when they fully understand their mission. They must try to complete their mission to the best of their ability. However, people will not listen to them and so they must use violence. The terrorism that the Muslim Brotherhood must engage in will not be understood and, most likely, the Brotherhood will be punished for the acts it commits. Al-Banna believes that he is supervising Allah's wishes and therefore terrorism is what Allah commands.

The terrorist sect of the Muslim Brotherhood, the Special Apparatus, was formed out of the Rover Scouts and the Battalions in approximately 1940. Several members from the Supreme Council of the Rover Scouts, such as Husayn Kamal al-Din, Mahmud Labib, and Abd al-Aziz Ahmad, were instrumental in the creation of the Special Apparatus. When al-Banna created the Secret Apparatus, he stated,

> provided that it is based on clean, strong Islamic military traditions; and provided that it is surrounded with complete secrecy, such that only it members shall know anything about it, and provided that it shall be financed by its own members, as it is an indication of the seriousness of an someone who offers his life to offer his money, as a sacrifice. [81]

The Secret Apparatus was an elite secret society within the Brotherhood and was only attainable for the most qualified and dedicated Brothers. The members of the Secret Apparatus had to submit their entire life histories to the headquarters and keep a daily journal of their activities, which was also submitted to headquarters. The members were required to swear their loyalty to the Brotherhood on a pistol and a Koran. The motto of the Brotherhood was "Absolute obedience without question, without hesitation, without doubting, and without shifting blame."[82] Halpern states:

> Thus the movement permits those who feel superfluous to participate, through various levels of initiation, in a powerful mystery within a group which deems itself the elite among Moslems. The powerless it thus keeps powerless by extinguishing their personality, but it also increases their sense of importance by creating an intense feeling of identification with the leader of the movement whose power, emotion, and style of living pantomime the yearning of his followers. Thus it stimulates an intoxicating sense of nihilism in which the willingness to sacrifice one's self becomes more important than the object for which the sacrifice is made. Those who are sent to death as robots have the illusion of dying as martyrs. [83]

Members of the Special Apparatus had to pray, fast, and complete rigorous physical training.[84] They shunned society and lived in secret. Certain sects of the Secret Apparatus were suicide sects created for the purpose of jihad. These zealous suicide sects were only sent out on extremely important missions.[85] Members were required to distribute pamphlets in secrecy and had to learn escape tactics such as jumping from three stories above the ground. The final test of the member was to see if he would buy the revolver that he needed to participate in the Special Apparatus with his own money. At this time, the Brothers were buying weapons from dealers in the desert and members of the Apparatus trained with these weapons.

When members of the Secret Apparatus had completed their training, they were instructed to pretend they had given up their membership in the Muslim Brotherhood and were told to join another organization active in religion or politics.[86] The purpose of this action was to absolve the Brotherhood from any act of terrorism. In fact, the members were supposed to corrupt these other organizations internally and take them over from the inside.

Although they had participated in violence in Palestine during war and in Egypt with assassinations, the Muslim Brotherhood only started committing several terrorist attacks in the late 1940s. Why were the declaration of war from al-Banna in 1938 and the actual terrorist attacks in the mid-1940s separated by so many years? The answer is clearly stated by al-Banna in 1938:

> When three hundred such units from amongst you are prepared, which are filled with belief and surety, fully equipped with knowledge and culture and have endured heat in the furnaces of exercise and practice, then demand of me and I will jump into waves of the seas with you. I will smash into the fortress of heaven and will break the paws of every tyrant and arrogant man.[87]

Al-Banna was waiting to build his forces to 300 units in the Secret Apparatus. When his secret terrorist sect was large enough, al-Banna would join them in the jihad to reform Egypt. Although it is difficult to ascertain the numbers, the members of the Secret Apparatus grew to the numbers that al-Banna had been waiting for.

Brothers were suspected in the assassination of Egyptian Prime Minister Ahmad Mahir in February 1945.[88] In 1946, the Brotherhood exploded a bomb at the King George Hotel, where the British Intelligence was stationed. In March 1948, two Brothers killed Judge Ahmad al-Khazindar because he had sentenced a Brother who blew up a British Officer's Club.[89] The Oriental Advertising Company was bombed in November 1948 and the Cairo Chief of Police, Salim Zaki, was assassinated in 1948.[90] On December 28, 1948, 'Abd al-Majid Ahmad Hasan assassinated Egyptian Prime Minister Mahmud Fahmi al-Nuqrashi Pasha.[91] When al-Nuqrashi passed through the Ministry of the Interior, Hasan shot him, putting one bullet in al-Nuqrashi's back and another into his chest when he turned to face Hasan. Hasan had been a member of the Muslim Brotherhood since 1944 and was a third-year veterinary student.[92]

Hasan al-Banna, after expanding the Muslim Brotherhood and recruiting new members, became frustrated when his attempts to reform Egypt were not successful. In response, he formed and trained militant sects of the Muslim Brotherhood. When the formation of these militant sectors again did not incite reform and were still too weak to fight the British and Egyptian armies, al-Banna formed the Secret Apparatus. The creation of the Secret Apparatus was the final execution stage of the Muslim Brotherhood. The Secret Apparatus used terrorist tactics to accomplish the Brotherhood's agenda. "It was terrorism which relieved the feelings of impotence and decay surrounding the organization which had driven members to it [terrorism]."[93]

CONCLUSION

The radicalization of the Muslim Brotherhood was due to three factors that, when combined, explain the use of terrorist tactics in the Brotherhood. The first of these factors was the charismatic leadership of Hasan al-Banna. Al-Banna fulfills the criteria of Weber's charismatic leadership. Al-Banna required obedience from his followers and they complied with his orders when he sanctioned the use of terrorist tactics by the Secret Apparatus. The second factor that led to the use of terrorist tactics was the radicalization of Hasan al-Banna. Al-Banna did not create the Muslim Brotherhood as a terrorist organization. It took several years for al-Banna to use terrorist tactics. The third factor that led to the radicalization of the Muslim Brotherhood was frustration. After the acquaintance and formation stages of the Brotherhood did not create any changes in Egyptian society, frustration grew to astronomical heights, ending in aggression. Al-Banna then consented to the execution stage of the Brotherhood when terrorist tactics would be used by the Secret Apparatus to punish and reform Egyptian society and the Egyptian government. In 1945, the Brotherhood committed its first terrorist attack, and the transformation of a social movement into a terrorist organization was complete.[94]

An area of research that needs examination concerning Muslim social movements is the factors that cause individuals to join these extremist movements and why individuals remained in these organizations after they have pursued terrorism. Some older literature, such as that completed by Eric Hoffer, examines this topic, but many conclusions rely on the personal psychological deficiencies of extremists. Quintan Wiktorowicz has begun some ground-breaking research on this area in his book *Radical Islam Rising*.[95] Wiktorowicz states that individuals are inspired to join radical Islamic movements because there is a cognitive opening that questions previously held beliefs. After this cognitive opening is addressed, the individual seeks to join, in his or her eyes, a legitimate organization that appears to have a scholarly interpretation of Islam. The individual, after joining this religious movement, is then socialized by the organization to participate in radical activities so that he or she may achieve salvation or a free pass to heaven. Consequences of violent action are then considered arbitrary if the passage into heaven is guaranteed. Wiktorowicz's work is solid but more research needs to be completed, especially concerning non-Islamic organizations.

What naturally follows from this research is the creation of possible policy implications. It is evident from this chapter that leadership is highly important in the radicalization of a social movement. If certain leaders are eradicated, this may temporarily incapacitate a radicalized social movement. Cronin[96] addresses this topic, but it would be interesting to see more literature concerning counterterrorism strategies and the number of terrorist attacks that follow. In the case of the Muslim Brotherhood, after Hasan al-Banna was killed, the Brotherhood did not fully recuperate for several years. Although Hasan al-Hudaybi[97] provided moderate leadership directly after al-Banna's death and tried repeatedly to dissolve the Secret Apparatus, he was not successful.[98] Sayyid Qutb was one of the most radical Muslim Brothers who rose to power in the 1950s and 1960s after al-Banna's death. Qutb's era gave the Brotherhood its real reputation as a terrorist organization.[99] However, the recent rise of the Egyptian Muslim Brotherhood to political power after the Arab Spring Revolution calls into question the intentions of the Brotherhood. Will the Egyptian Muslim Brotherhood again resort to violence or terrorism to accomplish their goals, and if so, what does the political future of Egypt look like?

NOTES

1. David J. Jonsson, *Islamic Economics and the Final Jihad: The Muslim Brotherhood to the Leftist/Marxist-Islamic Alliance* (Maitland, FL: Xulon Press, 2006), 433.
2. Ahmed Abdalla, *The Student Movement and National Politics in Egypt, 1923–1973* (London: Al Saqi Books, 1985).
3. Ishak Musa al-Husaini, *The Moslem Brethren, The Greatest of Modern Islamic Movements* (Westport, CT: Hyperion Press, 1981), 14.
4. Abel M. Sabit, *A King Betrayed, The Ill-Fated Reign of Farouk of Egypt* (New York: Quartet Books, 1989).
5. Sabit, *A King Betrayed*, and Bruce B. Lawrence, *Shattering the Myth* (Princeton, NJ: Princeton University Press, 1998).
6. Sabit, *A King Betrayed*, and Richard P. Mitchell, *The Society of the Muslim Brothers* (New York: Oxford University Press, 1969).
7. David J. Jonsson, *Islamic Economics and the Final Jihad: The Muslim Brotherhood to the Leftist/Marxist-Islamic Alliance* (Maitland, FL: Xulon Press, 2006), 433.
8. James Jankowski, *Nasser's Egypt, Arab Nationalism, and the United Arab Republic* (Boulder, CO: Lynne Rienner Publishers, 2002).
9. Dale F. Eickelman and James Piscatori, *Muslim Politics* (Princeton, NJ: Princeton University Press, 1996).

10. James Jankowski, *Nasser's Egypt, Arab Nationalism, and the United Arab Republic* (Boulder, CO: Lynne Rienner Publishers, 2002).

11. David S. Sorenson, *An Introduction to the Modern Middle East* (Boulder, CO: Westview Press, 2008).

12. Michael Haag, *The Timeline History of Egypt* (New York: Barnes and Noble, 2005).

13. Michael Haag, *The Timeline History of Egypt* (New York: Barnes and Noble, 2005).

14. Michael Haag, *The Timeline History of Egypt* (New York: Barnes and Noble, 2005), and Dale F. Eickelman and James Piscatori, *Muslim Politics* (Princeton, NJ: Princeton University Press, 1996).

15. Ishak Musa al-Husaini, *The Moslem Brethren, The Greatest of Modern Islamic Movements* (Westport, CT: Hyperion Press, 1981), 17.

16. Dale Eickelman, *The Middle East and Central Asia*, 4th ed. (Upper Saddle River, NJ: Pearson Education Inc, 2002).

17. Ishak Musa al-Husaini, *The Moslem Brethren, The Greatest of Modern Islamic Movements* (Westport, CT: Hyperion Press, Inc, 1981), 19.

18. David J. Jonsson, *Islamic Economics and the Final Jihad: The Muslim Brotherhood to the Leftist/ Marxist-Islamic Alliance* (Maitland, FL: Xulon Press, 2006).

19. Ishak Musa al-Husaini, *The Moslem Brethren, The Greatest of Modern Islamic Movements* (Westport, CT: Hyperion Press, 1981), 20.

20. Brynjar Lia, *The Society of the Muslim Brothers in Egypt, the Rise of an Islamic Mass Movement 1928–1942* (Reading, UK: Ithaca Press, 1998).

21. Michael Haag, *The Timeline History of Egypt* (New York: Barnes and Noble, 2005).

22. Quintan Wiktorowicz, *The Management of Islamic Activism* (Albany, New York: State University of New York Press, 2001).

23. Eric Larson, *Islamist Opposition and Political Opportunity: The Muslim Brotherhood in Egypt, 1928–1942* (unpublished master's thesis, University of South Carolina, Columbia, SC, 2004).

24. James Jankowski, *Nasser's Egypt, Arab Nationalism, and the United Arab Republic* (Boulder, CO: Lynne Rienner Publishers, 2002).

25. P. J. Vatikiotis, *Nasser and His Generation* (London: Croom Helm, 1978). 92.

26. Ellis Goldberg, "Bases of Traditional Reaction: A Look at the Muslim Brothers," *Mediterranean Peoples* 14 (1981), 79–96, and Brynjar Lia, *The Society of the Muslim Brothers in Egypt, the Rise of an Islamic Mass Movement 1928–1942* (Reading, UK: Ithaca Press, 1998).

27. Ellis Goldberg, "Bases of Traditional Reaction: A Look at the Muslim Brothers," *Mediterranean Peoples* 14 (1981), 80.

28. Brynjar Lia, *The Society of the Muslim Brothers in Egypt, the Rise of an Islamic Mass Movement, 1928–1942* (Reading, UK: Ithaca Press, 1998), 114.

29. Hasan al-Banna, *Memoirs of Hasan al-Banna Shaheed* (M. N. Shaikh, Trans.) (Karachi, Pakistan: International Islamic Publishers, 1981), 141.

30. Hasan al-Banna, *Memoirs of Hasan al-Banna Shaheed* (M. N. Shaikh, Trans.) (Karachi, Pakistan: International Islamic Publishers, 1981), 142.

31. Brynjar Lia, *The Society of the Muslim Brothers in Egypt, the Rise of an Islamic Mass Movement, 1928–1942* (Reading, UK: Ithaca Press, 1998), 117.

32. Zainab al-Ghazali, *Return of the Pharaoh, Memoir in Nasir's Prison* (Mokrane Guezzou, Trans.) (Leicester, UK: The Islamic Foundation, 1994), 26.

33. Zainab al-Ghazali, *Return of the Pharaoh, Memoir in Nasir's Prison* (Mokrane Guezzou, Trans.) (Leicester, UK: The Islamic Foundation, 1994), 27.

34. Afaf Lutfi al-Sayyid-Marsot, *Egypt's Liberal Experiment: 1922–1936* (Berkeley, CA: University of California Press, 1977), 236.

35. Brynjar Lia, *The Society of the Muslim Brothers in Egypt, the Rise of an Islamic Mass Movement, 1928–1942* (Reading, UK: Ithaca Press, 1998), 105.

36. As cited in Brynjar Lia, *The Society of the Muslim Brothers in Egypt, the Rise of an Islamic Mass Movement, 1928–1942* (Reading, UK: Ithaca Press, 1998), 105.

37. As cited in Brynjar Lia, *The Society of the Muslim Brothers in Egypt, the Rise of an Islamic Mass Movement, 1928–1942* (Reading, UK: Ithaca Press, 1998), 98.

38. Hafeez Malik, "Islamic Political Parties and Mass Politicization," *Islam and the Modern Age*, 3 (1972): 26–64.

39. Ishak Musa al-Husaini, *The Moslem Brethren, The Greatest of Modern Islamic Movements* (Westport, CT: Hyperion Press, 1981), 33.

40. Ishak Musa al-Husaini, *The Moslem Brethren, The Greatest of Modern Islamic Movements* (Westport, CT: Hyperion Press, 1981), 34.

41. As cited in Ishak Musa al-Husaini, *The Moslem Brethren, The Greatest of Modern Islamic Movements* (Westport, CT: Hyperion Press, 1981), 34.

42. Tewfik Aclimandos, "Revisiting the History of the Egyptian Army," in Arthur Goldschmidt, Amy Johnson, and Barak Salmoni (eds.), *Re-Envisioning Egypt, 1919–1952* (Cairo: The American University Press in Cairo, 2005), 68–93, 82.

43. Ellis Goldberg, "Bases of Traditional Reaction: A Look at the Muslim Brothers," *Mediterranean Peoples* 14 (1981), and Richard P. Mitchell, *The Society of the Muslim Brothers* (New York: Oxford University Press, 1969).

44. Robert Dreyfuss, *Devil's Game, How the United States Helped Unleash Fundamentalist Islam* (New York: Metropolitan Books, 2005).

45. Hasan al-Banna, *Memoirs of Hasan al-Banna Shaheed* (M. N. Shaikh, Trans.) (Karachi, Pakistan: International Islamic Publishers, 1981), 210.

46. Brynjar Lia, *The Society of the Muslim Brothers in Egypt, the Rise of an Islamic Mass Movement 1928–1942* (Reading, UK: Ithaca Press, 1998), 299.

47. Brynjar Lia, *The Society of the Muslim Brothers in Egypt, the Rise of an Islamic Mass Movement, 1928–1942* (Reading, UK: Ithaca Press, 1998), 119.

48. Hasan al-Banna, *Memoirs of Hasan al-Banna Shaheed* (M. N. Shaikh, Trans.) (Karachi, Pakistan: International Islamic Publishers, 1981), 208.

49. Hasan al-Banna, *Memoirs of Hasan al-Banna Shaheed* (M. N. Shaikh, Trans.) (Karachi, Pakistan: International Islamic Publishers, 1981), 204.

50. Franz Rosenthal, "The 'Muslim Brethren' in Egypt," *The Moslem World* 37 (1947), 278–291.

51. Brynjar Lia, *The Society of the Muslim Brothers in Egypt, the Rise of an Islamic Mass Movement, 1928–1942* (Reading, UK: Ithaca Press, 1998), 118.

52. As cited in Ishak Musa al-Husaini, *The Moslem Brethren, The Greatest of Modern Islamic Movements* (Westport, CT: Hyperion Press, 1981), 36.

53. As cited in Annamarie Edelen, *The Muslim Brotherhood's Quiet Revolution*. Unpublished doctoral dissertation, University of Wisconsin–Madison, 1999, 62.

54. As cited in Abedelaziz A. Ayyad, *The Politics of Reformist Islam Muhummad Abduh and Hasan al-Banna*. Unpublished doctoral dissertation, Georgetown University, Washington, DC, 1987, 41.

55. Abedelaziz A. Ayyad, *The Politics of Reformist Islam Muhummad Abduh and Hasan al-Banna*. Unpublished doctoral dissertation, Georgetown University, Washington, DC, 1987.

56. Hasan al-Banna, *Memoirs of Hasan al-Banna Shaheed* (M. N. Shaikh, Trans.) (Karachi, Pakistan: International Islamic Publishers, 1981), 33.

57. Hasan al-Banna, *Between Yesterday and Today* (Charles Wendell, Trans.) (Berkeley, CA: University of California Press, 1978), 31–33.

58. Hasan al-Banna, *Between Yesterday and Today* (Charles Wendell, Trans.) (Berkeley, CA: University of California Press, 1978), 31–33, 33.

59. Hasan al-Banna, *Between Yesterday and Today* (Charles Wendell, Trans.) (Berkeley, CA: University of California Press, 1978), 31–33, 34.

60. Hasan al-Banna, *Basic Teachings* (S.A. Qureshi, Trans.) (Karachi, Pakistan: International Islamic Publishers, 1983), 11.

61. Hasan al-Banna, *Memoirs of Hasan al-Banna Shaheed* (M. N. Shaikh, Trans.) (Karachi, Pakistan: International Islamic Publishers, 1981), 62, 32.

62. Hasan al-Banna, *The Concept of Allah in the Islamic Creed* (Sharif Ahmad Khan, Trans.) (Dehli, India: Adam Publishers and Distributors, 2000), 78.

63. Hasan al-Banna, *Basic Teachings* (S.A. Qureshi, Trans.) (Karachi, Pakistan: International Islamic Publishers, 1983), 33.

64. John Dollard, Neal E. Miller, Leonard W. Doob, O. H. Mowrer, and Robert R. Sears, *Frustration and Aggression* (New Haven, CT: Yale University Press, 1939).

65. As cited in Brynjar Lia, *The Society of the Muslim Brothers in Egypt, the Rise of an Islamic Mass Movement, 1928–1942* (Reading, UK: Ithaca Press, 1998), 172.

66. Ishak Musa al-Husaini, *The Moslem Brethren, The Greatest of Modern Islamic Movements* (Westport, CT: Hyperion Press, 1981).

67. Ishak Musa al-Husaini, *The Moslem Brethren, The Greatest of Modern Islamic Movements* (Westport, CT: Hyperion Press, 1981), 49.

68. Ishak Musa al-Husaini, *The Moslem Brethren, The Greatest of Modern Islamic Movements* (Westport, CT: Hyperion Press, 1981), 49.

69. Hasan al-Banna, *Memoirs of Hasan al-Banna Shaheed* (M. N. Shaikh, Trans.) (Karachi, Pakistan: International Islamic Publishers, 1981), 45.

70. Ahmed Abdalla, *The Student Movement and National Politics in Egypt, 1923–1973* (London: Al Saqi Books, 1985).

71. As cited in Brynjar Lia, *The Society of the Muslim Brothers in Egypt, the Rise of an Islamic Mass Movement, 1928–1942* (Reading, UK: Ithaca Press, 1998), 106.

72. Abd Al-Fattah Muhummad El-Awaisi, *The Muslim Brothers and the Palestine Question, 1928–1947* (London: Tarris Academic Studies, 1998).

73. Tewfik Aclimandos, "Revisiting the History of the Egyptian Army," in Arthur Goldschmidt, Amy Johnson, and Barak Salmoni (eds.), *Re-Envisioning Egypt, 1919–1952* (Cairo: The American University Press in Cairo, 2005), 68–93.

74. Brynjar Lia, *The Society of the Muslim Brothers in Egypt, the Rise of an Islamic Mass Movement, 1928–1942* (Reading, UK: Ithaca Press, 1998), 172.

75. Brynjar Lia, *The Society of the Muslim Brothers in Egypt, the Rise of an Islamic Mass Movement, 1928–1942* (Reading, UK: Ithaca Press, 1998), 173.

76. Karen Armstrong, *The Battle for God* (New York: Ballantine Books, 2000).

77. Hasan al-Banna, *Fifth Conference in (10 Years–1347–1357 Hijra)* (S.A. Qureshi, Trans.) (Karachi, Pakistan: International Islamic Publishers, 1983), 169.

78. Hasan al-Banna, *Fifth Conference in (10 Years–1347–1357 Hijra)* (S.A. Qureshi, Trans.) (Karachi, Pakistan: International Islamic Publishers, 1983), 182.

79. Hasan al-Banna, *Fifth Conference in (10 Years–1347–1357 Hijra)* (S.A. Qureshi, Trans.) (Karachi, Pakistan: International Islamic Publishers, 1983), 251.

80. Hasan al-Banna, *Memoirs of Hasan al-Banna Shaheed* (M. N. Shaikh, Trans.) (Karachi, Pakistan: International Islamic Publishers, 1981), 56–57.

81. Abd Al-Fattah Muhummad El-Awaisi, *The Muslim Brothers and the Palestine Question 1928–1947* (London: Tarris Academic Studies, 1998), 112.

82. As cited in Manfred Halpern, *The Politics of Social Change in the Middle East and North Africa* (Princeton: Princeton University Press, 1963), 141.

83. Manfred Halpern, *The Politics of Social Change in the Middle East and North Africa* (Princeton: Princeton University Press, 1963), 142.

84. Nachman Tal, *Radical Islam in Egypt and Jordan* (Brighton: Sussex Academic Press, 2005).

85. Nachman Tal, *Radical Islam in Egypt and Jordan* (Brighton: Sussex Academic Press, 2005).

86. Zvi Kaplinsky, "The Muslim Brotherhood," *Middle Eastern Affairs*, (December 1954), 377–385.

87. Hasan al-Banna, *Fifth Conference in (10 Years–1347–1357 Hijra)* (S.A. Qureshi, Trans.) (Karachi, Pakistan: International Islamic Publishers, 1983), 185.

88. Hafeez Malik, "Islamic Political Parties and Mass Politicization," *Islam and the Modern Age* 3 (1972): 26–64.

89. Donald M. Reid, "Political Assassination in Egypt, 1910–1954," *The International Journal of African Historical Studies* 15, vol. 4 (1982): 625–651.

90. Nachman Tal, *Radical Islam in Egypt and Jordan* (Brighton: Sussex Academic Press, 2005).

91. Manfred Halpern, *The Politics of Social Change in the Middle East and North Africa* (Princeton: Princeton University Press, 1963).

92. John Heyworth-Dunne, *Religious and Political Trends in Modern Egypt* (Washington: privately printed, 1950).

93. Ellis Goldberg, "Bases of Traditional Reaction: A Look at the Muslim Brothers," *Mediterranean Peoples* 14, (1981), 79–96, 90.

94. Abedelaziz A. Ayyad, *The Politics of Reformist Islam Muhummad Abduh and Hasan al-Banna*. Unpublished doctoral dissertation, Georgetown University, Washington, DC, 1987.

95. Quintan Wiktorowicz, *Radical Islam Rising, Muslim Extremism in the West* (Lanham, MD: Rowman and Littlefield Publishers, 2005).

96. Audrey Kurth Cronin, *How Terrorism Ends Understanding the Decline and Demise of Terrorist Campaigns* (Princeton: Princeton University Press, 2009).

97. Barbara H. E. Zollner, *The Muslim Brotherhood, Hasan al-Hudaybi and Ideology* (New York: Routledge, 2009).

98. Sayyid Qutb, *Milestones* (revised translation) (Indianapolis, IN: American Trust Publications, 1993) (original work published 1964).

99. Sayed Khatab, *The Power of Sovereignty, The Political and Ideological Philosophy of Sayyid Qutb* (New York: Routledge, 2006).

Chapter Two

Radicalizing Ekin

The Creation of Euzkadi ta Askatasuna (ETA)

"Frustration and above all, an intense hate. These are the two emotions that are most frequently found within those who have joined the ETA."[1] The predecessor to Euzkadi ta Askatasuna (ETA), Ekin, formed in Spain in 1952. Ekin was a social movement that wanted independence in the form of a Basque nation composed of territory in both France and Spain. Chapter 2 identifies what caused the radicalization of Ekin and the formation of ETA. Most importantly, the chapter further explains the takeover of ETA by radicals within the movement. Ekin was not founded on violence and ETA was hijacked by violent terrorists a few years after its inception. This chapter explains what caused the radicalization of Ekin and the formation of the terrorist group ETA.

THE HISTORY OF RELATIONS BETWEEN THE SPANISH GOVERNMENT AND ETA

Many scholars that are considered experts on ETA have blamed the state for the radicalization of Ekin or the formation of ETA. These scholars have looked at Franco and his dictatorship as the main reasons that Ekin was forced to resort to terrorism or become ETA. This section of the chapter goes against the grain of most contemporary scholarship concerning the Basque separatists. It is an attempt to offer an explanation as to why the Spanish Government is not the singular cause of Ekin's radicalization, as most Basque scholars have argued. This is not to say that Franco was not a cruel

53

dictator but to explain the causes of the radicalization of Ekin in an alternative manner.

After the civil war, Spain was still reeling from the effects of war. Insurgencies were still widespread. In 1947, the Decree-Law for Repression of Banditry and Terrorism was declared. This law constituted Franco's response to insurgency before 1960.

The Decree-Law on Banditry and Terrorism stated:

> "Crimes of military rebellion": the dissemination of false or tendentious information in order to cause disturbances in public order, international conflicts, or a decline in the prestige of the State, its institutions, the government, the army, of the authorities: the joining, conspiring or taking part in meetings, conferences, or demonstrations, intended to accomplish any of the above goals; strikes, sabotage, or any analogous act which has a political objective, or which causes serious disturbance of public order.
>
> "Terrorism": attacks against public security, terrorizing the inhabitants of a particular location, revenge or reprisals of a political or social character, or disturbing tranquility, order, or public services; causing explosions, fires, sinking of naval vessels, derailment of trains, interruption of communications, landslides, floods, or the employment of any other means or artifacts that can cause great damage; the deposit of arms and munitions, the possession of explosive apparatuses or substances, flammable items, or other lethal devices; the manufacture transport, or supply of any such items; the mere placing of any such substances or artifacts (even if they fail to explode or otherwise malfunction).
>
> "Armed attack and kidnapping": armed robbery, with or without any intention to employ the weapons to threaten or to harm the victims; the assault of any industrial or commercial establishment, or any person charged with the custody or transportation or any valuable items, or the holding captive of any such person; kidnapping.
>
> "Banditry": living in, or otherwise forming, groups of armed persons whose intent is to engage in banditry or social subversion; any act designed to take advantage of the fear of the disorder caused by any of the above proscribed acts, by threatening harm, or by exacting retribution in the form of money, jewels, of any other kind of goods, or by compelling any person to engage in any activity or to desist from any activity. [2]

The penalties for the crimes listed above were severe. A military court tried the accused. The death penalty was prescribed if any of those offenses resulted in the death of a person. Armed attack, kidnapping, or terrorism brought life terms. Military rebellion and banditry were given somewhat lesser prison sentences. [3] These judicial laws were instituted at least one year before ETA committed its first terrorist attack in 1961. ETA was aware of the penalties it would face for committing a terrorist attack.

Almost every scholar who writes about the Basques talks about their oppression by the Spanish government as their reason for using terrorist tactics.[4] Problematically, this oppression is only adequately explained because, in reality, scholars likely exaggerated the extent of the oppression since there is very little evidence to support this claim. Basques were not treated differently by Franco more than any other group of people, at least not on a national level.

Conversi's account of Basque repression by the Spanish government is the most complete that has been found. He states:

> From 1939 to 1945, the Basque country was subjected to a regime of state terror with no parallel in its history. Once they had occupied the Basque Provinces, Franco's troops initiated a campaign against any sign of Basque identity. Even innocuous aspects of popular culture, such as dance and music, were subjected to suspicion, inquiry, and proscription. A sketchy picture of this repression, which paralleled the Catalan one, is included in a message to UNESCO written in 1952 by José Antonio Aguirre (1904–60), then president of the Basque government in-exile. He denounced the following: closure of the Basque university; occupation by armed force of social and cultural associations; mass burning of books in Euskera; elimination of all use of Euskera in schools, on radio broadcasts, in public gatherings and in publications; suppression of Basque cultural societies and of all magazines, periodicals, and reviews in Euskera; prohibition of the use of Euskera during the celebration of Mass and other religious ceremonies; a decree requiring the translation into Spanish of all Basque names in civil registries and official documents; an official directive mandating the removal of inscriptions in Euskera from all tombstones and funeral markers.[5]

Conversi's claim is based on Clark's[6] explanation of Basque oppression, which is insubstantial to state the least and is based on Beltza's[7] inclusion of a letter from Aguirre, the president of the PNV (the Basque national political party). Ortzi,[8] a Basque scholar, also talks about Basque oppression and bases his argument of Basque oppression on a letter published by the PNV in 1960, not any historical law or evidence.

The basis of Basque oppression seems to stem from the prohibition of Euskera, the Basque language. However, other scholars state that there was never any real attempt made by Franco to prevent Basques from speaking Euskera and their observations are based on historical documents as opposed to personal letters. Sullivan states, "Contrary to the claim made by some nationalists, there was never any serious attempt to prohibit the use of spoken Basque."[9] There were a few isolated incidents where Euskera was forbidden but this did not include the entire Euskadi country. Sullivan found that the military governor of San Sebastián issued an order prohibiting the use of Euskera. In 1947, the Minister of Education stated that Euskera should not be used in the women's section of a Catholic bulletin.[10] Until 1976, use of Basque names at baptism or on gravestones was prohibited.[11] Clark adds,

"By the early 1950's the ability of Madrid to suppress the use of Euskera was beginning to erode."[12]

These few instances have been found relating to Basque oppression. The author has not found any evidence of Basques being physically hurt or reprimanded for using Euskera. Even Aguirre's letter does not talk about physical harm being done to the Basques. The Spanish government did not prohibit the use of Euskera throughout Basque country. The historical evidence of Basque oppression by the Francoist government is not substantial, although it has constantly been provided as the reason for the creation of Ekin and the radicalization of ETA.

There are several reasons as to why Basque was spoken regardless of these isolated local government policies. The first of these reasons is that many Basques, especially older generations, could not speak Spanish and certainly did not go to school to learn Spanish. These Basques had large farms to care for and were not inclined to learn another language in their spare time, if they had any.[13]

Another reason Euskera continued to be spoken in Basque country regardless of government interference was because the Catholic Church only sent priests fluent in Euskera to serve Basque parishes. At this time, Mass was performed in Latin until Vatican II in 1963.[14] These priests had to be fluent in Euskera because most Basques spoke Euskera in public and in church. Basques would reject any priest that could not speak to them in their native tongue. In addition, the Catholic Church helped to create Ikastolas in the early 1950s, which were schools that taught Euskera. These schools ceased to be clandestine in the late 1950s. In the 1960s, 75 percent of the people that wrote in Euskera were priests.[15] It is difficult to believe that usage of Euskera by both the Church and Basque people would be so blatant if the use of Euskera was truly outlawed.

In addition, Euskera was considered by extremists in the mid-twentieth century to be the defining characteristic of a Basque. Although most Basques supposedly have similar facial features, blood types, etc., the spoken use of Euskera was what made a person Basque, according to many ETA members. In fact, Basques are so attached to their language that they run marathons across Basque country for the sake of raising money to teach Euskera. These marathons have been in existence for several decades.[16] If Basques were not speaking Euskera, then the language would die. The oldest European civilization would probably not acquiesce to any government law that prevented Basques from speaking their language.[17]

Aside from the language issues, it does not appear that the Spanish attacked Basques any more than the Basques, in general, attacked the Spanish. Most of Basque and Spanish history appears to have been a cycle of tit for tat. Some Basques fought against Franco in the civil war. When Franco came into power after the Spanish Civil War, he punished those who fought against him, Basque or any other ethnicity. ETA began their violent activities before they were ever arrested or attacked by the Spanish police. ETA stated that they would use violence before they committed their first terrorist attack. Franco later instituted laws concerning terrorism one year before ETA committed its first terrorist attack. These laws clearly outlined the penalties for the crime of terrorism.

ETA's methodology for gaining independence was to use a strategy called action-repression-action spiral, which will be discussed in depth later in the chapter. ETA would provoke the government into attacking the Basque population by using terrorism. The Spanish government would then attack people in a retaliation cycle with ETA until the latent public rose up against the state. Then a revolution would begin.

It is true that Franco was extremely oppressive toward the Spanish people, but there is not much evidence that states Franco singled out Basques for oppression. Basque scholar Cameron Watson believes that Franco's treatment of the Basques was more symbolic violence than actual violence and that the Basque culture had accepted "resigned defeat" during Franco's regime.[18] Torture was used extensively in Spanish prisons on all races, not just Basques. This is not to excuse the act of torture but to state explicitly that Basques were not the only ones that were tortured. Franco idolized Adolf Hitler and believed in theories of racial supremacy. Basques and other races, in his opinion, were inferior. It is also important to remember that ETA specifically attacked members of Spanish police. Spanish police were the people that were torturing ETA members. It is understandable, although not excusable, that the police would want revenge for their lost brothers in arms.

Most importantly, ETA was not specifically fighting Franco's regime but was fighting Spain. In fact, Juan José Etxabe, a major leader, stated, "We are not anti-Franco, we are anti-Spanish."[19] Franco's dictatorship was difficult for every Spaniard, not just Basques. It is for the former reasons that have been mentioned that it is not likely that the Spanish government was responsible for the radicalization of Euzkadi ta Askatasuna (ETA).

Lastly, da Silva adds that Spanish Basques have had more autonomy than French Basques throughout history. Since 1789, the French Basques had been experiencing the same type of treatment from the French government that Spanish Basques endured from Franco. Franco came to power in the early 1940s. Da Silva states, "It would indeed be difficult to attribute the rise of Basque nationalism simply to the lack of democratic freedoms or to political oppression."[20] French Basques have been experiencing more political oppression than Spanish Basques for hundreds of years, and yet Basques in France have not turned to terrorism. A few French Basques have joined the Spanish ETA but this number is relatively small. There does not seem to be much of a case for Basque oppression caused by the Francoist regime.

Chapter 2

Wieviorka states, "ETA violence is primarily the result of the increasingly difficult task of simultaneously speaking in the name of the suppressed nation, social movements, and the revolution. It is aggravated by the fact that the meanings of each of these three components have themselves become diminished or deconstructed."[21] ETA originally had three purposes: to speak for the suppressed Basque nation, to sustain their own social movement with its political agenda, and to create a revolution. Over the years, the fundamental three purposes have become somewhat cloudy. Wieviorka states that ETA long ago lost its original purpose for committing terrorism. Zulaika and Douglass agree with Wieviorka's assessment of ETA.[22] This chapter will now proceed with the discussion as to why ETA turned to terrorism.

FUNDAMENTAL FOUNDING LEADERSHIP

One may question whether a student group such as Ekin, which later became ETA, can be classified as a social movement. Rucht writes that social movements consist of two components: "(1) networks of groups and organizations prepared to mobilize for protest actions to promote (or resist) social change (which is the ultimate goal of social movements); and (2) individuals who attend protest activities or contribute resources without necessarily being attached to movement groups or organizations."[23] Therefore, using Rucht's definition, social movements are groups of people that come together to agitate for social change.

There were several peaceful reasons for the creation of Ekin. Ekin was created to help mobilize Basque people to learn their own language because the use of Euskera was rapidly declining. The use of Euskera was the defining characteristic of a Basque for members of Ekin. Ekin also promoted pride in Basque culture and history by writing and disseminating literature. In addition, Ekin wanted to restore the independent Basque Republic. Ekin attended Basque events and protested. At times, Ekin protested silently through writing graffiti and other kinds of secret dissent for fear of Franco's retaliation. They protested the Spanish government and fought for social change for betterment of Basque people. It is evident that Ekin can be classified as a social movement because it promoted social change, the betterment of Basque people in Spanish society.

Ekin was created in 1952 by a group of approximately seven to thirteen young male students (the exact number differs according to founding ETA members) from a few universities (mostly Duesto University).[24] Most of these men were from upper-middle-class Spanish-speaking families. What bound these men together was a need to understand and perpetuate Basque culture and its language. Founding members of Ekin include José Luis Álvarez Emparanza (Txillardegui), Julen Madariaga, Benito del Valle, Alfonso Irigoyen, Joseba Elosegui, Gortiz, Gurutze Ansola, José Manuel Aguirre, Padre Rafa Albizu, Iñaki Larramendi, Sabino Uribe, Javier Bareño, and Iñaki Gainzarain.[25]

At first, Ekin meetings were rather benign; members would study a particular component of Basque history and would then share their research with the rest of the group. As Waldmann states, "In the early phase (1952–1956) they were a group that foremost was dedicated to the study of the language [Euskera], Basque history and the traditions and customs of Basque heritage."[26] Some of the founding members had spent time in other Basque student organizations so the need to do "something" to help save the Basque culture was already present. Julen Madariaga, a founder of ETA and Ekin, remembered the creation of Ekin in an interview. He stated:

> Little by little, we were put in contact—Txillardegi, Benito del Valle, Gortiz, Ansola, J.M. Aguirre, Albizu, etc.—the beginning embryo of Ekin—it's funny—we consisted of weekly reunions where we talked about literature, philosophy, and other topics.[27]

Madariaga states that members of Ekin were put into contact slowly through classes and that scholarly meetings were the original purpose of Ekin.

José Luis Álvarez Emparanza, another founding member (also known as Txillardegi or Txillardegui depending on whether one is using Spanish or Euskera) remembered founding members stating:

> At the moment when Ekin was born, we only counted two cells—one in Bilbao, formed by Benito del Valle, Alfonso Irigoyen, Iñaki Gainzarain, Julen Madariaga and José Manuel Aguirre, and another in Donostia, that we formed partly from Rafa Albisu, Iñaki Larramendi and I—in 1954, a strong path towards realization began developed, understood through short courses. These short courses contained various topics. The person that directed discussion would base their discussion on the themes from the first folder.[28]

From the previous two quotes from Txillardegui and Madariaga, both founders of ETA, it can be seen that Ekin was created for social and political purposes. Ekin wanted to help preserve and save Basque culture. Violence was not part of the original purpose of Ekin.

However, as time progressed Ekin began to radicalize. Txillardegui explains that Ekin later progressed toward a violent path as folders were given to those members who agreed with using violence. Txillardegui states:

> The groups in this first phase were composed of six or seven people who were considered sympathizers, those which passed through primary selection, received a second folder—exclusively for militants, with two new topics: "Ethics of resistance, patriotic ethics" and "Rules of Security."[29]

Only those members that were considered the most loyal and sympathetic to the Basque cause were given folders that began to prepare members of Ekin for military training. Txillardegui states in other literature that he was a proponent of the radicalization of Ekin from a social movement to a social movement that trained militants. Madariaga also explains that Ekin progressed toward violence "Later things became concrete and I arrived at a moment of objective maturity—if not all [members of Ekin], some were there—we began to state that we could not continue in a state of prostration before our people."[30]

It is important to state at this point in the chapter that Ekin was not created for violence, but instead continued to radicalize as time moved on. What initially drew Ekin members together was the need to do something, anything more than what they had been doing. Ekin members were required to take an oath swearing not to tell anyone about the existence of the group.[31] The liberal atmosphere and student networks in Spanish universities provided the environment for an organization that later chose to accomplish its goals through violence. At time progressed, the leaders believed that something more needed to be done to accomplish self-determination for the Basque people. Scholarly meetings and protests were not enough to accomplish the goals of Ekin. To be clear, Ekin's successor, ETA, was created in 1959 for the purpose of violence, although terrorism was not chosen by everyone within Ekin at this time. The group progresses from conversational meetings to short courses where students studied violence. Ekin was born in 1952 and by the late 1950s, Ekin already had cells that were being trained for militant action.

Many of those members that founded Ekin were responsible for the first acts of violence that ETA committed. These people were part of the Executive Committee of ETA. The first Executive Committee was formed in either 1959 or 1960 from core members of Ekin: Julen de Madariaga, Benito del Valle, José Luis Álvarez Emparanza (also known as Txillardegui), Ignacio Irigaray, and Barrenño Omaechevarría.[32]

These men were either professionals or students. The Executive Committee consisted of Basques who held upper-middle-class jobs. Madariaga was a lawyer who taught maritime law at major English-speaking universities in Spain. José María Benito del Valle, Ignacio Irigaray, and José Luis Álvarez Emparanza were engineers. Lastly, Barreño Omaechevarría was an administrator. These four ordinary Basque men were responsible for planning ETA's first terrorist attack. However, these men were not as radical as the members of ETA that would later execute many large-scale violent attacks.

On July 18, 1961, ETA derailed several trains carrying supporters to San Sebastián to celebrate Franco's war victory. According to ETA's own publications, the small-scale attack had been ordered by the Highest Director of ETA, Txillardegui, and planned by the Executive committee.[33] However, no one was hurt because members had tried to take precautions to kill as few people as possible. Spanish authorities were quick to round up over 100 members. Some ETA members were sentenced to as many as twenty years in prison. However, some of the founding members, Txillardegui, Madariaga, Benito del Valle, Irigaray, and Elosegui, had just completed a short jail sentence in France for inciting rebellion and got out the same day the train was derailed. They stayed in France in exile while other members that carried out the attack were arrested and placed in jail.[34]

In 1962, the Executive Committee, consisting of founding members, issued a statement: "ETA is a clandestine organization whose only objective is to obtain as rapidly as possible and using all means possible—including violence—independence of Euzkadi."[35] In 1962, ETA confirmed that it was a terrorist organization or an organization that would use violence to accomplish its political agenda. This transition took less than ten years to occur; Ekin transformed from a harmless social movement to a terrorist organization.

Below in figure 2.1, the hierarchy of ETA is shown. This diagram differs little from the initial structure of ETA in the early 1960s. It appears that one man is in charge of ETA but the diagram is ambiguous in it actual representation of ETA. As one can see, power within ETA was divided among different positions that were in charge of certain aspects of the organization. Power was shared among seven members of the Executive Committee, which includes responsibilities for various offices. The Highest Director, or Máximo Dirigente, however, did not have absolute power and was more of a public figurehead for the organization. ETA elected the Highest Director in its national assemblies and was in this sense a democratic organization.

The main reason that ETA's power was shared among the Executive Committee as opposed to lying in the hands of the Highest Director was because the group was scattered throughout Basque land. This structure increased security of the organization because any one person from the Executive Committee was capable of running the organization if the Highest Director was killed or captured. It is more difficult to destroy an organization if power is shared among several members living all over the country and even in other countries. In addition, the power was shared among several members because several men created the organization. No one person embodied or represented the organization.

When the leaders wrote letters or published documents, they used the words "we" or "us." Rarely was the word "I" used to describe the actions of leadership. The Executive Committee in the first years of ETA consisted mostly of the founding members. Madariaga was responsible for the Political Branch. Benito del Valle was responsible for the Economic Branch. Imaz Garay, who was not a founding member of ETA, was in charge of the Military Branch. Txillardegui was in charge of the Cultural Branch. As stated

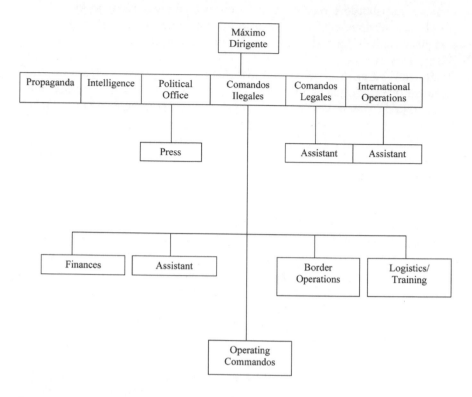

Figure 2.1.   The Hierarchy of ETA in 1981. Source: Clark, *The Basque Insurgents ETA, 1952–1980,* **213.**

previously, Emparanza was the Highest Director.[36] ETA published several items stating that it was bent on pursuing violence, although at this time it appears that violence was not the only perceived vehicle through which to secure Basque independence.

The importance of the initial leadership in the radicalization of Ekin into ETA is important because many of these men from the same group of students that established Ekin were the same group of young professionals that advocated the first use of terrorism in ETA in 1961. It is clear that these men radicalized throughout time. Txillardegui ordered the first attack and the Executive Committee helped to plan it according to ETA's personal publications. Without the leadership of these six or seven students, the social movement Ekin would not have radicalized into the terrorist organization ETA. By their own admissions, these men chose violence. The founding leaders personally transformed Ekin, the social movement, into ETA, a terrorist organization.[37]

José María Portell was a journalist from Bilbao who had close ties with ETA. As a side note, ETA later assassinated Portell in 1978. In his book, Portell asks, "Who were the initiators of the most violent Spanish clandestine movement in the last thirty years?" He answers his own question, stating that Julián de Madariaga, José María Benito de Valle, Ignacio Irigaray, José Luis Álvarez Emparanza (Txillardegui), and Barreño Omaechevarría were the initiators of ETA violence.[38] Portell's conclusions were that the four members of Ekin—Julián de Madariaga, José María Benito de Valle, Ignacio Irigaray, and José Luis Álvarez Emparanza—were the masterminds behind initial ETA terrorism and were the founders of ETA. The other man Portell remembers, Barreño Omaechevarría, is rarely, if ever, mentioned in ETA history. Although other members of ETA, such as Luis Zabilde, later carry on and expand the terrorist strategy, the founders first used terrorism in 1961, thus making ETA a terrorist organization.

EKIN, EGI, AND ETA: THE ESCALATION OF FRUSTRATION

Several issues caused frustration for members of Ekin throughout its existence from 1952 to 1959. The Basques had hoped after World War II that Western powers would intervene to expel fascist Franco from Spain. "There was—at least from the Basque perspective—an implicit agreement between the Basques and the Allies during the war, whereby the Basques supplied intelligence and espionage services as well as combat troops, and the Allies agreed to intervene against Franco once the war was over."[39] This was an understanding, according to the Basques, between the PNV (Basque political party) and American representatives known as the "Umbe Pact."

The Basques did several things either to attract attention for their nationalist cause, or to appease the Americans. PNV gathered information concerning Franco for the CIA. In 1947, Basque resistance and union members launched a seven-day strike against Franco's government. The strike was brought to an end by President José Antonio de Aguirre's (President of the Basque Republic) when it was not effective. The Basque government even expelled suspected communists from President Aguirre's Cabinet in 1948 when the Americans asked them to expel communists. Another workers' strike was launched against Franco in March 1951. "In fact, before long the 1951 strike would be seen as the 'last shot' to be fired by the [Basque] resistance."[40] Aguirre even went to the State Department in 1952 to plead for assistance from the United States. In 1956, Aguirre held a World Basque Congress in Paris, which would have some 363 attendees, although to no avail.

Franco signed a treaty with the Americans in Madrid in 1953. Spain would receive foreign aid if the United States could build some military bases in Spain. In addition, the Americans would recognize Franco's government. Basques had hoped that Americans would eventually overthrow the dictatorship and create a democratic Spain. A democratic Spain would be more likely to allow the secession of an independent Basque nation. Since the end of World War II, Franco had been ostracized by democratic nations. Unfortunately, Basques were stuck with Franco for at least two more decades. Txillardegui, a founder of Ekin and ETA, stated, "The American desertion had been the end of hope that had been built for many years and it was evident that they [Basques] were passing through a crisis."[41] The "last shot," or second strike that was launched in 1951, was closely followed by the formation of Ekin in 1952.

United States support of Franco's regime was a crushing blow to dreams of Basque nationalism and a serious testimony to the ineffectiveness of PNV. The whole ordeal was incredibly frustrating to Ekin. At this point, violence was not a realistic possibility for members of Ekin; they were still seeking Basque independence through political solutions. "The leadership of Ekin was more prone to follow Arana's[42] (a founder of Basque nationalism) mandate of passive resistance at a time when echoes of Gandhism were still in evidence."[43] Gandhi had won Indian independence from the British using a pacifist stance. However, Gandhi had peacefully faced the British, whereas Basques were facing a dictatorship after a civil war and a world war.

Ekin had created militant sectors but they were not yet physically trained to use violence nor did they have the weaponry they needed. They also did not have money to buy weapons at this point. Ekin had distributed folders to members concerning how to use violence but actual physical training did not come until later. In addition, Ekin had not reached a group consensus to use violence. Some wanted to pursue a political means of Basque separatism while others wanted to use violence to accomplish Basque separatism. Violence did not become the unanimous strategy until many moderate members later left ETA. The student leaders had envisioned violence as a possibility but the entire organization was still unsure as to whether violence was the correct path. Most likely, Ekin would not have engaged in violence yet if it had the resources; there were still other options besides violence during this period.

In 1956, Ekin joined the youth group of PNV, the Basque nationalist political party. Ekin had been created to make waves in a stagnant political situation. PNV had held a monopoly over Basque politics since its creation in the late 1800s. If someone wanted to do something, he or she would approach PNV or join the party. Instead of challenging PNV, Ekin joined the youth movement of PNV, the Euzko Gaztedi (EGI), to help PNV accomplish its agenda.

José Antonio Extebarrieta, an early ETA member, states that Ekin joined PNV for the following reasons:

1. From childhood, nationalism, PNV, Paris government, etc., represented to us nearly the same thing.
2. PNV had not taken any interest in us; we were practically unknown to them.
3. The strength of PNV was apparent in those days and given that we would like to create an organization that included all Basque nationalists, we would begin through PNV.[44]

By the 1950s, many Basques had given up on the formation of an independent Euzkadi, if they ever supported it and were financially benefiting from Franco's regime. Why would PNV create conflict with the Spanish state when Basque people were profiting from Franco? In addition, the members of PNV knew that an independent Basque nation could not successfully survive. PNV believed Basques had very little land and not enough economical resources to become an independent country. Basques' lives were improving under Franco's regime.[45] PNV represented the dominant views of Basque people.

After Ekin joined EGI, it soon realized that PNV, like the majority of Basques, was insistent upon not creating problems for Franco. Frustration continued to grow. Members of Ekin wanted to vent "frustration at the inability or willingness of the PNV to wage a more active campaign against Spanish domination."[46] PNV was stingy in its distribution of money to EGI and was controlling. The EGI was thought of as more of a young social group than a political action group by the PNV. There was tremendous suspicion between EGI and PNV. The PNV became very disturbed by Federico Krutwig's speech in which he advocated violence to help create an independent Basqueland. In addition, Madariaga and Benito de Valle had tried to begin a small clandestine group that would plant bombs and throw firecrackers. The PNV wanted nothing to do with violence. One regional branch of the PNV proposed the expulsion of Benito de Valle. Before de Valle could be reinstated, it was requested that he publicly recognize the hegemony of the PNV as the supreme Basque party. EGI refused to have de Valle apologize. In the end, EGI was forced to go back to its former efforts, although the lack of closure left large wedges within the group. Those who agreed with the use of violence supported Ekin while the peaceful members supported the PNV. Ekin then broke from EGI in 1959 once they realized that PNV would not change its strategy.[47] Ekin members were forced again to find another strategy to complete their agenda of achieving Basque rights and independence.

Violence became much more attractive for former Ekin members. "The new group had concluded that the PNV had become ossified in its approach. Consequently, it decided to adopt a more radical and dramatic course of action."[48] An expert ETA historian, Robert P. Clark believes that future ETA members tried other options first, and turned to violence only when other options appeared to be futile. [49] The future ETA members were most of the former Ekin members. Ekin left PNV with most, if not all, of their original members.

The formation of ETA on July 31, 1959, coincided with the anniversary of the formation of the PNV. ETA conceived the idea that members would use terrorism in the Basque nationalist struggle. ETA members soon realized, after having encountered many latent Basques, that violence was the only means to get their agenda accomplished. Frustration had grown to the point that political processes would no longer serve their purposes. [50] ETA was formed to commit terrorist acts.

One ETA member replied:

> Why ETA and not EGI, say, since that could be considered one of the options? Because I felt you had to do something more, if you know what I mean. To do something more than all that folklore, what simply wasn't getting done in those days. The way I saw it, the PNV, EGI were doing absolutely nothing. That is, they were well organized and all, but there wasn't any . . . any task they were carrying out. And those other guys, well, at least they were pretty dynamic, you know? When you're young, it's easier to get hooked by something dynamic, something along those lines right? [51]

In a document from the 1970s that was written by an ETA member, the purpose of the formation of ETA is made clear:

> After a period of formation and study [1959–1961], there is an intent to shake the traditional parties from their drowsiness . . . signifying the obligation for immediate action, clearly understood by those members in the ETA. There is little internal doubt that some violence is necessary. The ETA, while on the terrorist path realized that the working class must also be included in the struggle for Basque independence. [52]

After their first terrorist attack in 1961 and Franco's debilitating response, ETA grew more vocal even while it was underground. In November 1961, after the first attack, ETA issued a statement stating:

> ETA has chosen the path that they should choose, the path of resistance until the end. All Basques know that the moment had already arrived when the ETA must be classified as heroes or traitors. We are destroying that which has destroyed. Neither the situation of the Basques nor the secret martyrdom of our prisons will permit any other alternative. [53]

ETA then had to rebuild. "In the short run, their efforts would have to be devoted to consolidating their position, to recruiting trusted members, to flushing out the spies and informers that had infiltrated the movement, and to acquiring weapons and training members in their use." [54] An issue of *Zutik*,

ETA's newsletter, in 1961, stated, "Violence is necessary—a contagious, destructive violence that supports our struggle, a good struggle, one that the Israelis, Congolese, and Algerians have taught us."[55]

In summary, frustration was present during the lifespan of Ekin and continued to rise until ETA was formed. The United States would not come to the rescue of Basque nationalists to help them create a democratic Spain nor an independent Euzkadi. The PNV would not do anything even when Ekin joined it to try to create some political action because Basques were proliferating under Franco and were not interested in fighting for an independent Basqueland. Things were getting better for Basque people but not for ETA because Basques did not have an independent nation of their own. Ekin split from PNV in 1959 and ETA formed a few months later in 1959. Their first terrorist attack followed shortly after in 1961. The accumulation of frustration led to aggression in the form of a terrorist attack.

THE VIOLENT ETA MEMBERS ASCEND TO LEADERSHIP POSITIONS

It has already been demonstrated previously in this chapter that founding members of Ekin and ETA were responsible for the initial use of terrorist tactics. However, in the mid-1960s, ETA was hijacked by more radical members who were bent on a much more destructive path. The story begins at the First Assembly in May 1962, which was the first general meeting for ETA. Immediately after the First Assembly, some dissenters questioned whether ETA should continue to pursue violence because there were still some members in the organization that did not completely agree with using violence. The leaders, specifically the Highest Director Txillardegui had originally decided to use violence because they had planned the first terrorist attack in 1961.

The moderates, who are not known by name and were not in leadership positions within the organization, argued that violence would lead to repercussions for ETA and the Basque people. The moderates came to the following conclusions: 1) Franco's dictatorship is strong. Attacking him will create violence in Basque territory. 2) Franco's regime is held accountable to European public opinion. 3) Many Basque Christians favor nonviolent methods. 4) A nonviolent strategy would permit more patriots to join the fight for independence. 5) The number of ETA members would increase notably if ETA did not use violence.[56] The conclusions and reasoning of the moderates was based on experience and common sense. It would be best to deal with a ruthless dictator like Franco with peaceful methods. In addition, most people favor peaceful methods of change rather than violence regardless of whether they are Spanish spectators or Basques.

Of course, the moderates were pushed out or quickly learned to tolerate the use of violence. Julen Madariaga, one of the founders, believed that nonviolent methods could only work in civilized regimes, not in the case of Spain. "This is not the situation in Euzkadi where burning one flag of the invading country results in regret for sixty years, not sixty days."[57] Madariaga believed that the Franco regime could not be dealt with peacefully and that violence was a necessity. Violence must be met with violence in his opinion. He had previously tried to establish a clandestine group that would be responsible for planting bombs and using firecrackers, although the clandestine group never materialized.[58] Madariaga used a recently published book by Federico Krutwig to publicly justify his position.

Krutwig's book *Vasconia*[59] was written under the pseudonym Fernando Sarrailh de Ihartza. The book examined guerrilla tactics Krutwig believed Basques should use to overthrow the Spanish government. Krutwig was not ethnically Basque but he had been working to create a regionally understood dialect of Euskera. Krutwig believed in the superiority of violent tactics. He had once given a speech in front of the PNV in the mid 1950s to advocate the use of violence and had later been highly criticized for his belief in the use of violence. He had studied revolutions of developing nations, specifically Algeria, and believed that these guerrilla tactics were the most useful tactics to obtain Basque independence. In addition, the Cuban revolution, the recent successes of Che Guevara in Latin America, the Tupamaros in Uruguay, Mao Tsetung in China, and Vietnam had created a revolutionary world political environment that gave inspiration to the Basque cause. The tactics that that these guerillas used to achieve their successes also provided education for men like Krutwig. Using the research he had collected from other revolutions, Krutwig invented what he called the "action-repression-action cycle."

The action-repression-action cycle starts when guerrillas attack the government. The government then indiscriminately attacks the population, not knowing who the guerrillas are. The guerrillas then attack the government again, thus creating a retaliatory cycle. The guerrilla war would conclude with a revolution after repeated instances of government abuse toward Basques and Basque retaliation. This would bring about desired Basque independence through the uprising of Basque people in conjunction with ETA support and leadership.

The use of the action-repression-action cycle is actually what defined ETA as a terrorist organization. If a group uses violence to attack noncombatants within the population purposefully, then that organization is hurting the people it claims to protect to further its own goals. A terrorist group wants to abuse a population so that the population gets angry at the government for not protecting them and their property. Thus the government looks incompetent in its inability to protect its population.

Krutwig was the one person who provided the strategy of violence for ETA. Krutwig was a brutal individual who believed the Spanish should suffer for their oppression of the Basques.

> The measures that the enemy uses against our guerillas or our population should always be received with an exemplar response on the part of the Basques. When it does not represent a danger to the guerillas, the torturers should be eliminated by torture. If the forces of the occupier use methods of torture, one should never doubt to employ in retaliation the torture of their friends and family and the civil or military agents of authority.[60]

Krutwig believed in punishing the Spanish.

Krutwig officially joined ETA in 1966, but his ideas had already influenced ETA by the time he joined the organization. Jose Zabilde wrote *Insurreción en Euskadi* under the pseudonym K. de Zumbeltz in 1963, which was based on Krutwig's ideas concerning the action/repression/ action cycle. Zabilde endorsed the cycle as ETA's strategy for Basque independence. The strategy had four parts: 1) conquer the population, 2) destroy the organization of the colonizing oppressor, 3) make the methods that they enemy uses fail, 4) finally, take power.[61]

In his book *Insurreción en Euskadi,* Zabilde

> criticized the organization for having tried to skip over the required stages for the making of revolutionary war. The 1961 train-derailing episode, he argued, was a grave error, because it reflected a mistaken belief that ETA would be able to wage war against Franco and the Spanish army without proper preparation. Revolutionary war, he asserted advanced in stages.[62]

Zabilde, whose code name was Goiztiri, was not satisfied with the initial terrorist attack that ETA had planned. More people needed to die and more collateral damage needed to transpire. Zabilde advocated that Basques conduct a dirty war against Spain. ETA militants were to corrupt the state both psychologically and physically. Even Basque women were to be widowed if they chose to have relations with Spaniards. Zabilde stated:

> In the revolutionary war of Euzkadi it is an absolute necessity for us to employ all arms, tricks, and procedures that utilize the aggressor; even though, naturally, we are adding our own supply. Using humanitary motives or moral considerations is as stupid as it is absurd. The violence, wrote Engels is the midwife of the birth from an old society to a new society.[63]

Zabilde goes on to state:

> Corrupt the enemy with all the best things, with offers, presents, and promises. Disturb trust provoking and fomenting the shameful and vile acts of their best

deputies; then give it maximum publicity. Maintain secret relations between the enemy and the multiple numbers of these agents. Confuse the government adversary. Sow discord between bosses exciting envy and distrust. Provoke indiscipline; Reasons proportional to the discontent lives that they will live and the ammunition that does not arrive or arrives when they are retreating; that the sensual music penetrates the softness in their hearts; widow easy women that have been corrupted. Make sure the soldiers are never where they should be. Give false alarms and false advice. Win over the administrators and the enemy government officials. [64]

Influenced by Zabilde and his supporters, ETA officially adopted the action/repression/action strategy in April and May 1964 at the Third Assembly. [65] By the end of 1965, the original Executive Committee had dispersed throughout the world. Txillardegui, a founder of ETA, was expelled from France on January 2, 1965, and went to Belgium. Julen Madariaga and Eneko Irigaray, two other founders were expelled from France on January 7, 1965. Others from the Executive Committee were not heard from again. This left positions open for new members that wanted to fill the shoes of the exiled members of the Executive Committee.

Continuing with the story, Escubi, Bareño, and Bilbao Barrena spent September 1965 preparing for the Fifth Assembly with help from Krutwig and Madariaga. In 1966, ETA held the Fifth Assembly. The internal debates within the organization that had plagued ETA for the last few years finally came to a head. Txillardegui, who had led the culturalists, the original ideology of ETA, had been president since ETA's inception in 1959 and was voted out in 1965. The culturalists believed that the use of *Euskera* and preservation of Basque culture were the most important goals of ETA. Etxebarrieta brothers and Escubi, who were not founders, took control of the Fifth Assembly. Zabilde took control of the presidency September 24, 1965. Many of the founding members were not allowed to vote at this assembly so that the newer factions in ETA, led by Zabilde, could take control of ETA.

The original founders of ETA had lost control of ETA because they had been away from the organization. What had followed in between the dispersions and expulsions of the founders was literally a hijacking by terrorists bent on extreme violence. It is believed that the original founders and members of ETA had progressed toward the use of violence. They were not originally inclined to use violence, especially when Ekin was created, but as peaceful actions were not successful, frustration increased and ETA was created. Even when they used violence to derail a train, they made sure that no one would be killed and no one was killed. ETA was not a very violent terrorist organization until it was hijacked by Zabilde. It was not until Zabilde took over that ETA really became an extreme terrorist organization.

The moderates had lost the battle and many that did not agree with the use of violence had already left the organization. However, some moderates were still hopelessly vying for peaceful methods until 1967 when a group called Aintzina left ETA to form a radical party that condemned ETA's use of violence. Another group, Saioak, left in 1968 for the same reasons and joined the Spanish Communist party. In fact, those who did not agree with the use of violence struggled from 1966 to 1975 against the leadership to use peaceful methods but were not victorious.

ETA robbed a bank on June 7, 1968, to get funds needed for terrorist attacks. Two *etarras* were stopped at a roadblock and one killed a civil guard in a panic. A gunfight then erupted but the car managed to escape. At the second roadblock, two ETA members were dragged out of the car and shot. One of these men was Txabi Etxebarrieta, then the President of ETA. This was the spark that ETA had been waiting for to resume attacks.

Etxebarrieta became a Basque hero and Basques took to the streets to protest his death. Priests said Mass in his memory for weeks after his death. ETA wanted revenge and their first planned assassination took place in 1968 with the murder of Police Commissioner Melitón Manzanas. Manzanas was shot outside his house in front of his wife; this was a revenge attack because Manzanas was suspected of torturing several people. Again, Franco was swift in rounding up ETA members, beating them, and intimidating them. The first phase of action/repression/action had begun.[66] Since its first terrorist attack in 1961, ETA has continued to use terrorism to accomplish the political agenda of Basque independence.

One earlier ETA member describes the use of violence is contagious and has been ETA's mode of operation since its inception:

> A heap of people, I believe that there are many people from ETA that participated during the period 1976–1978. When we, us or myself began to question the efficacy of the armed struggle, the moral validity, politics, strategy, well some people I believe that . . . I don't know, the people . . . it's easy, it's normal to succumb to the prominent idea or something where you see overwhelming enthusiasism, it's contagious.[67]

Those who questioned the use of violence were persuaded toward the predominant line of thinking; violence accomplishes goals.

Many of the original founders of ETA such as Txillardegui and Madariaga agreed with and advocated violence. These founders of ETA even planned the first ETA terrorist attack. However, when ETA founders were sent into exile, other violent personalities such as Zabilde, Krutwig, and Etxebarrieta took over and continued to implement terrorist strategies. The action/repression/action cycle was created by violent personalities like Krutwig and Zabilde. Zabilde's terrorism strategy was officially passed at the Third Assembly. It became the official strategy of ETA and was a much more virulent strategy than the unsuccessful train derailment that founders had planned in 1961. Terrorists had hijacked ETA.

CONCLUSION

Three factors were responsible for the radicalization of Ekin and later the violent terrorist attacks of ETA. The first of these was the initial leadership, which was responsible for the first round of ETA violence. The second factor that led to the radicalization of ETA was frustration. The lack of success that Ekin members or Basque nationalists had kept increasing their frustration until terrorism became their preferred option. It took nine years for ETA to use terrorism. The third factor that led to the radicalization of ETA was the ascendance of violent personalities in the organization. Many of the original founders of ETA and Ekin were prone to violence, but the ascendance of people like Luis Zabilde, who later became president of ETA, expanded and strengthened ETA's use of terrorism.

Charismatic leadership was not a factor in the radicalization of Ekin or the formation of the ETA. This may be because the organization was set up with horizontal leadership, meaning that there were many powerful members within the group and one person was not the primary leader of ETA or Ekin. No one person embodied either Ekin or ETA. Leadership was certainly important in the radicalization of the group but several people were responsible for this radicalization. Perhaps later this is why ETA experienced a leadership coup where all the original members were kicked out of the organization and the violent members took over, making it more violent than ever.

NOTES

1. Fernando Reinares, *Patriotas de la Muerte* (Madrid: Grupo Santillana de Ediciones, 2001), 121.
2. Robert Clark, *The Basques: The Franco Years and Beyond* (Reno, NV: University of Nevada Press, 1979), 178–179.
3. Page Von Tangen, *Prisons, Peace, and Terrorism* (Chippenham, Wiltshire: Antony Rowe, Ltd, 1998).
4. Robert Clark, "Euzkadi: Basque Nationalism in Spain since the Civil War" in Charles R. Foster (ed.), *Nations without a State, Ethnic Minorities in Western Europe* (New York: Praeger Publishers, 1980). Daniele Conversi, *The Basque, the Catalans, and Spain, Alternative Routes to Mobilisation* (Reno: University of Nevada Press, 1997). Macdougall J. Hislop, *Spanish State Policy, Basque Nationalism and ETA Terrorism* (unpublished master's thesis) Edmonton, Alberta, Canada: University of Alberta, 1995. Cameron J. Watson, *Basque Nationalism and Political Violence: The Ideological and Intellectual Origins of ETA* (Reno, NV: University of Nevada Press, 2007).
5. Conversi, *The Basque, the Catalans, and Spain, Alternative Routes to Mobilisation*, 80.
6. Clark, *The Basques: The Franco Years and Beyond*, 78–179.
7. Beltza (pseudonym of Emilio López), *El Nacionalismo Vasco En El Exilio 1937–1960* (San Sebastían: Editorial Thertoa Plaza de las Armericas, 1977).
8. Ortzi (pseudonym of Francisco Letamendia), *Los Vascos, Sítesis de Su Historia* (Donostia: Hordago Publicaciones, 1978).
9. John Sullivan, *ETA and Basque Nationalism, The Fight for Euskadi, 1890–1986* (New York: Routledge, 1988), 34.
10. Sullivan, *ETA and Basque Nationalism, The Fight for Euskadi, 1890–1986*, 20–21.

11. Sullivan, *ETA and Basque Nationalism, The Fight for Euskadi, 1890–1986,* 34.

12. Clark, *The Basques: The Franco Years and Beyond,* 137.

13. Peter Janke, "Spanish Separatism: ETA's Threat to Basque Democracy," *Conflict Studies* 123 (October 1980), 1–20.

14. Ortzi (pseudonym of Francisco Letamendia), *Historia de Euzkadi* (Aleconnaise: Ruedo Ibérico, 1975), 291.

15. Shlomo Ben-Ami, "Basque Nationalism between Archaism and Modernity," *Journal of Contemporary History* 26 (3/4) (September 1991), 493–521, 503–504.

16. Jeremy MacClancy, "The Culture of Radical Basque Nationalism," *Anthropology Today* 4 (5) (October 1988), 17–19.

17. Jacqueline Urla, "Ethnic Protest and Social Planning: A look at Basque Language Revival," *Cultural Anthropology* 3 (4) (November 1988), 379–394. Jacqueline Urla, "Cultural Politics in an Age of Statistics: Numbers, Nations, and the Making of Basque Identity," *American Ethnologist* 29 (4) (November 1993), 818–843.

18. Cameron Watson, *Basque Nationalism and Political Violence, The Ideological and Intellectual Origins of ETA* (Reno: University of Nevada Press, 2007), 214.

19. Patxo Unzueta, *Los Nietos de la IRA, Nacionalismo, Violencia en el País Vasco* (Madrid: Ediciones El País, S. A., 1988), 91.

20. Milton M. da Silva, "Modernization and Ethnic Conflict," *Comparative Politics* 7 (2) (January 1975), 227–251, 248.

21. Michel Wieviorka, *The Making of Terrorism* (Chicago: University of Chicago Press, 1993), 178.

22. Joseba Zulaika and William A. Douglass, *Terror and Taboo, The Follies, Fables, and Faces of Terrorism* (New York: Routledge, 1996), 58.

23. Dieter Rucht, "The Impact of National Contexts on Social Movement Structures: A Cross-Movement and Cross-National Comparison," in Doug McAdam, John D. McCarthy, and Mayer n. Zald (eds.), *Comparative Perspectives on Social Movements* (Cambridge, UK: Cambridge University Press, 1996), 185–204, 186.

24. Robert P. Clark, *The Basque Insurgents ETA, 1952–1980* (Madison, WI: University of Wisconsin Press, 1984).

25. José María Garmendia, Gurutz Jáuregui, and Florencio Domínguez Iribarren, *La Historia de ETA* (Madrid: Temas' de Hoy, 2000). Ortzi (pseudonym of Francisco Letamendia), *Historia de Euzkadi,* 298.

26. Peter Waldmann, *Radicalismo Étnico* (Madrid: Ediciones Akal, S.A., 1997), 63.

27. J. N. Nicolas and Paxto Unzueta, *Documentos Y* (Vol. 1) (Itxaropena, Spain: Hordago S.A., 1979), 11.

28. Nicolas and Unzueta, *Documentos Y* (Vol. 1), 12.

29. Nicolas and Unzueta, *Documentos Y* (Vol. 1), 12.

30. Nicolas and Unzueta, *Documentos Y* (Vol. 1), 12.

31. Cameron Watson, *Basque Nationalism and Political Violence, The Ideological and Intellectual Origins of ETA* (Reno: University of Nevada Press, 2007), 192.

32. José María Portell, *Los Hombres de ETA* (Barcelona: Dopesa, 1974).

33. Nicolas and Unzueta, *Documentos Y* (Vol. 1), 367.

34. Ortzi (pseudonym of Francisco Letamendia), *Historia de Euzkadi.*

35. Clark,*The Basque Insurgents ETA, 1952–1980,* 37.

36. Ortzi (pseudonym of Francisco Letamendia), *Historia de Euzkadi,* 300.

37. Later in its history, the composition of ETA changed and less than 10 percent of ETA was composed of students throughout the period 1978–1992. See Florencio Domínguez Iribarren, *ETA: Estrategia Organizativa y Actuaciones 1978–1992* (Bilbao, Spain: Universidad del País Vasco, 1998), 47. Also see Florencio Domínguez, *Dentro de ETA, La Vida Diaria de Los Terroristas* (Madrid: Santillana Ediciones Generales, S. L., 2002), for literature on more recent ETA members. Fernando Reinares, *Patriotas de la Muerte, Quiénes Han Militado en ETA y Por Qué?* (Madrid: Grupo Santillana de Ediciones S. A., 2001).

38. José María Portell, *Los Hombres de ETA* (Barcelona: Dopesa, 1974).

39. José Antonio de Aguirre, *Escape Via Berlin* (Reno: University of Nevada Press, 1991), 10.

40. Aguirre and Lecube, *Escape Via Berlin*, 11.

41. Patxo Unzueta, *Los Nietos de la IRA, Nacionalismo, Violencia en el País Vasco* (Madrid: Ediciones El País, S. A., 1988), 93.

42. For more on Sabino Arana Goiri, see Ludger Mees, *Nationalism, Violence, and Democracy, The Basque Clash of Identities* (New York: Palgrave Macmillan, 2003).

43. Daniele Conversi, *The Basque, the Catalans, and Spain, Alternative Routes to Mobilisation* (Reno: University of Nevada Press, 1998), 88.

44. Nicolas and Unzueta, *Documentos Y* (Vol. 1), 19.

45. Fracisco J. Llera, "ETA: Ejercito Secreto Y Movimiento Social," *Revista de Estudios Politicos* 78 (October–December 1992), 161–193.

46. Robert Clark, "Euzkadi: Basque Nationalism in Spain since the Civil War," in Charles R. Foster (ed.), *Nations without a State Ethnic Minorities in Western Europe* (New York: Praeger Publishers, 1980), 92.

47. Francisco J. Llera, "ETA: Ejercito Secreto Y Movimiento Social."

48. Milton M. da Silva, "Modernization and Ethnic Conflict," *Comparative Politics* 7 (2), (January 1975), 227–251, 233.

49. Clark, *The Basque Insurgents ETA, 1952–1980.*

50. José María Garmendia, Gurutz Jáuregui, and Florencio Domínguez Iribarren, *La Historia de ETA* (Madrid: Temas' de Hoy, 2000).

51. Fernando Reinares, "Who Are the Terrorists? Analyzing Changes in Sociological Profile among Members of ETA," *Studies in Conflict and Terrorism* 27 (2004), 465–488, 475.

52. José María Garmendia, *Historia de ETA*, 2 vols (San Sebastián: L. Haranburu, 1979 and 1980), 19.

53. Gurutz Jáuregui Bereciartu, *Ideologia y Estrategia Politica de ETA, Análisis de su evolución entre 1959–1968* (Madrid: Siglo Veintiuno Editores, 1981), 137.

54. Clark, *The Basques: The Franco Years and Beyond*, 159.

55. As cited in Cyrus Ernesto Zirakzadeh, *A Rebellious People, Basques, Protests, and Politics* (Reno, NV: University of Nevada Press, 1991), 162.

56. Gurutz Jáuregui Bereciartu, *Ideologia y Estrategia Politica de ETA, Análisis de su evolución entre 1959–1968* (Madrid: Siglo Veintiuno Editores, 1981), 209.

57. Bereciartu, *Ideologia y Estrategia Politica de ETA, Análisis de su evolución entre 1959–1968*, 209.

58. Cameron Watson, *Basque Nationalism and Political Violence, The Ideological and Intellectual Origins of ETA* (Reno: University of Nevada Press, 2007), 198.

59. Federico Krutwig, *Vasconia* (Buenos Aires: Ediciones Norbait, 1962).

60. Krutwig, *Vasconia*, 339.

61. J. N. Nicolas and Paxto Unzueta, *Documentos Y* (Vol. 3) (Itxaropena, Spain: Hordago S.A., 1979), 48–50.

62. Clark, *The Basques: The Franco Years and Beyond*, 159.

63. Nicolas and Unzueta, *Documentos Y* (Vol. 3), 30.

64. Nicolas and Unzueta, *Documentos Y* (Vol. 3), 45.

65. Bereciartu, *Ideologia y Estrategia Politica de ETA, Análisis de su evolución entre 1959–1968*, 236.

66. Conversi, *The Basque, the Catalans, and Spain, Alternative Routes to Mobilisation.*

67. Fernando Reinares, *Patriotas de la Muerte* (Madrid: Grupo Santillana de Ediciones, 2001), 105.

Chapter Three

Forsaking Colombia

The Creation and Radicalization of the Fuerzas Armadas Revolucionarias de Colombia (FARC)

In winter 2009, right before Christmas, I went on a cruise for a week to the Caribbean with my husband. After a long day of exploring Honduras, my husband and I went to relax in the ship's hot tub. Stuck in close proximity of one another, I struck up a conversation with a Colombian woman named Sandra. Ecstatic to meet a Colombian, I began questioning her about the state of her country, and most particularly, the FARC. Sandra lamented that the FARC was once "for the people." However, as time progressed, "the FARC became a terrorist organization and a drug cartel." Having been friends with someone who rehabilitated FARC guerrillas and reintroduced them to society, Sandra explained that the former FARC members' only skill is fighting. "These people are difficult to employ because the only thing that they know how to do is start fights." In addition, Sandra stated that President Uribe was extremely successful in combating the FARC. While Western nations criticized the president for his human rights abuses, Sandra stated that it was only because of President Uribe that Colombians were able to live in and visit their own country without fear of the FARC.

The previous interlude creates the perfect introduction to a chapter that explains the radicalization of the FARC. The FARC was once part of a political party that fought for the peasants, but as time progressed, the FARC became a terrorist organization that financed itself through drugs and kidnappings. In 1966, amid the violent turmoil in the dense mountainous jungles of Colombia, the Fuerzas Armadas Revolucionarias de Colombia (FARC) was born. Although it is currently known as one of the most dangerous, formidable terrorist groups in the world, the FARC was originally part of the Com-

75

munist Party of Colombia. This chapter tells the story of the radicalization of a political party that has successfully challenged both the United States and Colombian governments. Surrounded by dense jungle canopies with villagers living on the outskirts of encampments acting as "human shields," the FARC is often impossible to locate or attack.[1] Because it has controlled approximately up to one-half of Colombian territory at times and become one of the largest drug cartels in the world, the FARC continues to remain the major adversary of the Colombian government.[2]

The chapter will begin with an analysis of the relationship between the Colombian government and the FARC. Other groups within the population that were contemporaries of the FARC will also be included within the analysis. The chapter will then present a theory as to why the FARC became the terrorist organization it is today. Lastly, the chapter will look at the current state of the FARC and its dominant position in Colombia.

THE HISTORY OF THE RELATIONSHIP BETWEEN THE COLOMBIAN GOVERNMENT AND THE FARC

One word can be used to describe the history of Colombia: violent. "After the fourteen years of the Independence Wars, there were eight national civil wars, fourteen local civil wars, many small revolts, two wars with Ecuador, and three coups d'état."[3] It can be said that violence was the only way Colombians knew how to with deal with conflict. According to Rochlin, "Colombia is the only country in the world to have the academic discipline of "Violentology," which is actually a small field within academia where experts study the violent history of Colombia and its people.[4]

Much of this violence first took root when the Spanish colonized Colombia. In 1509, the first Spanish settlement was created, and explorers such as Alonso de Lugo, Gonzalo Jimenez de Quesada, Sebastian de Belalcazar, and Nicolas Fedderman continued to create cities and settlements across most of what is modern-day Colombia. The Spanish treated the indigenous peoples of Colombia with great cruelty; Quesada himself went on a rampage of murder and torture to establish the city of Santa Fé de Bogotá (currently Bogotá) in 1538. Bogotá became a major source of gold and indigenous peoples were enslaved to help mine the gold; later, African slaves were brought in because local populations were decimated and slaves from Africa were typically tougher and stronger. The Spanish continued to exploit Colombia, gaining profit from goods such as tobacco, brandy, and gold.

After witnessing several nationalist uprisings from disgruntled peasants, Simon Bolivar, the son of a wealthy Spanish landowning family in Caracas, assembled revolutionary forces to defeat the Spanish. Bolivar was successful and on December 17, 1819, the Republic of Colombia was established, comprised also of Venezuela and New Granada. In 1821, Gran Colombia, an expansion of the Republic of Colombia, was created consisting of Venezuela, Colombia, Panama, and Ecuador. Although Bolivar wanted to keep these four independent countries united under one government, most of his peers knew that these countries would eventually secede from the conglomerate nation. Bolivar became known as a tyrant after he established himself as a dictator to quell the dissent against him. As his health was poor, Bolivar eventually died in 1830 from tuberculosis.

Francisco de Paula Santander was Bolivar's vice president; Santander had been exiled to New York after an assassination attempt on Bolivar's life. Santander later returned and organized modern Colombia. Santander created a system of laws, organized schools systems, created a finance system, and reduced the influence of the church in education.

As history progressed, the United States dominated the southern hemisphere after the creation of the Monroe Doctrine on December 2, 1823. The construction of the Panama Canal became a major issue in U.S. foreign policy toward South America. With Colombian embroiled in a civil war called the "War of a Thousand Days" (1899–1902), the United States was easily able to secure Panamanian independence. In President Theodore Roosevelt's mind, Panama was the best place to create a canal and little more was needed to start a Panamanian revolution. Panamanian independence was secured with 441 firemen and 500 Colombian troops, who had been bribed. The United States provided cruisers for support. Panama seceded from Colombia in 1903 with little effort.[5]

What followed in Colombia were several decades of tenuous swings between democracy and dictatorship interspersed with periods of civil war. Of course, these periods of democracy were not very democratic; wealthy landowners controlled politics and 99 percent of the land in Colombia. This left the peasants in Colombia the option of sharecropping or renting land from the wealthy. Colombia was a country whose politics were dominated by the latifundia lifestyle. Peasants would work the land and swear absolute loyalty to their landowners. Hence, social mobility did not exist and could not exist until a more egalitarian society was created.

The Communist Party first organized peasants into armed militias to fight the military and Conservatives in 1947. At this time, Conservative large landowners were trying to retake land that peasants had been squatting on and the military became involved in the conflict. Conversely, some peasants became informants for the military. Everyone was fearful for their lives. The Communist Party, Conservatives, and the military all killed thousands of peasants. Many peasants lost their homes and land; some would simply start farming abandoned land. Peasants killed wealthy landowners or ran for their lives. The Communists also created safe zones and declared independent governments throughout Colombia, thus claiming land as their own throughout Colombia.

La Violencia (1948–1953; 1958–1965), two periods of tremendous bloodshed and civil war in Colombia, was caused by vast economic inequalities and social injustices. La Violencia began in 1948 with the assassination of leftist Liberal Party leader Jorge Eliécer Gaitán. Gaitán, originally a member of the Liberal Party, helped peasants to fight off large landowners from both the Liberal and Conservative Parties. These landowners had employed the police to suppress peasant insurrections that began after landowners began increasing their property holdings. Although peasants, shop owners, and unionists had chosen Gaitán as their president, the Conservative and Liberal Parties considered him an enemy.[6] It is a mystery as to who killed Gaitán in 1948; the list of suspects includes the Conservative and Liberal Parties, the United States, and the Communist Party. After Gaitán was assassinated, Bogotá swelled with riots and angry mobs looted, and burned the city. The violence later spread to the countryside and La Violencia had begun.[7]

Violence became so rampant that President Ospina Perez declared a state of emergency in 1950 to control crowds that had been protesting Gaítan's assassination. People used La Violencia to punish cheating husbands, annoying neighbors, unfair bosses, or crooked landlords. Rape, torture, crucifixion, the mutilation of pregnant women and male reproductive organs, burning, looting and a host of other unimaginable offenses lead to the death of over 200,000 people. Colombians created an entire creative litany of ways to leave a body as an example for others to see; one of the most popular methods was called the Colombian necktie wherein the victim's chin would be carved and his or her tongue would be pulled out through the lower jaw. Those that lived through the era were ultimately traumatized by what they witnessed or what acts of passion they had committed.

Liberals and Conservatives fought throughout the country, pulling everyone to one side or the other. Both sides used tremendous violence to kill their opponents. The Conservatives used paramilitary death squads, while the Liberals used guerrilla groups. The Communist Party used whatever was available at the time. Some leaders within the Catholic Church even became involved.

The Bishop of Santa Rosa de Osos, Msgr. Miguel Angel Builes, viewed La Violencia as a Liberal strategy of revolution aimed at destroying the Church. Therefore, some leaders encouraged direct involvement in defense of the Conservatives and the Catholic Church. "Safe conduct" passes were given to those parishioners who could declare themselves loyal Conservatives. Conservatives party ballots were also given out in the parishes. However, other Church leaders, such as Archbishop Msgr. Ismael Perdomo from Bogotá, forbade the Catholic Church from choosing any side and wanted priests to give nonpolitical sermons.[8]

There was a short hiatus in the violence when Pinilla took power. Rojas Pinilla assumed power on June 13, 1953, in a military coup with the Liberal Party's support and some support from the Conservatives. Pinilla's dictatorship actually stopped La Violencia for a few years although it resumed as soon as Pinilla left office. His administration's slogan was "No more bloodshed, no more degradation." Pinilla's overarching goal was to pull a war-torn country toward unity and peace. This objective was very difficult. Pinilla restored some of the political liberties that had been destroyed previously during Arbeláez's administration. He lifted the censure of the press and reestablished the Supreme Court as a bipartisan branch of government. The most important thing that Pinilla did to reunite the country was to provide amnesty to guerrillas, including the Communist guerrillas. He also gave the peasants, or *campesinos*, a pay increase, something that was important to the Communists, but the Communists refused to lay down their arms.[9] However, it was rumored that some of those who laid down their weapons were assassinated.

The Communists negotiated a relative peace with the Liberals in the early 1950s and vowed to give logistic support such as manpower to areas where the war would be inevitable. However, this relationship between the Communists and the Liberals went sour. There was a disagreement between the Communist guerrillas and the Liberal landowners.[10]

The bloodshed resumed when a new military coup assumed power. In 1957, the unsuccessful dictatorship of Rojas Pinilla was overthrown by the military and replaced by democratically elected president, Alberto Lleras Camargo. In an effort to stop the bloodshed, the National Front, an agreement between the Liberals and Conservatives to share power, was implemented in 1958. The National Front was also formed to stop Pinilla's reelection.[11] Under the National Front, the presidency would alternate between parties and Liberals and Conservatives would split the legislative bodies equally. According to Hoskin, the National Front lasted until 1986 when Virgilio Barco was elected.[12] In the context of the Cold War, the Liberals and Conservatives would unite to defeat the Communists. The Communist Party had already been outlawed in 1954 although the Communist guerrillas were still fighting throughout the country.

After the National Front was created in 1958, both of the parties decided to try to improve the situation of the peasantry. A few programs were created to help mitigate the impoverished situation of the peasantry. The Special Commission for Rehabilitation was given up to 100 million pesos to help the poor. In 1960, President Camargo instituted a series of tribunals dedicated to equity and conciliation for the peasantry. A small business institute was created, as were the Tribunals for Conciliation and Equity. At first, these social programs were placed in areas that the administration considered areas of political support, but later eight more Tribunals for Conciliation and Equity were created across the country.[13]

The Communist Party had become the greatest enemy of both the Liberal and Conservative Parties at this point and with the help of the United States government, the Colombian government regardless of party sought to eradicate communism. However, the National Front did not lead to an efficient state apparatus. . . . Clientelism replaced secretarianism as the source of support for political parties."[14] Neither Liberals nor Conservatives were able to agree on much of anything else besides removing Communists from the political sphere.

Shortly after the Bay of Pigs incident in 1964, the Colombian government launched Plan Lazo with the help of training and military weaponry from the United States. The Colombian government was trying to reestablish control over the independent peasant republics. The Communist Party had evacuated the elderly, women, and children, anticipating an attack by the government. Forty-four peasants remained to defend Marquetalia.[15] Some 16,000 Colombian troops surrounded the valley of Marquetalia, the major stronghold of the guerrillas, and their supporters, while the Colombian airforce carpet-bombed the region. Very few peasants died and the aftereffect created a network of Communist guerrillas that was built throughout the country. It is estimated that only 500 guerrillas existed at this time.[16]

In response to the attack on Marquetalia, in September 1964 the Block of the South Conference was held and the FARC was unofficially created at this conference with approximately 350 members. The FARC was a radical sect of the guerilla movement of the Communist Party, which will be explained later in the chapter. In 1966, a second conference occurred, which is the formal creation date of the group.

Several scholars have pointed to the Colombian government as a cause for the creation of the FARC. As just one example, Stokes states, "The FARC . . . grew out of rural inequality, state violence, and the failure of Colombia's political system to accommodate any moves democratically to redress Colombia's vastly unequal distribution of natural resources."[17]

There are some problems with this assertion that the state is a cause of the FARC's radicalization to a terrorist organization. Foremost, neither the Conservative nor Liberal Parties controlled the Colombian government at length. The FARC was created one year after a period of intense civil war that had been going on for decades. Although the government was one actor within this civil war, different people and parties also controlled it. There has been consistent and constant regime change throughout Colombia's history. In other words, one dictator or political party did not monopolize power. Violence was the norm in Colombia and everyone used violence against everyone to accomplish their agendas. The Conservative or Liberal governments did not specifically target the Communist Party, the forerunner to the FARC.

Instead, the members and supporters of what later became FARC remained adversaries for both parties because they remained a threat to political power monopolization.

Secondly, the Communist Party, directly after Gaitán's assassination in 1948, began its version of a Proletarian revolution complete with looting, burning, and the destruction of religious structures. Therefore, the Communists were also actors within the civil war; they were not victims. It is understandable that the government would want to outlaw a party that contributed to massive violence throughout Colombia and publicly called for more violence.

Thirdly, the guerrilla groups that later became the FARC took over large areas of land in Colombia, declaring those areas under FARC control. In fact, the government viewed these areas as "independent republics" because they had no control over the areas that were controlled by the FARC. The government's only choice then would be to react and take back land that is sovereign Colombian territory.

The explanation of the radicalization of the FARC that is offered in this chapter is not to underestimate or excuse the rabid violence in Colombia perpetrated by political parties or the military. However, the government of Colombia is not a single explanatory cause for the radicalization of the Communist Party or the creation of the FARC. Other factors may better explain the radicalization of the Communist Party and the creation of the FARC such as charismatic leadership, frustration-aggression theory, and the ascendance of violent personalities.

CHARISMATIC LEADERSHIP

Pedro Antonio Marin, later known as Manuel Marulanda Vélez or Sureshot (Tirofijo), was born on May 12, 1930, or May 12, 1928. The date discrepancy exists because Marulanda's father and Marulanda disagreed about the year of his birth. Pedro Antonio Marin personally adopted the name Manuel Marulanda Vélez after one of the many times he was pronounced dead by the newspapers. Vélez assumed the name of a dead man to create anonymity. Manuel Marulanda Vélez was given the name "Sureshot" as his nom de guerre. However, Vélez was not given this nickname because his aim with a gun was superb; rather, it is because Vélez liked to shoot his victims by putting the gun directly against the victim's forehead.

Sureshot was the oldest of five brothers and sisters and came from a working-class family. At the age of nineteen, he joined the conflict and became a Liberal guerrilla with the other men from his village. During this time, Marulanda roamed throughout the country slaying as many Conservatives as he could. "Marín [Marulanda] also killed people who helped the

Conservatives—those who gave them shelter, women who slept with them, owners of restaurants they patronized."[18] Marulanda participated in the bloodbath at length and learned many skills that would later help him take command of the FARC. He found himself in command of 150 men when the Communists entered the Liberal zone in approximately 1947. The Communists had rapidly expanded their influence throughout the area and Sureshot cooperated and participated at times with Communist squadrons. In the late 1940s, Liberals and Communists worked together to defeat a government controlled by Conservatives.

There were several differences between the Communists and Liberals concerning military discipline. The Liberals did not maintain a well-disciplined trained army with a clear hierarchy; decisions were often made on the go. The Communists, however, were model revolutionaries and created an army that was both hierarchically organized and highly disciplined. In fact, Marulanda makes comments often in his biography about the Communists' preoccupation with the military command hierarchy. While criticizing the Liberals, Marulanda stated, "There were no barracks with which to perform the functions of a military training in the morning, the afternoon, during the 24 hours. They [Liberals] did not exercise strict control over their men in arms."[19]

However, the collaboration between the Communists and Liberals was soon cut short. In 1952, after the First National Conference of the Liberation Movement, Marulanda was told by his superior, Gerardo Loayza, to separate himself from the Communists. Loayza wanted the Liberal guerrillas to go to their Liberal zones of control and wait for further instructions. Loayza stated, "We have the support of colonels in the army that are going to give us weapons and munitions to fight the Communists within our zones. The moment has arrived to end communism."[20] The Liberals betrayed the Communists in order to create a political monopoly over the country. Besides the Conservatives, the Communists would be the last political party the Liberals would have to contend with politically.

This decision was tough for Sureshot to accept. He had fought next to the Communists and had become brothers in arms with them. Sureshot fit in well with the Communists because his main goals were land reform, the nationalization of industries, and the destruction of the American imperial domination. Eventually Sureshot decided to defect to the Communists in light of the Liberal betrayal. As the war went on, a new war began between the Communists and Liberals. Sureshot was chosen as a representative for El Davis to lead peace talks between the two groups; as this was too difficult for Sureshot to attend, his brother Jésus represented Davis in his place. The groups literally decided to leave one another alone at this point, although fighting between the two groups eventually resumed.

In mid-1956, at a guerrilla conference in Marquetalia, thirteen men were elected as leaders of Estado Mayor. Marulanda was one of these men and he was placed in charge of the military. Often in these early years before the creation of the FARC, Marulanda often led the guerrilla groups with the assistance of a man named Charro Negro, whose real name was Jacobo Prías Alape. Charro Negro was killed by the military on January 11, 1960, and this was difficult for Marulanda because Charro Negro was one of Marulanda's best friends. Marulanda suspected that the U.S. government had a hand in the assassination of Charro Negro, although this has never been proven. As time passed, Marulanda took complete command of what would become the FARC in 1964.

Traditionally, two people have been identified as founders of the FARC. Jacobo Arenas is known as the intellectual founder who has written many of the official statements pertaining to the group and has refined the group's political ideology. Arenas was one of the early Communist guerrillas under Marulanda's command. Manuel Marulanda is typically portrayed as the military commander of the FARC. In his book, Arenas identifies Marulanda as the main leader and founder of the FARC. Throughout his book *Diario de la Resistancia de Marquetalia*, Arenas reveres Marulanda. In one scene in the book, Arenas is speaking with the soldiers and Marulanda interrupts. Marulanda makes a brilliant comment and Arenas replies, "Salud comandante! I responded . . . jumping up like a squirrel in a flash to stand at attention."[21] Arenas not only salutes Marulanda but also acts subordinate to Marulanda while in his presence. In addition, Arenas states that Marulanda was at first the commander of the guerrillas, but then later became the chief commander of the Southern Block and leader of the masses of Nudo de la Cordillera Central.[22] The Southern Block is the area where the Communist guerrillas had a conference and created the FARC. In another book he wrote, Arenas refers to Marulanda as the highest leader of the FARC.[23] In addition, Gallego quotes in his book, "the Communist Party created by Comrade Manuel Marulanda Vélez, commander of the guerrillas of FARC."[24] It can be ascertained that Marulanda is the primary leader and founder of the FARC.[25] For these reasons, this part of the analysis will focus on Marulanda as the charismatic leader in the FARC who was mainly responsible for the complete radicalization of the Communist Party leading to the creation of the FARC.

Table 3.1 summarizes Marulanda's capacity as a charismatic leader according to Weber as explained in the introductory chapter. Each characteristic will be explained in the following pages in the order that it was placed in the table.

One of Weber's primary criteria for charismatic leadership is for the leader to believe that his authority came from God. This is rather problematic when looking at a Marxist because Marxists are not only atheists stereotypi-

Table 3.1.   Charismatic Leadership and Manuel Marulanda

Max Weber's Criteria for Charismatic Leadership	Characteristic of Manuel Marulanda
Authority of Higher Being for Mission?	Yes but with caveat
Complete Obedience of Followers?	Yes
Brings Followers Material and Social Rewards?	Yes
Charismatic Leader Directs and Organizes Organization?	Yes
Delegates Power to Followers?	Yes
Seeks to Defray Costs from His Own Pocket?	Yes
Develops an Army Trained and Equipped by Leader?	Yes
Rejects Personal Profit from Organization and Has No Rational Economic Behavior?	Yes
Followers Do Not Elect Him?	Yes
Leadership Is Not Stable?	No
Charismatic Leader Selects His Successor?	Yes

cally, but also believe that religious institutions reinforce a class system. Some recent literature on the FARC explains that

> while religious practices such as prayer, are not actually forbidden in the rebel forces, they are not allowed any public expression and can only take place in solitude and in private. In general, there is little tolerance of religion or understanding of spiritual needs. Neither of the two largest guerilla forces [M-19 and the FARC] supports religious practice in any form. [26]

The FARC is not tolerant toward religion; in fact, religious practice is forbidden by the FARC.

For these reasons, the higher being referring to a god-like entity was replaced with the common people. For Marxists, the Proletariat Revolution is for the good of the people to break down class inequalities and to create an atmosphere where every citizen has enough resources. The people or the welfare of the people replace a spiritual entity. It can then be said that Marulanda believed that he had the permission of the people to start a Marxist revolution in Colombia. "Marín [Marulanda] said that if the government had spent even a fraction of the money it used equipping soldiers to help needy farmers and build roads and schools, it might well have avoided decades of trouble with the FARC."[27]

It is evident that Sureshot had the complete obedience of his followers. "Sureshot could no longer lead the charge into battle. He was far too old for that. Fortunately, he didn't have to, he had a second generation of ferocious young Turks to do that for him. He could now orchestrate the war from afar."[28] In addition, "The man [Sureshot] refused to use his troops as fodder, and this added to his legend."[29]

One of his men described Sureshot, stating, "He arrived and said something, and everyone would consider or support it. . . . When he said: I need a commission to go to this part, everyone would follow his orders. With him, we would go wherever. He had a natural gift of command."[30] Jacobo Arenas stated, "As for his concept of justice, since the movement he has had law, a code of regulations, and a disciplinary regime and rules of command, for him all of this is military doctrine. He enforces the rules and he wants others to apply the rules rigorously."[31] There are many similar quotes such as the previous quotes that demonstrate Sureshot's command over his men and their obedience to him.

FARC members also received both material and social rewards for their membership within the FARC. For one, FARC members were paid better most of the time than the Colombian Army they fought against in the jungles. Ruiz writes, "After all, Sureshot took comfort in knowing his FARC soldiers were better trained and better paid than the regular Colombian Army."[32]

Life in the FARC was often better than life at home for most of the men. These men were properly clothed and had a pair of boots to protect their feet from the difficult Colombian climate. Food was a lot more abundant than at home. Peasants often provided the men with necessities and many peasants idolized the men for the participation in the FARC.

One chronicler described the FARC's role in Colombia

> In the heart of Colombia, there is another completely independent country, whose extension is three thousand square kilometers and they call it El Pato. There is not even a police inspector here. The law is imposed by more than 1200 men, who call themselves the FARC. If someone robs, kills, violates, smokes marijuana or commits some other offense, the FARC judges and the person is mostly likely condemned to death, exiled or forced to work on the estate of the victim. All of the children born in this forest were delivered by the hands of the guerilla doctors and guerilla professors have taught them to read and write but not in the sense of learning to read without, "The origin of the family, private property, and the 'state' of Fredrich Engels."[33]

The FARC viewed themselves as the protector of the common people and many citizens looked to the FARC as their savior. There was certainly some pride and social prestige attached to the role of protector and provider for the Colombian people.

Sureshot was the charismatic leader who directed and organized the FARC. Arturo Alape, Sureshot's personal biographer, describes the founding of the FARC as based on Marulanda's ideas. "The vision that Marulanda had as a guerrilla in the year 66 created the conditions for the foundation of the FARC."[34] Alape states that Sureshot created the ideology of the FARC.

After he became older, Sureshot did not participate much in the fighting. "But I did not participate personally in as many battles that the FARC has fought because it is a dangerous life and in this sense among leaders from the FARC there are many people that are able to do it with skill."[35] When Marulanda first entered the war, he fought alongside his men, but as time progressed, Marulanda commanded his forces from the sidelines.

As seen in the figure 3.1 below, the FARC is a hierarchical organization. "Ultimate authority is vested in a six-member general secretariat led by Marulanda."[36] The Secretariat is composed of five members along with two rotating members. The Estado Mayor Central has approximately 25 members who are in charge of different blocs distributed according to Colombia's geography. Each of the blocs is then in charge of and divided into fronts.

Sureshot also delegated his power. Sureshot explained after the Constitutive Congress in 1966 how and where the military forces should be organized.

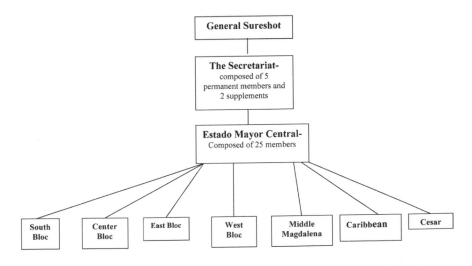

Figure 3.1.   The Hierarchy of the FARC. This figure is a reconstructed drawing from Yaziz Artetam, Commander of the Eastern Bloc in Nazih Richani, *Systems of Violence, the Political Economy of War and Peace in Colombia* (New York: State University of New York Press, 2002), 77.

Scatter the forces, for example a detachment sent towards El Pato, under mine and Jacobo's direction; another force sent towards Cordillera Central under the direction of Joselo; a small group sent towards the center of Tolima directed by Abanico; create a national finance commission commanded by Gilberto and create another commission so that Ciro travels to Calda and Quindío to establish the movement . . . to send destruction and to maintain forces in several places. [37]

In the previous quote, Sureshot distributes his forces throughout different areas in Colombia in order to begin the creation of the Communist country "Estado Mayor." In addition, certain men are named as commanders of forces sent to these other areas.

There was no information found that could conclude that Manuel Marulanda used his own finances to establish and maintain the FARC in the beginning. Considering that Sureshot came from a lower-class family, it is evident that he did not possess money necessary to transform a political party into a terrorist organization. Little money was earned in guerrilla organizations. However, as time progressed and the FARC made massive amounts of money in the drug trade and extortion, that money was used to finance the FARC. Sureshot would control the profits from illicit activities because he was the main leader of the organization.

Sureshot was the primary leader responsible for training and equipping his own personal army. Arturo Alape, the biographer of Manuel Marulanda, tells of Marulanda's development of his private army:

As a result of his experience in innumerable situations, Manuel Marulanda understood the imperious need to always have under his command an elite group of combatants, that he had selected, prepared, and watched over like a teacher; a group with mutual trust, united in their virtues and their flaws; with a formidable physique and profound disciplinary action, that responded to critical circumstances and in that moment assumed without fear the commands they were given. [38]

This group of men that Sureshot kept around him was known as his trusted men. As time passed, Sureshot's forces would multiply. Sureshot would often "spend at least an hour a day indoctrinating by his radio his eighteen thousand soldiers all over Colombia." [39] As time passed, Sureshot became more of a professor or teacher for his soldiers.

Besides his own group of trusted men, Sureshot also directed his larger army of guerrillas. He created schools with which to train his men. At the sixth conference he stated:

The specializations that are natural in an army have already appeared. I believe that we have over 1000 men at this moment with at least 100 to 200 commands. At this conference, we propose the means of communication; to leave the mistakes we have mentally made. We are talking about workshops, we are talking about command schools not only for guerrillas but schools for commanders of companies, for commanders of fronts. [40]

Marulanda's creation of workshops involving military training attests to his preferred training over his soldiers and his military.

Manuel Marulanda spent most of his life in the jungles of Colombia fighting with various other Colombian entities. Arturo Alape, Marulanda's biographer, comments on Marulanda's sparse lifestyle. He states that Marulanda is a "man of the mountain. . . . He has lived like a refugee in a hurried escape attempt. He has breathed in an auspicious space for the war and for peace."[41] Marulanda never lived a lavish lifestyle. Raúl Reyes, who is one of Marulanda's friends within the FARC stated that "he [Marulanda] is a man that represents the peasant particularly because he comes from peasant origins and he is a man that has always lived in the field and for these reasons he understands the needs of the peasants."[42] In the encampments, Marulanda lived among his soldiers with the same food and living quarters. Marulanda certainly did not gain wealth from a terrorist organization. If anything, his behavior was somewhat economically irrational. In the later years, the FARC began to finance itself through drug operations, but Marulanda still lived among his soldiers, moving throughout the jungle. The point is that Sureshot did not profit from the FARC even though he could have in the FARC's later years. There has never been any mention in any of the FARC literature of Marulanda owning any type of extravagant possessions. It appears as though Sureshot created and managed the FARC because he actually believed in the purpose of the organization, not to make any type of profit.

In the earlier years when the Communists were still participating in the guerrilla movement and the FARC had not yet been created, Marulanda was elected at some of the earlier conferences to lead the troops. However, after the FARC was created, this element of democracy no longer existed. Sureshot took command of the FARC. There were no signs of democracy after the FARC had been created. The FARC is set up like the military; there is a strict chain of command and soldiers are expected to follow their commanders. Commands that are not followed can result in death or physical deformation for the soldier. Sureshot was not democratically elected to the position of the supreme commander of the FARC.

Unlike other terrorist organizations, the leadership in the FARC was stable. The FARC was created by Jacobo Arenas, the intellectual founder, and Manuel Marulanda, the military commander. Both of these men remained in leadership positions until their deaths in 2008 and the highest leadership positions never changed. The military tried constantly to assassinate Marulanda but was never successful. Even when Marulanda was presumed dead by the military (this happened numerous times) and Marulanda went into hiding, Marulanda's troops were commanded by his chosen commanders such as Balín. Marulanda would remain in hiding, writing letters to his troops until he was able to return to his command. There appears to have been no attempts to usurp command by any of his men; indeed this was a close-knit group of soldiers who respected and revered their commander. Marulanda remained the supreme commander of the FARC from 1966 to 2008; his forty-two years of leadership within the FARC are rather remarkable. Although he chose his commanders and successors, it appears that the FARC never experienced any serious leadership instability.

Lastly, it is evident that Sureshot chose his successor, known to the public as Mono Jojoy, who was killed by the Colombian military in 2010. If Marulanda was the revered founder of the FARC, then Mono Jojoy was the new and improved guerrilla model. Robin Kirk, a journalist who had spent much time in Colombia describes Mono Jojoy as a "jolly, vicious, fun-loving murderer who drives a flashy vehicle with his pistol on his hip, girls on the running boards, and a rum bottle at the ready."[43]

According to Weber's criteria, two factors are unknown. Foremost, it is unknown whether Sureshot financed the FARC with his own money. It appears that Marulanda did use money that the FARC earned for the benefits of the FARC. In addition, Sureshot remained the leader of the FARC from the founding of the organization to his death. Leadership struggles may have occurred, but these struggles have not been found. Despite these two possible inconsistencies, for the most part, it appears that Marulanda was a charismatic leader.

The charismatic leadership of the Manuel Marulanda is important because it helped lead to the radicalization of the Communist Party and the formation of the terrorist organization the FARC. It is evident that without the strong control and leadership of Marulanda over the FARC, the organization would never have chosen to use terrorist tactics. In the beginning, during La Violencia, Marulanda stated,

> I said to myself: this situation is very complicated, it seems that everything has changed, so I must find a solution. So I said to myself: who will search for it with me? Who will help? Weapons, where are they, how do we get them? If we just remain calmly in place, they will kill us all. But I could not bear more humiliation.[44]

Marulanda's leadership takes the FARC from a guerrilla defense organization to an offensive war organization, bent on destroying the Colombian government. In 1984, under Marulanda's command, the FARC produced a statement stating: "The FARC will no longer wait for the enemy in order to ambush them, but instead will pursue them in order to locate, attack, and eliminate them."[45] Even though the FARC had used terrorism before 1984, it was during the early 1980s that the FARC really began to grow and become much more violent.

FRUSTRATION THAT LEADS TO AGGRESSION

In the introductory chapter of this book, I present theories which state that frustration leads to aggression. In the case of the FARC, frustration that leads to aggression is an explanatory factor for the use of terrorism. It is evident that after repeated attempts to create a Communist revolution or create a strong Communist Party that is competitive in Colombian politics, the Communist Party decided to use violence to accomplish its agenda. The radicalization of the Communist Party becomes apparent in the creation of the FARC, created by Manuel Marulanda and, to a lesser extent, Jacobo Arenas. The FARC then becomes the violent terrorist organization that it is today. The radicalization of the Communist Party will be explained according to what occurred during three specific eras throughout Colombian history. The first era encompasses 1948 to 1953, beginning with Gaitán's assassination and ending with the last year of Roberto Urdaneta Arbeláez's presidency. The next era begins with the first year of Gustavo Rojas Pinilla's military dictatorship, which began in 1954. This includes the request of the Communist Party for the guerrillas to create autodefense groups in 1957 and ends just before the creation of the FARC in 1963. The final era begins in 1964 with the creation of the FARC and continues up until the present period. These time periods were selected as they are used in Jacobo Arena's book *El Diario de la Resistancia de Marquetalia* to describe the evolution of the FARC.

First Era, 1948–1953

The assassination of Jorge Eliécer Gaitán in 1948 was the first incident in a long line of events that caused frustration within the Communist Party. Fluharty summarizes the frustration and anger felt by common people after Gaitán was assassinated. He states:

> The people were the helpless pawns in the struggle for power. To understand the dynamics of the events of April 9, 1948, and the violent times, which grew out of them, one must look at the hungry, the dispossessed, the misery-ridden, who had pinned their slim hopes on Gaitán. It was their revolution that had failed, and it was their price which was exacted for that failure.[46]

The Communists saw themselves as the representatives of these peasants or the common people. The party was deeply affected by Gaitán's death even though Gaitán had been a member of the Liberal Party. One former guerrilla stated, "I have long believed that the guerrillas developed because the Liberal Party leaders turned their backs on their peasant followers and kept silent as the Conservatives went about violently dismantling all forms of independence and Liberal rural organization."[47] Many have pointed to the Liberal Party turning its back on the peasants as a reason for peasant defection to the Communist Party and as a reason for the violence.

However, there is much speculation that Gaitán was a Communist or had Communist sympathies. The Communist Party viewed Gaitán's assassination as part of an anticommunist declaration that had been passed at the Pan-American Conference. The mantra of the Communists became "Against the reactionary violence, the violence organized by the masses."[48]

Shortly before the assassination of Gaitán, in the final days of 1947, the Communist Party created the organization Popular Autodefense. These groups were created in response to other guerrilla groups that the Liberal and Conservative Parties had set up throughout the country. The violence throughout Colombia was rampant and everyone on every side was participating in the violence. "The Autodefense was a popular armed organization of the peasants and was under the direction of the Communist Party in the agrarian region under the Party's control."[49] This organization was created by the Communists to support the peasants but it was not necessarily controlled by the Communist Party. It seems the Communist Party came up with the idea of the organization and allowed the peasants to do as they pleased. Arenas stated, "In reality, it [the Autodefense] was a strong movement formed by multitudes of peasants."[50] After Gaitán's death and the violence that followed perpetrated by the Communists, the Communist Party organized the guerrillas of Davis located to the south of Tolima.[51] The purpose of these guerrilla groups, according to the Communist Party, was to defend the peasants against the Colombian military. The defense groups created by the Communists in 1948 became "guerrilla groups . . . that were of new quality."[52] The guerrilla groups were virulent and received what was equivalent to military training to fight forces controlled or allied with the Liberals or the Conservatives. Gaitán's death frustrated the Communists and so in order to protect the masses from the government, the Communists sent out Communist guerrillas to defend the masses.

Second Era, 1954–1963

The Communist Party was outlawed in 1954. At this point in the analysis, it is important to state that history must be studied through the glasses that witnessed history. The FARC is essentially a product of the Cold War. During the Cold War, the United States led the fight against communism. In America's eyes, any political system including brutal military dictatorships such as that of Augusto Pinochet's were better than another Communist country in America's backyard. After the fall of the Berlin Wall in 1989, the world knew without a doubt that communism was not a viable political system. In addition, communism directly led to the deaths of approximately 300 million people under the auspices of Mao Zedong and Joseph Stalin. Historians do not really know how many people were killed in China and the USSR because censuses were not taken; the death toll could be far greater or even less. The cries of the dead were drowned by the famines, purges, and gulags. In all, communism was a political system that "looked great on paper" but could never quite get past the maniacal, murdering dictator who distributed the goods to the people.

With the former information in mind, it is possible to understand why the Communist Party was outlawed in 1954 by the military government of General Gustavo Rojas Pinilla, formed in 1953. Pinilla had a difficult job in mending the Colombian society after several years of bloody violence. He outlawed the Communists because he considered them a greater danger to Colombian society. They had been publicly calling for a Proletarian revolution since 1948.

The prohibition of the Communist Party in 1954 was one major source of frustration that led to the creation of the FARC. The prohibition of the Communist Party was the government's and Colombia's population's final exclusion of the far left and one can imagine the frustration the Communists must have felt when their ability to use the political process was denied. Both the Liberal and Conservative Parties had ganged up on the Communist Party and banned it from power. General Pinzón Caicedo of the FARC summarized the situation when he stated:

> The commander of the army has asked the opinion of the citizens, conscious of their civic duties to finally understand that the war presents a war not only against the public. . . . This is without embellishment or clichés the great war between democracy and communism, carried out in the Colombian theater. [53]

The exclusion of the Communists because of their radical political ideologies had created a war between a fledgling struggling democracy like Colombia and the Great Iron Curtain of Communism. After the dictatorship of General Rojas ended in 1957, the Communist Party asked the guerrillas to become autodefense units and remain in an alert status. [54]

In another attempt to exclude the Communist Party and consolidate its political power, the Liberal and Conservative Parties created the National Front in 1958. This was an agreement to share power between the Liberals and Conservatives. The two parties would alternate the presidency and share Congress equally. It infuriated the Communists that a supposed democratic system could allow two political parties to share power equally regardless of what the people wanted or voted for in elections. At first, the guerrillas were actually prepared to cooperate with the National Front in the hopes that they could gain some political power. Manuel Marulanda, the leader of the FARC along with other guerrillas stated:

> As patriots, who have struggled during the years prior to 10 May 1957 against despotic dictatorships which sowed ruin in the countryside and towns, we are not interested in the armed struggle and we are willing to collaborate in any way we can, with the task of pacification which the present government of Doctor Alberto Lleras Camarago is prepared to implement.[55]

However, the Communist Party quickly realized that the Conservatives and Liberals would not share power with Communists; it was difficult enough to work together as two separate parties.

In addition, the United States played a large role in creating the frustration that led to the creation of the FARC. Manuel Marulanda stated in 1964, "Imperialism is our biggest enemy. The forces that we fight here in these forests are nothing more than troops commanded by the imperialists. . . . The imperialist Yankee is not only our enemy but the enemy of the entire world."[56] Marulanda saw the United States as a greater enemy than the Colombian government and it created frustration that led to the creation of the FARC.

In addition, President John F. Kennedy created the Alliance for Progress in 1961. The Alliance for Progress was a ten-year plan that was meant to bring about economic progress and political freedom in Latin America. In the case of Colombia, the United States provided $298.1 million just in military assistance from 1953 to 1961 and $2,091.4 billion in military assistance alone from 1946 to 2007. A lot of this military assistance went toward fighting the FARC and communism.[57]

Colombia was "the first country in Latin America to adopt U.S. CI [counter-insurgency] measures in relation to its perceived problems of insurgency and civil unrest and also hosted the first Latin America counterinsurgency training school."[58] The goal of the U.S. military to indoctrinate the Colombian military with anticommunist rhetoric was clear.

> From the beginning it was considered that in order to adequately influence and capture the minds of present and future [Colombian] Armed Forces leaders, with the objective of orientating them to western democratic concepts and precepts, much more was required than just obvious simple publications expounding on the virtues of western democracy and the evils of communism. It was deemed necessary to use the gentle indirect approach, which would expand their mental horizons and imbue them with the spirit and great universal thoughts of great thinkers and writers of all ages, who believed in the virtue of a free society in all fields of endeavor. . . . Coupled with the above an approximate total of 225,000 copies of direct anti-Communist type of literature and security was distributed to the Armed Forces unites and personnel as well as

civilians during various civic action 'Jornadas' of many military units. . . .
Another media [*sic*] was the utilization of numerous movies, depicting the
tragedy, misery, and inhumanness of communism. These were distributed for
showing in every Army headquarters and unit down to and including company
level. [59]

Furthermore, the Colombian military was significantly influenced by the
training its cadets and officers were receiving at The School of the Americas
in Fort Benning, Georgia. [60] The School of the Americas was created in 1946
to teach military strategy, fight insurgencies, and create military profession-
alism in Latin American militaries. [61] Washington refused to allow another
Cuba to be created and the Cuban revolution was an inspiration to the
FARC. [62] Arenas stated, "The people of Cuba gave us a great example for our
continent." [63]

In addition, the Colombian government intensified its attacks on the
Communists in 1964 because the Communists had taken over five municipal-
ities. Plan Lazo was launched with the help of training and military weaponry
from the United States. In an effort to incorporate the "bullets and beans"
strategy, the United States would provide economic stimulus to poverty-
stricken areas while using bullets to take care of the Communist areas. Some
16,000 Colombian troops surrounded the valley of Marquetalia while the
Colombian air force carpet-bombed the region. Most of the peasants escaped
and networks of Communist guerrillas were built throughout the country. In
total, only a few Communists lost their lives and the Communists had actually won the battle. If anything, the Colombian government had only rein-
forced the idea that Communists could and should protect the peasants from
the government.

It is evident that the Marquetalia incident was one of the greatest causes
of frustration to the Communist guerrillas. In a biographical book pertaining
to Marulanda, Arenas states, "The FARC has its origins in the resistance
from Marquetalia." [64] In the introduction of Arenas' book, an unknown writer
asserts that the Marquetalia attack is the beginning of a new era in the
relationship between the guerrillas and the government. "This phase, initiated
by an attack which is the third time the Colombian army has attacked Marquetalia has unfurled the plans of Colombia. This has created a new stage in
the war." [65] It was also stated later by Arenas that "because of Marquetalia,
they [Communist guerrillas] believed in the resistance." [66] After Marquetalia,
Arenas began to think big, "create the Southern Bloc and seize power for the
people." [67] Marulanda stated, "Only now, after 34 years of permanent armed
confrontation, the three powers [United States, Colombia, and France] and
society start to realize the seriousness of the Marquetalia attack." [68]

After Plan Lazo, the Communist Party wrote letters and messages to all
the democratic organizations and personalities in Colombia explaining what

had occurred in Plan Lazo. They had created such a stir that some French intellectuals such as Jean Paul Sartre, Simone Beauvoir, and Jacques Duclós wrote a letter to the Colombian government denouncing the violence. [69] Some organizations such as the Catholic Church came to investigate but the Colombian government, according to the Communists, would not allow them access to the areas. Plan Lazo was the final straw for the Communist Party; it began to believe that violence against the government and those civilians that did not agree with it was the only way to accomplish the Proletarian Revolution. It was then that the Communists decided to become professional guerrillas. [70]

Third Era, 1964 to Today

In September 1964, the Block of the South Conference was held and the FARC was created at this conference. In his book *Diario de la Resistancia de Marquetalia,* Jacobo Arenas includes documents concerning the initial creation of the FARC. In these documents, the FARC summarizes the reasons why it chose to radicalize and use violence. The Document Agrarian Program of the Guerrillas explains:

> We are the core of a revolutionary movement that started in 1948. . . . We have been victims of the politics of "blood and fire" preconceived and carried out by the oligarchy in power. Against us, in the last fifteen years, four wars have been unleashed. . . . We have been the primary victims of the fury of the large landowners because here in this part of Colombia, their interests are predominate. . . . For these reasons, we have suffered physically and spiritually all the bestialities of the rotten regime seated high above the monopoly of the large landowners and the production and the exportation under the United States. It is for these reasons that we fight against our troops, planes, special forces, and especially the North Americans.
>
> We have arrived at a place where multiple doors have been destroyed in the procurement of aid to lead an anticommunist crusade, an unpatriotic crusade against our people, a long and bloody battle. We are revolutionaries fighting for a change in the regime. But it would please us to fight this battle using the means least painful for our people: the peaceful way, the democratic fight of the masses, and through the legal means that the Colombian Constitution has provided. This way has been violently closed to us and we are revolutionaries that have responded to history, obligated by the circumstances previously mentioned, we have chosen the other way, the path of the armed revolutionary fighting for power. [71]

On March 17, 1965, the FARC committed its first known terrorist attack. "Pedro Antonio Marín (alias Tirofijo), and his band of about 100 men assaulted the village of Inzá in the department of Cauca. They murdered sixteen villagers, including the local mayor, two policemen, several peasants, and two nuns."[72] The nuns were supposedly an accident.

In May 1966, a second conference occurred and this is the official creation date of the FARC. Camilo Echandía states, "The FARC alone was responsible for organizing itself like Communist guerrillas in 1966 that were guided by goals to take political power."[73] The actual statement is written in the *Declaracion Politica de la Segunda Conferencia Guerrillera del Bloque Sur*. It states:

> We have united at this Conference and constituted Las Fuerzas Armadas Revolucionarias de Colombia (F.A.R.C.), that begins a new era of the fight and of unity with all the revolutionaries in our country, with all the workers, farmers, students and intellectuals, with all our people, in order to drive the fight of the masses making the insurrection popular and taking the power for the people.

It is evident that after repeated incidences, the frustration of the Communist Party continued to grow and violence became the method of choice for dealing with a Colombian population that did not fully support communism and a government that would not allow the Communist Party to participate in politics. Although the Communist Party had taken almost half of the Colombian territory by force, it still expected to remain a legitimate political contender. One cannot expect to be taken peacefully if one is slowly taking over a country. Few believed that the Communist Party had peaceful intentions. In addition, obviously the Communist Party did not have a large following or popular support because very few people voted for the Communists in elections and, most importantly, a Proletarian Revolution never started. The Colombian people never rose up and overthrew the government. Nothing happened after several years of trying to create political change in a more peaceful manner. Terrorism relieved the feelings of impotence that the Communist Party must have felt and thus led to the creation of the FARC.

The numbers of members in the FARC at the time of its creation are estimated to be approximately 350 people. Most of the people who became members of the FARC were peasants from the Marquetalia region and came from the Southern Block in the southern region of Colombia. The FARC's major areas of influence included areas where sharecropping and squatters were prevalent. The FARC operated out of the old peasant republics. They were successful in gaining support and guerrillas from poorer, rural areas. Wickham-Crowley found that all areas of Colombia with double-digit sharecropping numbers were areas of guerrilla influence such as Tolima, Santander, Caldas, Valle, Meta, and Antioquia.[74] The FARC is actually one of few terrorists groups that consist of impoverished people. FARC members saw themselves as the creators and purveyors of equality. One former member of the FARC who shared her thoughts about the FARC stated:

We shared our dreams about the Colombia we wanted, but without the theoretical controversies of the university. We were united by a deep respect for armed groups and the conviction that change in the country needed armed support. Up until then the socialist project had been the clearest option for radical change from a country led by the privileged few to one in which social justice prevailed.[75]

Problematically for the FARC, a capitalist economic system helped to improve the economy from 1964 to 1978. "In 1964, the top 10 percent of the population controlled 45.5 percent of the country's total wealth, falling to 37.6 percent of total national wealth in 1978. The bottom 50 percent of the population saw their share of national wealth increase from 14.8 percent in 1964 to 18.6 percent in 1978."[76]

THE RADICALIZATION OF THE COMMUNIST PARTY AND THE ASCENDANCE OF VIOLENT PERSONALITIES

The radicalization of the Communist Party is a long and complicated story. In summary, the Communist Party (PCC) was created in 1930 from the ashes of the Revolutionary Socialist Party.[77] The Communist Party did not radicalize until 1948, when they began using violence. For approximately 16 years, the Communists functioned as both a political party and a guerrilla force. A priest-contemporary-turned-guerrilla in the Army of National Liberation (ELN) recounts in the early 1960s, "After forty years of political activity, the Communist Party had its cells [guerrillas] operating in every corner of the country."[78] Finally, in 1964, the FARC, the terrorist organization was formed from a radical guerrilla sect of the Communist Party.

With numbers reaching only 8,000 people at the most, the Communists were a minor party in the midst of the power struggle between the Conservatives and the Liberals in the mid-1940s in Colombia. The Conservative Party regained power when Mariano Ospina Pérez was elected president in 1946. In that same election, the Communists fared well in the Congressional elections, gaining 25,000 votes, and electing one Senate and one House member. Problematically, in the election of 1946, dissent grew within the Party because the Party had disagreed on whom to elect to the presidency. Some members of the Party supported Gaitán; Augusto Durán led these people. The other members supported Turbay for president; Gilberto Vieira led these Communists.

However, in 1947 the Communists squandered what little legislative power they had when the Party split. The Party met in Bucaramanga in July 1947 to try to reconcile its differences. Durán blocked the Party's efforts to make Vieira the Secretary General of the Party. The meeting in Bucaramanga actually exasperated the conflict within the Communist Party and the Party could not resolve its problems. The Party then officially split into two parties; Vieria founded his own Colombian Communist Party, while Durán sponsored the Colombian Workers Party. Most historians consider the Colombian Communist Party the authentic Colombian Communist Party, and so many historians state that the Colombian Communist Party was formed in 1948 although the Communists had been active in Colombia for several years beforehand.

Vieria pursued more violent paths in the Colombian Communist Party. Osterling states, "The PCC divided itself into various factions which ranged from those who supported the achievement of revolutionary goals through peaceful means, to those who encouraged the use of violence and military-type strategies to achieve power."[79] In the final days of 1947, the Central Committee of the Colombian Communist Party sent small groups of guerrillas throughout the areas where they maintained control.[80] Then after Gaitán's death in 1948, the Communist Party created more violent, professional guerrilla groups. Arenas states, "It is to say [they are] combatants of a new type, professionals from the Cause, that fight above all for power."[81] Rather than the typical peasant guerrillas that have previously consisted of the Communist forces, these guerrillas had received some military training from Communist commanders.

In the beginning, these guerrilla groups were rather isolated from the Communist Party and the Liberal Party paid them little attention. Sureshot stated,

> When we began the revolution, the rumor never arrived nor did communication from the Liberal leaders . . . later, in Sur del Tolima we did nothing without a fight with the honest Liberals; we left El Davis and spent almost two solitary years in El Charro, roaming through the mountain with little contact with the party [Communist Party].[82]

At this point, the Communist Party was receiving aid from several sources. The USSR was supportive by giving the Colombian Communists aid and political instruction. Russian diplomats would throw lavish parties at the Soviet Legation in support of the Communist Party. Moscow sent several delegates to Colombia and Colombia sent some in return. In addition, Russia provided some monetary aid to the Communists. However, most of the monetary aid the Communist Party received came from Venezuela.

Many Communists from Venezuelan President Romulo Betancourt's cabinet were exiled to Baranquilla, Colombia, for the period 1929 to 1936. When they later returned home to Venezuela, they kept their political ties with the Communists. These men had been part of the "Baranquilla Plan," which was a plan to liberate Colombia, Ecuador, and Peru from economic feudalism. Ammunition and arms were sent over the Venezuelan border and given to the Colombian Communists. These weapons were traced by their serial numbers back to Venezuela. President Betancourt denied all involvement when the scandal broke, stating that the ammunition and weaponry were stolen from Venezuela. Although one would hesitate to call the Communist Party well financed, it is certainly true that the Communist Party was receiving aid from both Venezuelan and Russian sources.

The most influential initial incident that led to the radicalization of the Communist Party was the assassination of one the most important Colombian leaders in history. On April 9, 1948, when he was going to lunch, Gaitán, a member of the Liberal Party who was considered a Communist sympathizer, was assassinated. Both sects of the Communist Party were outraged. Although he had supported Turbay for president, the leader of the official Colombian Communist Party, Gilberto Vieira, stated:

> My party considers that the new political conditions created in the country require a full revolutionary battle of the working class and of the people, in order to speed up the belligerent action of the masses and to defend democratic liberties, as well as to defeat the . . . Conservative plans for reaction which confirm to the slogan of Minister Jose Antonio Moltavo, "Blood and Fire."[83]

What followed Gaitán's assassination was tremendous violence. There is strong evidence that the Communists planned and carried out the violence after Gaitán's death. The Communist Party wrote a letter on April 4, 1948, five days before the violence ensued, talking about a revolt in Latin American countries that was assisted by the Venezuelan government. Several Communists were also seen leading the riots. The Communists also made announcements over the radio calling for violence or influencing others to commit violence. A writer in *El Tiempo*, the Bogotá newspaper, wrote,

> To spread terror, to create panic are fundamentals of the Communist offensive strategy. Looting, steal things that might be useful, can be understood. But why destroy the Palace of San Carlos; why throw workers and modest employees out of work? Because this enters into the Communist plan: creation of panic, of desperation, of disorientation, the spreading of hunger among workers.
>
> On the radio, we heard them urging on the incendiarists. And we saw them at the head of the mobs which set the torch to the governmental palace, which was just of the beginning of the barbarism. Then, another Communist tactic, the jails were thrown open, bringing six thousand more malefactors into the wild melee and the wild hordes.
>
> Is it possible to doubt the Communist direction of the uprising? Whoever listened on the radio would have been sufficiently convinced. They had everything ready and were prepared. They called over the radio to cities and towns, to specific individuals in those places to whom they gave specific orders and

directions; and on the radio appeared the name of the mysterious "Doctor X," as head of the movement. [84]

In addition, there were certain Communist characteristics to the violence that displayed the Communist beliefs in obliterating religion from an oppressed class society. The Communists called over the radio that the priests were launching a war against the people. Priests were taken out of the church, and stoned or beaten to death.

> Those who ran into the churches broke the stained glass windows and turned the pews into firewood. They wrecked the gilded altars, pulled down the statue of the Virgin Mary, and wrenched the holy cross from the altar. Some defecated there. . . . Throughout the afternoon and early evening men assaulted convents and cloisters, no doubt seeking to fulfill deeply hidden sexual fantasies on defenseless nuns and young virgins. [85]

Killing members of the Catholic Church is highly uncharacteristic of the Colombians who traditionally have shown great respect and reverence for the Catholic Church. Although the Communist Party was blamed by some for the assassination of Gaitán, this was never proven. It is still unknown who assassinated Gaitán. Historians are certain that the Communists helped instigate violence after Gaitán's death. [86]

In an interesting side note, Fidel Castro participated in the rioting that occurred in Bogotá. Castro was supposed to meet with Gaitán that same afternoon that Gaitán was shot and of course, Gaitán never made it to the meeting. Castro "quickly joined a small group of men that was attacking a police station. Inside, he took a tear-gas gun, donned military boots, shirt, cap, grabbed a rifle and sixteen bullets, and ventured out again." [87] What is interesting is that the FARC that was formed in 1964 modeled its violent revolution after Castro's Communist revolution in Cuba.

As the years passed, the Communists continued to create underground cells, recruiting peasants in their efforts. Jacobo Arenas was one of the Communists picked to lead the guerrillas. Jacobo Arenas stated that

> the central management of the Communist Party needed to strengthen the presence of their framework in the theater of future events. To Hernando González and myself, we accepted the grand honor to be commissioned to complete this work, to represent the young Communists and the secondly, the Communist Party. [88]

The violent nature of Colombia never changed as new presidents took office. The end of Ospina's presidency was marked by a shootout between the Liberals and Conservatives in Congress on September 8, 1949. As he continued to lose power, Ospina escalated the violence between the Liberals and the Conservatives. He used the army to harass and attack the Liberals and he dissolved Congress. After Ospina left, the Conservative dictator Laureano Gómez took over on November 27, 1949.

Gómez continued the violence and attacked both Liberals and guerrillas. Gómez once stated:

> Liberalism has died and their supporters are being colonized by communism and now there are two worlds on this planet, communism and anticommunism and this [fight] finally has inscribed its names on the Conservative leaders, the fight until death has joined [Conservatives and anticommunism] in the end and in this country.[89]

Many Liberals fled to other countries or cowered in their homes. Gómez used repression to improve the economy of Colombia and was quite successful. Roberto Urdaneta Arbeláez became the acting president in 1951 after Gómez had a heart attack. Urdaneta was Gómez's puppet president and was cast aside when Gómez's presidency was threatened. Gustavo Rojas Pinilla finally ousted Gómez in a bloodless coup in 1953.

Pinilla was a military dictator who stopped the anarchic bloodshed between classes and the Liberals and Conservatives. His dictatorship created a period of less violence and was the break between the eras of La Violencia. While trying to help the masses, he alienated the oligarchy and wealthier classes by taxing them. He closed two newspapers because they were encouraging conflict through their publications, although he reopened them later. He created a third party called the Third Force. Most importantly, Pinilla gave amnesty to the guerrillas; in his efforts to unite society, Pinilla not only tried to end the violence but also increased the wages of the peasants. Pinilla's government also created some social welfare programs to assist the peasants.

One specific incident, the killing of some students on June 13, 1954, caused a military campaign that lasted a year. This campaign was the first time the Communist guerrillas and the Autodefense units united to fight the military. In 1956, the Communist Party called for a peaceful revolution, thus forcing many young guerrillas to look for a more drastic solution. "The Colombian Communist's Party support of resolutions passed by the Twentieth Soviet Congress in 1956, which called for a peaceful road to revolution, disappointed many young Colombians, leading them to break from the Party in order to follow the more radical Cuban model."[90]

Pinilla was overthrown by a military coup in 1958. The Liberals and Conservatives had created the National Front to share power in 1958 so that Pinilla would not be reelected. The Communists were firmly opposed "to the bipartisan system jointly commissioned by the 'national front' oligarchy, which we consider anti-democratic and antinational."[91] At this point, the Communist Party was still involved with the Communist guerrillas, which they considered a useful resource in case they wanted to create a coup against a military dictatorship.[92] In 1958, "in Marquetalia, another guerrilla conference occurred with assistance from a member of the central Communist Party."[93]

Albertos Lleras Camargo from the Liberal Party took over the presidency after Pinilla was ousted. Camargo launched attacks against the independent republics, the agrarian resistance, and the Autodefense. The independent republics were not only economic but also military in nature. The independent republics were in the southern area of Tolima and were created by famous guerrillas such as Tirofijo, Charro Negro, Ciro Castaño, and Isauro Yosa. Many of these men were later killed, except for Tirofijo, who became the leader and founder of the FARC.[94] In 1960, Jacobo Prías Alape, or Charro Negro, the commander of the revolutionary guerrillas, was assassinated by Liberal troops commanded by José de Jesús Oviedo, otherwise known as Mariachi.[95]

In 1964, with the official creation of the FARC, Jacobo Arenas later stated:

> This conference has the importance of knowing that in these moments the armed resistance movement is growing, in this moment that these fundamental detachments waiting for the Communist conference, this is their conference, new formulations concerning the armed fight call for the elaboration of a strategy and military tactics from guerrillas that create new successes and to the growth of their prestige, that is the greatest prestige of the party [Communist], the prestige of the marxist-leninist ideas, the prestige of the revolution and communism.[96]

By 1966, the Communist Party was ready to wash its hands of the guerrillas. Many Communists had seen the break between Communist China and the USSR in the early 1960s and had decided that Soviet assistance was needed to create a revolution through peaceful means. Violence was not the best strategy anymore. The guerrillas were not only groups created and dispersed by the Communist Party but were also a military extension of the Communist Party.

> Within the Marxist PCC as well as within the PCML [Marxist-Leninist Communist Party that split from the PCC] there were militants who advocated the use of violence to achieve change. These radical members organized themselves into two guerrilla organizations: the Marxist "Southern Block" soon renamed the "Colombian Revolutionary Armed Forces (FARC) . . . and the EPL.[97]

By 1966, the FARC had split from the Communist Party, becoming the terrorist organization it is today. The Communist Party made an effort to separate themselves from the newly created FARC, stating:

> Our party . . . nevertheless considers that there is no revolutionary situation in Colombia as yet. It does not consider armed struggle in cities because such a struggle can be little more than a series of isolated events accomplished by little groups. . . . The guerrilla struggle at present is not the principal form of battle.[98]

The FARC had been born and shortly afterward was abandoned by its parents.

The radicalization of the Communist Party is an important explanatory factor in the creation of the FARC. Had the Communist Party not turned to violence, the FARC would not have been created. Marulanda would not have left the Liberal guerrillas to join the Communist guerrillas and would not have consolidated his leadership in the FARC.

CONCLUSION

The creation and radicalization of the FARC can be attributed to three factors. The charismatic leadership of Marulanda was important in the creation of the FARC and its resort to terrorist tactics. Frustration that resulted from several incidents helped turn the FARC toward violent tactics that could help accomplish its agenda. Lastly, the radicalization of the Communist Party and its use of guerrilla groups helped to create a guerrilla organization that eventually became a terrorist organization.

In its early days, the FARC was relatively weak and was more of a defensive organization. The FARC was harassed by the Colombian military and by large cattle ranchers who were looking to take land back from the peasants. Gradually, the FARC grew and was able to offer protection to peasants, to take fresh territory, and to provide basic services to areas under its control. Instead as time progressed, the idea of defending oneself from the government grew, and so did the FARC.

> They [FARC] were always the underdogs who with their will could defeat the enemy. . . . Glorifying the self-defense groups strengthened the guerrilla side of the organization. Inevitably the self-defense groups replicated themselves and the FARC grew. The political side, the Communist Party tried to maintain control, but soon the rebels began taking the offensive. With military victories came more political power for the FARC. Soon it was clear that the rebels were becoming the leaders of the organization.[99]

However, the FARC and other guerrilla groups did not always protect all the peasants; indigenous peoples who comprise a part of the peasantry were often attacked. Appelbaum states:

The principal guerrilla armies (known by their Spanish acronyms as the FARC, ELN, and EPL) have all operated in the mountains of western Caldas and Risaralda, claiming to support indigenous land rights. Indigenous leaders do not want to antagonize either side in the armed conflict and have attempted to stake out a public position of neutrality. But this stance has not protected them from repression. Military personnel and paramilitaries, allegedly backed by landowners and politicians, have murdered indigenous activists, a pattern that has been repeated across the country. [100]

In addition, Kline talks about how areas of FARC control were generally areas that the Colombian government considered independent republics because the FARC was in complete control of these areas. There was no rule of law in these areas. The FARC would take over areas where peasants were growing illegal crops. As the FARC continued to face greater pressure from Colombian troops that were financed by the U.S. government, they began to engage in more actions that were meant to harm civilians, such as land mines, gas cylinder bombs, hijackings of airplanes, assassinations of journalists, peace activists, and elected officials, and attacks on family parks. These attacks against noncombatants only decreased its popularity among the peasants, yet the FARC kept accumulating more territory. In retaliation, the Colombian military would train and equip peasants who wanted to defend themselves from the FARC. These groups were created to provide self-defense against the FARC. [101]

From 1964 to about 1966, the FARC experienced some major setbacks in their numbers. In 1964, the Colombian government launched Plan Lazo. Plan Lazo included 16,000 troops that surrounded the valley of Marquetalia, the major stronghold of the FARC and its supporters while the Colombian Airforce carpet-bombed the region. Plan Lazo, in addition to some other Colombian military actions, caused the FARC to lose 70 percent of its armaments and a large portion of its soldiers from 1966 to 1968. However, most scholars state that the FARC and the peasants were not strongly affected by the aftermath of Plan Lazo. After 1966, the FARC embarked on a major program to build mobile and secretive guerrilla groups. By 1978, the FARC's forces had grown to over 1,000 soldiers. [102] It was not until the 1980s that the FARC became a formidable terrorist group.

NOTES

1. James Rochlin, *Social Forces and the Revolution in Military Affairs, The Cases of Colombia and Mexico* (New York: Palgrave Macmillan, 2007).
2. Camilo Echandía, "Expansión Territorial de las Guerrillas Colombianas," in Malcolm Deas and María Victoria Llorente (eds.) *Reconocer la Guerra para Construir la Paz* (Bogotá, Colombia: Cerec, 1999), 107. Look at the map to determine the extent of FARC territorial control.
3. Geoff Simons, *Colombia, A Brutal History* (London: SAQI, 2004), 39.

4. James Rochlin, *Social Forces and the Revolution in Military Affairs, The Cases of Colombia and Mexico* (New York: Palgrave Macmillan, 2007), 22.

5. J. Fred Rippy, *The Capitalists and Colombia* (New York: The Vanguard Press, 1931). See chapter 5.

6. John W. Green, *Gaitanismo, Left Liberalism, and Popular Mobilization in Colombia* (Gainesville, FL: University Press of Florida, 2003).

7. Steven Dudley, *Walking Ghosts, Murder and Guerrilla Politics in Colombia* (New York: Routledge, 2004).

8. Daniel H. Levine, *Religion and Politics in Latin America, The Catholic Church in Venezuela and Colombia* (Princeton, NJ: Princeton University Press, 1981), 64.

9. Camilo Granada, "La evolución del gasto en seguridad y defensa en Colombia, 1950–1954" in Malcolm Deas and María Victoria Llorente (eds.), *Reconocer la Guerra para Construir la Paz* (Bogotá, Colombia: Cerec, 1999), 548.

10. Donny Meertens, *Ensayos Sobre Tierra, Violencia, y Género* (Colombia: Universidad Nacional de Colombia, 2000).

11. Reza Rezazadeh and Joseph Mac McKenzie, *Political Parties in Colombia, Continuity in Political Style* (Ann Arbor, MI: University Microfilms International, 1978).

12. Gary Hoskin, "The State and Political Parties in Colombia" in Eduardo Posada-Carbó (ed.), *Colombia, The Politics of Reforming the State*, 45–70 (New York: St. Martin's Press, 2000), 46.

13. Donny Meertens, *Ensayos Sobre Tierra, Violencia, y Género* (Colombia: Universidad Nacional de Colombia, 2000), 196–198.

14. Harvey F. Kline, *Showing Teeth to Dragons, State Building by Colombian President Álvaro Uribe Vélez, 2002–2006* (Tuscaloosa, AL: The University of Alabama Press, 2009), 11.

15. Nazih Richani, *Systems of Violence, The Political Economy of War and Peace in Colombia* (New York: State University of New York Press, 2002), 62.

16. Luis Alberto Matta Aldana, *Colombia y las Farc-EP Origen de la lucha guerrillera. Testimonio del Comandante Jaime Guaraca* (Naffaroa, Colombia: Txalaparta, 1999).

17. Doug Stokes, *America's Other War, Terrorizing Colombia* (New York: Zed Books, 2004), 78.

18. Robin Kirk, *More Terrible Than Death, Violence, Drugs, and America's War in Colombia* (Cambridge, MA: Public Affairs, 2004), 30.

19. Arturo Alape, *Las Vidas de Pedro Antonio Marin Manuel Marulanda Velez Tirofijo* (Bogotá, Colombia: Planeta, 1989), 152.

20. Arturo Alape, *Las Vidas de Pedro Antonio Marin Manuel Marulanda Velez Tirofijo* (Bogotá, Colombia: Planeta, 1989), 161.

21. Jacobo Arenas, *Diario de la Resistencia de Marquetalia* (Colombia: Ediciones Abejón Mono, 1972), 35.

22. Jacobo Arenas, *Diario de la Resistencia de Marquetalia* (Colombia: Ediciones Abejón Mono, 1972), 56.

23. Jacobo Arenas, *Cese el Fuego, Una Historia Politica de las FARC* (Bogotá, Colombia: Editorial Oveja Negro, 1985), 15.

24. Carlos Medina Gallego, *Autodefenses, Paramilitaries and Narcotrafficking in Colombia* (Bogotá, Colombia: Editorial Documentos Periodísticos, 1990), 133.

25. Osterling also identifies Marulanda as the leader of the FARC and states that Arenas is the successor to Marulanda. Jorge P. Osterling, *Democracy in Colombia, Clientelist Policies and Guerrilla Warfare* (New Brunswick: Transaction Publishers, 1989), 294.

26. Human Rights Watch, *You'll Learn Not To Cry, Child Combatants in Colombia* (New York: Human Rights Watch, 2003), 51.

27. Robin Kirk, *More Terrible Than Death, Violence, Drugs, and America's War in Colombia* (Cambridge, MA: Public Affairs, 2004), 53.

28. Bert Ruiz, *The Colombian Civil War* (Jefferson, NC: McFarland and Company, Inc., Publishers, 2001), 6.

29. Bert Ruiz, *The Colombian Civil War* (Jefferson, NC: McFarland and Company, Inc., Publishers, 2001), 23.

30. Arturo Alape, *Tirofijo: Los Sueños y Las Montañas* (Bogotá, Colombia: Planeta Colombiana Editorial S.A., 1994), 73–74.

31. Arturo Alape, *Tirofijo: Los Sueños y Las Montañas* (Bogotá, Colombia: Planeta Colombiana Editorial S.A., 1994), 214.

32. Bert Ruiz, *The Colombian Civil War* (Jefferson, NC: McFarland and Company, Inc., Publishers, 2001), 6.

33. Arturo Alape, *Tirofijo: Los Sueños y Las Montañas* (Bogotá, Colombia: Planeta Colombiana Editorial S.A., 1994), 174.

34. Arturo Alape, *Tirofijo: Los Sueños y Las Montañas* (Bogotá, Colombia: Planeta Colombiana Editorial S.A., 1994), 67.

35. Arturo Alape, *Tirofijo: Los Sueños y Las Montañas* (Bogotá, Colombia: Planeta Colombiana Editorial S.A., 1994), 187.

36. Human Rights Watch, *You'll Learn Not To Cry, Child Combatants in Colombia* (New York: Human Rights Watch, 2003), 23.

37. Arturo Alape, *Tirofijo: Los Sueños y Las Montañas* (Bogotá, Colombia: Planeta Colombiana Editorial S.A., 1994), 84.

38. Arturo Alape, *Las Vidas de Pedro Antonio Marin Manuel Marulanda Velez Tirofijo* (Bogotá, Colombia: Planeta Colombia Editorial S.A., 1989), 214.

39. Juanita León, *Country of Bullets, Chronicles of War* (Albuquerque, NM: University of New Mexico Press, 2009), 83.

40. Arturo Alape, *Tirofijo: Los Sueños y Las Montañas* (Bogotá, Colombia: Planeta Colombiana Editorial S.A., 1994), 105.

41. Arturo Alape, *Tirofijo: Los Sueños y Las Montañas* (Bogotá, Colombia: Planeta Colombiana Editorial S.A., 1994), 107.

42. Arturo Alape, *Tirofijo: Los Sueños y Las Montañas* (Bogotá, Colombia: Planeta Colombiana Editorial S.A., 1994), 212.

43. Robin Kirk, *More Terrible Than Death, Violence, Drugs, and America's War in Colombia* (Cambridge, MA: Public Affairs, 2004), 69.

44. Robin Kirk, *More Terrible Than Death, Violence, Drugs, and America's War in Colombia* (Cambridge, MA: Public Affairs, 2004), 29.

45. Robin Kirk, *More Terrible Than Death, Violence, Drugs, and America's War in Colombia* (Cambridge, MA: Public Affairs, 2004), 116.

46. Vernon Lee Fluharty, *Dance of the Millions* (Pittsburgh: University of Pittsburgh Press, 1957), 89.

47. Herbert Braun, *Our Guerrillas, Our Sidewalks, A Journey Into the Violence of Colombia* (Niwot, CO: University Press of Colorado, 1994) 9.

48. Jacobo Arenas, *Diario de la Resistancia de Marquetalia* (Colombia: Ediciones Abejón Mono, 1972), 11.

49. Jacobo Arenas, *Cese el Fuego, Una Historia Politica de las FARC* (Bogotá, Colombia: Editorial Oveja Negro, 1985), 75.

50. Jacobo Arenas, *Cese el Fuego, Una Historia Politica de las FARC* (Bogotá, Colombia: Editorial Oveja Negro, 1985), 75.

51. Jacobo Arenas, *Diario de la Resistancia de Marquetalia* (Colombia: Ediciones Abejón Mono, 1972).

52. Jacobo Arenas, *Cese el Fuego, Una Historia Politica de las FARC* (Bogotá, Colombia: Editorial Oveja Negro, 1985), 77.

53. Jacobo Arenas, *Diario de la Resistancia de Marquetalia* (Colombia: Ediciones Abejón Mono, 1972), 13.

54. Jacobo Arenas, *Diario de la Resistancia de Marquetalia* (Colombia: Ediciones Abejón Mono, 1972), 12.

55. As cited in Jenny Pearce, *Colombia: Inside the Labyrinth* (London: Latin American Bureau, 1990), 64.

56. Jacobo Arenas, *Diario de la Resistancia de Marquetalia* (Colombia: Ediciones Abejón Mono, 1972), 54.

57. U.S. Agency for International Development (USAID), "U.S. Overseas Loans and Grants: Obligations and Loan Authorizations, July 1, 1945–September 30, 2007 (1945–2007)." Retrieved December 23, 2009, from http://gbk.eads.usaidallnet.gov/.

58. Doug Stokes, *America's Other War, Terrorizing Colombia* (New York: Zed Books, 2004), 5.

59. As cited in Doug Stokes, *America's Other War, Terrorizing Colombia* (New York: Zed Books, 2004), 71.

60. James Rochlin, *Vanguard Revolutionaries in Latin America* (Boulder: Lynne Rienner Publishers, 2003), 99–100.

61. Richard F. Grimmet and Mark P. Sullivan, "United States Army School of the Americas: Background and Congressional Concerns," 2005. Retrieved December 23, 2009, from www.globalsecurity.org/intell/library/reports/crs/soa.htm.

62. James Rochlin, *Vanguard Revolutionaries in Latin America* (Boulder: Lynne Rienner Publishers, 2003).

63. Jacobo Arenas, *Diario de la Resistancia de Marquetalia* (Colombia: Ediciones Abejón Mono, 1972), 56.

64. Arturo Alape, *Tirofijo: Los Sueños y Las Montañas* (Bogotá, Colombia: Planeta Colombiana Editorial S.A., 1994), 80.

65. Jacobo Arenas, *Diario de la Resistancia de Marquetalia* (Colombia: Ediciones Abejón Mono, 1972),12.

66. Jacobo Arenas, *Cese el Fuego, Una Historia Politica de las FARC* (Bogotá, Colombia: Editorial Oveja Negro, 1985), 84.

67. Robin Kirk, *More Terrible Than Death, Violence, Drugs, and America's War in Colombia* (Cambridge, MA: Public Affairs, 2004), 55.

68. Cristina Rojas, "Elusive Peace, Elusive Violence: Identity and Conflict in Colombia," in Cristina Rojas and Judy Meltzer (eds.), *Elusive Peace: International, National, and Local Dimensions of Conflict in Colombia*, 209–237 (New York: Palgrave Macmillan, 2005), 220.

69. Jacobo Arenas, *Cese el Fuego, Una Historia Politica de las FARC* (Bogotá, Colombia: Editorial Oveja Negro, 1985), 83.

70. Arturo Alape, *Tirofijo: Los Sueños y Las Montañas*. (Bogotá, Colombia: Planeta Colombiana Editorial S.A., 1994), 25.

71. Jacobo Arenas, *Diario de la Resistancia de Marquetalia* (Colombia: Ediciones Abejón Mono, 1972), 128–130.

72. James L. Payne, *Patterns of Conflict in Colombia* (New Haven, CT: Yale University Press, 1968), 313.

73. Camilo Echandía, "Expansión Territorial de las Guerrillas Colombianas," in Malcolm Deas and María Victoria Llorente (eds.), *Reconocer la Guerra para Construir la Paz* (Bogotá, Colombia: Cerec, 1999), 104.

74. Timothy P. Wickham-Crowley, *Guerrillas and Revolution in Latin America* (Princeton: Princeton University Press, 1992.

75. María Eugenia Vásquez Perdomo, *My Life as a Colombian Revolutionary, Reflections of a Former Guerrillera* (Philadelphia: Temple University Press, 2005), 45.

76. James Rochlin, *Vanguard Revolutionaries in Latin America* (Boulder: Lynne Rienner Publishers), 99.

77. Jenny Pearce, *Colombia: Inside the Labyrinth* (London: Latin American Bureau, 1990), 26.

78. Walter J. Broderick, *Camilo Torres, A Biography of the Priest-Guerrillero* (Garden City, New York: Doubleday and Company, Inc, 1975), 279.

79. Jorge P. Osterling, *Democracy in Colombia, Clientelist Policies and Guerrilla Warfare* (New Brunswick: Transaction Publishers, 1989), 186.

80. Jacobo Arenas, *Cese el Fuego, Una Historia Politica de las FARC* (Bogotá, Colombia: Editorial Oveja Negra, 1985), 75.

81. Jacobo Arenas, *Cese el Fuego, Una Historia Politica de las FARC* (Bogotá, Colombia: Editorial Oveja Negra, 1985), 78.

82. Arturo Alape, *Las Vidas de Pedro Antonio Marin Manuel Marulanda Velez Tirofijo* (Bogotá, Colombia: Planeta Colombia Editorial S.A., 1989), 20.

83. Vernon Lee Fluharty, *Dance of the Millions* (Pittsburgh: University of Pittsburgh Press, 1957), 101.

84. As cited in Vernon Lee Fluharty, *Dance of the Millions* (Pittsburgh: University of Pittsburgh Press, 1957), 102.

85. Herbert Braun, *The Assassination of Gaitán, Public Life and Urban Violence in Colombia* (Madison: University of Wisconsin Press, 1985), 161–162.

86. David Bushnell, *The Making of Modern Colombia, A Nation in Spite of Itself* (Berkeley: University of California Press, 1993), 203.

87. Herbert Braun, *The Assassination of Gaitán, Public Life and Urban Violence in Colombia* (Madison: The University of Wisconsin Press, 1985), 177.

88. Jacobo Arenas, *Diario de la Resistancia de Marquetalia* (Colombia: Ediciones Abejón Mono, 1972), 16.

89. Arturo Alape, *Las Vidas de Pedro Antonio Marin Manuel Marulanda Velez Tirofijo* (Bogotá, Colombia: Planeta Colombia Editorial S.A.), 48.

90. Gary M. Leech, *Killing Peace, Colombia's Conflict and the Failure of US Intervention* (New York: Information Network of the Americas [INOTA], 2002), 14. Jorge P. Osterling, *Democracy in Colombia, Clientelist Policies and Guerrilla Warfare* (New Brunswick: Transaction Publishers, 1989).

91. Jacobo Arenas, *Diario de la Resistancia de Marquetalia* (Colombia: Ediciones Abejón Mono, 1972), 17.

92. Eduardo Pizarro, "Revolutionary Guerrilla Groups in Colombia," in Charles Bergquist, Ricardo Peñaranda, and Gonzalo Sánchez (eds.), *Violence in Colombia, The Contemporary Crisis in Historical Perspective* (Wilmington, DE: SR Books, 1992), 169–193.

93. Arturo Alape, *Las Vidas de Pedro Antonio Marin Manuel Marulanda Velez Tirofijo* (Bogotá, Colombia: Planeta Colombia Editorial S.A.), 257–258.

94. Alfredo Molano, "Violence and Land Colonization," in Charles Bergquist, Ricardo Peñaranda, and Gonzalo Sánchez (eds.), *Violence in Colombia, The Contemporary Crisis in Historical Perspective* (Wilmington, DE: SR Books, 1992), 195–216.

95. Jacobo Arenas, *Cese el Fuego, Una Historia Politica de las FARC* (Bogotá, Colombia: Editorial Oveja Negro, 1985).

96. Arturo Alape, *Tirofijo: Los Sueños y Las Montañas* (Bogotá, Colombia: Planeta Colombiana Editorial S.A., 1994), 80.

97. Jorge P. Osterling, *Democracy in Colombia, Clientelist Policies and Guerrilla Warfare* (New Brunswick: Transaction Publishers, 1989), 187.

98. As cited in Jenny Pearce, *Colombia: Inside the Labyrinth* (London: Latin American Bureau, 1990), 167.

99. Steven Dudley, *Walking Ghosts, Murder, and Guerrilla Politics in Colombia* (New York: Routledge, 2004), 10.

100. Nancy P. Appelbaum, *Muddied Waters, Race, Region, and History in Colombia, 1846–1948* (Durham, NC: Duke University Press, 2003), 201.

101. Harvey F. Kline, *Showing Teeth to Dragons, State Building by Colombian President Álvaro Uribe Vélez, 2002–2006* (Tuscaloosa, AL: The University of Alabama Press, 2009), 13.

102. James F. Rochlin, *Social Forces and the Revolution in Military Affairs* (New York: Palgrave Macmillan, 2007).

Chapter Four

Ceylon Tigers

The Creation and Radicalization of the Liberation Tigers of Tamil Eelam (LTTE)

According to the LTTE, "There are two ways of going about things. . . . There is the passive democratic way, and then there is the armed struggle."[1] The LTTE, or the Liberation Tamil Tigers of Eelam, were founded in 1975. Like many nationalist terrorist organizations, the Tamils Tigers were once part of a larger social movement to create an independent Tamil homeland in the state of Sri Lanka. What is somewhat different from the Tamils Tigers in regard to other terrorist groups is that Tamil people did experience tremendous persecution and oppression from the Sri Lankan government. Unlike those populations represented by the Muslim Brotherhood, the ETA, and the FARC, the Tamil people were truly repressed by their own government, the Sri Lankan government. Although state subjugation can be a sufficient condition for the radicalization of a social movement to a terrorist organization, it is not a necessary condition.

What follows in this chapter is a story of a people, a people that have been pushed into oblivion by their state. The Tamils were once a social movement that fought peacefully for their rights. However, as time progressed radical elements of the social movement like Prabhakaran took control and used unmitigated violence toward his own Tamil people and the greater Sri Lankan population. The purpose of this chapter is to explain why the LTTE radicalized from a social movement into the terrorist organization it is today.

Most scholars point to the Sri Lankan government as a cause of the radicalization of the Tamil people and the creation of the LTTE. DeVotta states in one of the final chapters in his book *Blowback*, "The preceding chapters have shown how Sinhalese ethnocentrism [as defined by government policies] transformed pacific Tamils into terrorists."[2] Although this explanation certainly has merit and it is true that the government did play a part in the radicalization of the LTTE, there are other explanations worth examining. This chapter looks at the role of 1) the radicalization of S. J. V. Chelvanayagam and the Tamil Federal Party (FP), 2) the frustration that led to the formation of the LTTE, and 3) the role that the charismatic leadership of Veluppillai Prabhakaran played in this transition.

THE RELATIONSHIP BETWEEN THE SRI LANKAN GOVERNMENT AND THE LTTE

Currently, the Sinhalese make up less than 75 percent of the population of Sri Lanka, while Indian Tamils and Sri Lankan Tamils make up about 9 percent of the population.[3] Although some scholars contend that animosity has always existed between the two ethnic groups, there is no consensus concerning the history of the relationship between the Tamils and the Sinhalese people. On one side, Hellmann-Rajanayagam states, "Problems between the Tamils and the Sinhalese are not a phenomenon of the 1980's. According to one's approach, one can trace them back over 20, 50, 100 or even 2000 years."[4] Conversely, Pfaffenberger states:

> There is nothing about the traditional cultures of the Tamil and the Sinhalese people of Sri Lanka that prevent them from living in amity. Far from isolated in precolonial times, the Tamil and Sinhalese peoples of Sri Lanka were in sufficiently close communication to have deeply influenced the sentence structure of each other's languages, the minutiae of their strikingly similar kinship classification systems, the structure and organization of their caste systems, and the details of village rituals. . . . But it was precisely because the two groups dwelt in amity for so long that their cultures bear some remarkable similarities to one another.[5]

One journalist states that the conflict began directly after independence when Tamils began demanding 50 percent representation in government even though they only made up 23 percent of the island's population. Of course, the Sinhalese became uneasy after these demands and the conflict began.[6] However, there is some consensus concerning when the problems between the two groups began. From most scholars' accounts, it appears that the most serious problems between the two ethnicities occurred almost a decade after independence (1948) when Sinhala was declared the official language of Sri Lanka in 1956. DeVotta states, "The 1956 election was the first to indicate that the country lacked strong norms that could withstand political opportunism, and the ethnic outbidding practiced by the UNO and SLFP [Sinhala political parties] especially evidenced this."[7]

It began with two political actors that were mostly responsible for instituting the Sinhala-only policy in the 1956 parliamentary elections. Both men compromised principles to gain political power. The first political actor was S.W.R.D. Bandaranaike, a cabinet member in the ruling United National Party (UNP) (who later changed parties and joined the Sri Lanka Freedom Party [SLFP]) who proposed the Sinhala-only policy even though he could not even read or write in Sinhala. Bandaranaike came from a wealthy family who had changed religions constantly throughout history to suit their political goals as often as necessary. According to one relative, "The son of Maha Mudaliyar [S.W.R.D. Bandaranaike] leaped to political power by identifying himself with the 'everybodies' and 'anybodies' to whom the post-Independence era was giving a decisive vote and by spurning the 'somebodies' of his own clan whom Independence had displaced."[8] Bandaranaike had realized the political power he could harness by establishing Sinhalese as the official language and his aspirations to become the prime minister were great. His counterpart for the prime minister position, John Kotelawala from the UNP Party, also jumped on the Sinhala-only-policy bandwagon. The outcome was the inauguration of Bandaranaike on April 12, 1956, as the Prime Minister of Sri Lanka and the passage of the Official Language Act of 1956.

The reasons for instituting the Official Language Act ran far deeper than a quest for political power. Since the British colonization of Ceylon (as Sri Lanka was originally called), English was the official language of the island. Tamils stereotypically tended to have higher fluency rates in English, although their literacy rates overall were historically lower. As a result, Tamils held many jobs in the civil service sector because fluency in English was required for government jobs. In tough economic times, these civil service jobs were highly coveted because of job security and good pay. In addition, the Sinhalese were becoming increasingly literate in English and were obtaining education at higher rates. In an effort to assert their racial dominance in Sri Lanka, several Sinhalese began calling for Sinhala to be the official language of Sri Lanka. Because the Tamils comprised less than one sixth of the population, the majority party, the UNP, passed The Official Language Act of 1956 without much trouble and with Bandaranaike's influence.

The Official Language Act of 1956 stated:

a. That Sinhalese should be made the medium of instruction in all schools.
b. That Sinhalese should be made a compulsory subject in all public examinations.
c. That Legislation should be introduced to permit the business of the State Council to be conducted in Sinhalese.
d. That a Commission should be appointed to choose for translation and to translate important books of other languages into Sinhalese.

e. That a Commission should be appointed to report on all steps that need to be taken to affect the transition from English into Sinhalese. [9]

As one might imagine, this policy struck the Tamils hard. Tamils were forced to learn in Sinhalese at school. All official state transactions would be conducted in Sinhalese. Tamils would be required to speak Sinhalese in order to obtain the government post they relied on. Tamils were crippled both socially and economically by the act. As administrative changes were slowly implemented, riots began. Two hundred Tamils began protesting peacefully across from parliament on June 5, 1956. Shortly after, Sinhalese protestors led by Junior Minister Rajaratna attacked the Tamils and began pelting them with rocks. Then urged on by Mettananda to boycott Tamil businesses, the Sinhalese dispersed to loot Tamils businesses and create mayhem. Riots then spread throughout the country and thousands of Tamils were murdered. Tamils noticed that the Sinhalese police were often bystanders when needed by Tamils or would even arrest Tamils that had been injured. [10] A compromise was reached in July 1957 between Tamils and Sinhalese to allow the use of Tamil in Tamil districts through regional councils and to give the Tamils power in land resettlement schemes. [11] This B-C Pact, as it was called, was never implemented. Shortly after, on May 23, 1958, anti-Tamils riots began after a train carrying delegates to the Federal Party Convention was derailed. Tamils were taken out of the train and beaten. Mob violence spread throughout the country and became rampant. [12]

Anti-Tamil rioters were often above the law; the police were helpless to stop rioting when parliamentary members would demand the release of their subordinates after they were arrested. Some Tamils did retaliate by burning Sinhalese property. Although the Tamil Language (Special Provisions) Act was passed, allowing Tamil to be used in education and government in Tamil areas, the act was never implemented. Although Bandaranaike's government passed the bill, he was assassinated shortly thereafter by a Sinhalese monk. Bandaranaike's quest for absolute political power brought about his demise in the end.

Bandaranaike's wife then took over and pursued pro-Sinhalese policies for the SFLP Party. In 1962, it was declared that all entrance exams should be conducted in Sinhala, which was called the standardization policy. Mrs. Bandaranaike's government was defeated in the March 1965 elections by the UNP Party. Prime Minister Dudley Senanayake, who followed Mrs. Bandaranaike, somewhat perpetuated the pro-Sinhalese government that he had replaced. However, in 1965 the Dudley-Chelvanayagam Pact, or D-C Pact, was introduced. This pact would allow Tamils to use their language for administrative purposes and to communicate with the government, in addition to allowing school to be taught in Tamil throughout Tamil provinces. Those Tamils in government service would not experience hardship while learning

Sinhala. Again, there was much backlash against the pact and it was never implemented.

Mrs. Bandaranaike was then reelected from 1970 to 1977. The Bandaranaikes' policies were single-handedly the most disruptive and damaging to Tamil society. In addition, during her reign, the Sinhala Army slaughtered 15,000 to 20,000 Sinhala youth in a revolt.[13] In 1972, Bandaranaike's government created a new constitution. The Tamils considered this constitution to be degrading to Tamils. The constitution banned Tamils from traveling to south India, banned the import of Tamil writings, and the Sinhalese took over the news industry. In response, the Tamils formed the Tamil United Front, which combined the FP and the Tamil Congress. Then in 1974, quotas were introduced into the university system. Although the system was created to decrease the acceptance rates of the elite urban students, the Tamils viewed the quotas as solely discriminating against Tamils.[14] In 1977, another constitution replaced the 1972 constitution.

In 1977, the government actually got it right with the introduction of a presidential system. Majoritarian representation was replaced with proportional representation. Proportional representation provides a much more representative vote for the entire population. By counting voters' second and third choices, minorities had more impact on the election process. The Tamil language was also recognized as a national language.

The 1977 constitution provided many of the rights that the Tamils had been asking for, but it was too late. The Tamils wanted a separate Tamil nation at this point and were focusing on self-determination. The new constitution did not address any territorial ambitions of the Tamils. The Sri Lankan government was not interested in losing any territory to the establishment of another country and the self-determination of the Tamils.

In 1978, another constitution was created that favored the Sinhalese in a unitary government, giving the president dictatorial powers. Although laws were instated to give political equality, these changes did not seem to be implemented into society. In addition, Tamils sincerely doubted the ability of the Sinhalese to create a fair government. Since the UNP was in power at this time, it adopted pro-Western stance because of aid from the IMF, World Bank, and Western countries. Thus, the UNP cut food subsidies, privatized government-owned industries, decreased the number of state workers, reduced tariffs, deregulated financial markets, and created free trade. In essence, the government adopted a more capitalist economy. The Sinhalese suffered from this free trade and the Tamils prospered from it because of their new relationship with India.

It is true that the Sinhalese-dominated government in Sri Lanka played a large part in the radicalization of the Tamil social movements. The Sinhalese governments did not listen to the Tamil people nor did they acknowledge any of the Tamils' problems. The Tamils were stereotypically a peaceful people and it might be said that the LTTE would not have been created if the Sinhalese had addressed Tamil rights. However, what most definitely can be said is that the radicalization of S. J. V. Chelvanayagam and the Federal Party (FP) and the leadership of Prabhakaran played a large role in radicalization of the Tamil people and the creation of the LTTE.

THE RADICALIZATION OF S. J. V. CHELVANAYAGAM AND THE FEDERAL PARTY (FP)

Theories like the violent society theory or the authoritarian personality theory suggest that people choose violence because they are part of a violent culture. Thus, the explanation becomes, "Because I am constantly exposed to violence, I view violence as a legitimate means of solving my problems. Therefore, violence becomes my mode of operation." Theories such as these, while perhaps valid in explaining the actions of Hamas or Hezbollah, are a poor explanation for the radicalization of Tamil society, or more specifically, the Tamil Federal Party (FP).

Traditionally, Tamils have not been known as a violent people. In fact, they were more often looked upon as meek. Shortly after independence there were studies completed concerning the ethnic perceptions of Sri Lankans. The Sinhalese viewed the Tamils as egotistical, compassionate, crafty, frugal, proud, intelligent, and clannish, while the Tamils thought the Sinhalese were slothful, haughty, and courageous.[15] Never was it even considered that the Tamils were violent or could use violence. In fact, the Tamils would use Gandhi's *satyagraha* methods as a means of nonviolent protests and had been doing so since independence as a response to Sinhalese domination. However, as Sinhalese suppression of the Tamil people continued to grow, so did the resentment of the Tamil people. The radicalization of the founder of the Tamil Eelam movement, S. J. V. Chelvanayagam, and the radicalization of his party, the FP, played a major part in the creation of the LTTE. Figure 4.1 will provide the reader with the clarification of the parties in Sri Lanka for a reference tool.

S. J. V. Chelvanayagam is considered the founder of the Tamil Eelam movement. Chelvanayagam entered parliament in 1947 with the aspiration to be the "dour guardian of Tamil interests."[16] Chelvanayagam formed the Tamil Federal Party (FP), the actual Tamil political party, with two other Ceylon parliamentarians, C. Vanniasingham and Senator E. M. V. Naganathan in 1949. The FP had four objectives. The first objective sought to federalize the Sri Lankan state. The FP wanted to create a federal union of Ceylon comprised of the two Tamil-speaking Northern and Eastern provinces. Secondly, the Sinhalese were to immediately stop their colonization of the Tamil provinces. The third objective was the unity of all Tamil-speaking

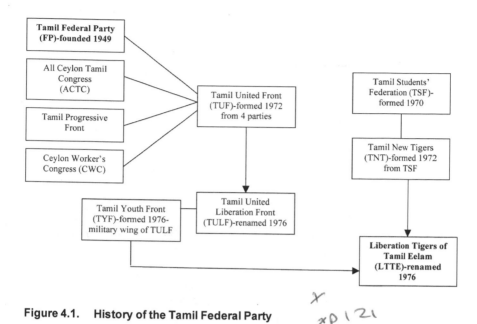

Figure 4.1. History of the Tamil Federal Party

people throughout Sri Lanka. The final objective was for Sinhala and Tamil
to be recognized equally as official state languages.[17]

During the years 1950–1955, Chelvanayagam became "a prophet" to the
Tamil people and became their "saviour and protector."[18] Problematically, in
its first elections in 1952 the FP did not do well; most Tamils at this time
believed that their future was vested with a unitary government. In 1955,
Chelvanayagam became the official national Tamil leader. In the 1956 election the following year, the FP achieved victory in the Tamil areas. On June
6, 1956, the FP started *satyagraha*, or peacefully protested the Official Language Act. This protest was halted by angry Sinhalese mobs and then soon
after the FP organized a peaceful march. Then on August 19, 1956 at the
Trincomalee Convention, the FP constructed a resolution amongst Tamil
people asking that the Tamil people be placed in a federal unit where they
would enjoy "the widest autonomous and residuary powers." This resolution
was ignored by the Sinhalese government.

In the B-C Pact created on July 29, 1957, the FP asked for the same thing,
although the B-C Pact was never implemented.[19] The purpose of the B-C
Pact was to allow Tamil to be the official language of Tamil areas and to give
greater autonomy to Tamil areas through regional councils. Wilson states,

> Again this Pact was evidence enough that the Tamils desired only to preserve
> their identity. They wanted no more than territorial homelands, not even
> merged in one unit, as a way of living in peaceful coexistence with the Sinha-

lese. Up till thus point, there was still no claim to self-determination or even partial statehood. The goal was to attain some autonomy within the framework of quasi-nationalism. [20]

At this point, it is evident that there were no ideas of secession or violence in the FP. "Chelvanayagam was able to channel protest along the non-violent path as long as he held the political stage."[21] Tamils were still content to be part of Sri Lanka although they wanted their own provinces, governed by Tamils. Chelvanayagam and others from the FP went to Tamil villages to explain how a federal system would protect the Tamil interests and language.

In the election of 1960, the FP gained enough seats to win the balance of power. The National Language Act was fully implemented on January 1, 1961, and at this point Mrs. Bandaranaike was the prime minister from the governing SLFP. In response to the implementation of the National Language Act, which made Sinhala the national language (including government and judiciary), the FP planned two extra parliamentary protests. The first protest went well, although the crowds were eventually dispersed by the police. The second protest was a campaign for Tamils to conduct business in Tamil and to write letters concerning their complaints to the Sinhala-dominated government. Of course, the government had some difficulty reading and replying to these letters because few could speak Tamil other than the Tamils. Either way, the Tamils' problems were not addressed.

In December 1964, Mrs. Bandaranaike's government was defeated. In the elections of 1965, the FP again held the balance in parliament. In attempt to revive the B-C Pact, the new government headed by Dudley Senanayake (UNP) created the Dudley Senanayake-Chelvanayagam Pact (or D-C Pact) of 1965. Senanayake agreed to the District Development Councils that were overseen by the central government. Second, Senanayake agreed that the Tamil provinces would not receive any more colonization efforts by the government. Third, the Language Act would be altered to make Tamil an official language and the language of the courts in Tamil provinces. Lastly, Tamil government employees who had not obtained fluency in Sinhalese would be protected. It looked as though the FP would finally accomplish something. However, bureaucratic infighting halted the implementation of the D-C Pact and the SLFP goaded the UNP into scrapping the D-C Pact. Senanayake actually apologized to the FP and told them that he could not pass the pact. His only alternative was to resign, but the FP asked him to remain in power.

In the period from 1965 to 1968, the FP and the UNP were able to work together. The FP helped pass the Tamil Regulations in 1966, which provided for Tamil to be the language of administration and of the courts in the Northern and Eastern provinces. In addition, Tamil public servants were given some relief. Senanayake then became extremely ill, which left the

Sinhala parties to work together. At this point, the FP left the government in disgust. Parliament was dissolved in 1970 because of other infighting amongst the Sinhalese parties.

Mrs. Bandaranaike's United Front (UF), composed of the SLFP and Marxists, took power after the UNP was defeated. As seen in her previous government experience, Mrs. Bandaranaike was not sensitive to Tamil issues, and thus the Tamils were dead in the water. "The actions of the UF government left the FP and the Tamils with no alternative but to turn their backs on the single federalized island entity they had striven for . . . Chelvanayagam, who till then had been supportive of a federal state, now reluctantly switched his stand to call for a separate statehood."[22] Before calling for a separate statehood, Chelvanayagam had tried desperately through his party to create a federalist country in Sri Lanka, giving the Tamils autonomy over their own provinces. To call for an independent state was a large step for Chelvanayagam.

At first, Chelvanayagam tried peaceful protests to create his Tamil state, but young Tamils quickly learned that guns were more effective. Chelvanayagam resigned from his parliamentary seat on October 2, 1972 over the new constitution that was passed, which further decreased Tamil rights. At this point in his life, he was slowly dying from Parkinson's disease. Chelvanayagam stated, "We have abandoned the demand for a federal constitution. Our movement will be all nonviolent. . . . We know that the Sinhalese people will one day grant our demand and that we will be able to establish a separate state from the rest of the island."[23] At this point Chelvanayagam is still calling for a separate Tamil state, but he is politely demanding that the Sinhalese government recognize his request.

What began to occur afterward was a slow consolidation of Tamil political groups. On May 14, 1972, mainstream Tamil political parties met in Trimcomalee and joined in what was known as the Tamil United Front (TUF). The FP joined the TUF and was the leading political party and figurehead for the organization. In addition, the All Ceylon Tamil Congress (ACTC), the Tamil progressive Front, and the Ceylon's Workers Congress also joined the TUF.[24] In 1973, the FP began to publicly advocate for a separate nation for the Tamil people as part of the TUF and Chelvanayagam was elected the leader of the TUF.

In 1974, Chelvanayagam was one of few moderates left in the TUF. He stated to an interviewer, "My presence in the movement is itself a check on extremism."[25] By 1975, Chelvanayagam had radicalized. He stated, "There is no other alternative for the Tamils to live with self-respect other than fight to the end for a Tamil Nadu' [Tamil country]."[26] What he had avoided all along was violence yet it was violence that became his final weapon for the creation of the Tamil nation.

In 1975, the TUF changed its name to the Tamil United Liberation Front
(TULF). "What was more significant about the changes leading to the formation of united fronts was the decisions of the leaders of the major Tamil
groupings to sink their differences and work for the common cause of the
emancipation of the Tamil people."[27] Finally, at the first National Convention of the TULF led by Chelvanayagam on May 14, 1976, the Vaddukoddai
Resolution was passed. The Vaddukoddai Resolution was a monumental act.
It stated, "The Tamil Nation in general and the Tamil youth in particular to
come forward to throw themselves fully in the sacred fight for freedom and
to flinch not till the goal of a sovereign socialist state of Tamil Eelam is
reached."[28] Prabhakaran, the founder of the LTTE, was actually at this convention.
    Shortly after the passing of the Vaddukoddai Resolution, Appapillai
Amirthalingam and M. Sivasithamparam created the military wing of the
TULF, called the Tamil Youth Front (TYF). Wilson states:

> In the last year or two of his [Chelvanayagam] life, he functioned as a patron
> of the movement, forcefully expressing his views on vital questions. But his
> party colleagues were increasingly associating with the militant youth ele-
> ments and this was something over which he could not exercise any control
> because of his age and failing health . . . He trusted his party men, especially
> Amirthalingam, and did not know that they were hand-in-glove with people
> who were involved in violent acts and preparing for armed confrontation with
> the state.[29]

Amirthalingam used the military wing as a threat to exact concessions from
President Jayewardene. Unfortunately, Jayewardene was old and was not
interested in dealing with the Tamils. His attitude toward the situation was to
let the Tamils simmer out until they got tired of fighting and protesting.
However, there were many people such as Kathiravetpillai warning the
TULF that unless Jayewardene gave some concessions soon, the young Tamils would explode.
    The Tamil Students' Federation formed in 1970, which was shortly there-
after called the Tamil New Tigers (TNT). In 1975, the TNT was christened
the LTTE. The connections between the various predecessors to the LTTE
and the TULF are evident in that many of the young men that belonged to the
military wing of the TULF, the Tamil Youth Front (TYF), also belonged to
the Tamil Students' Federation (TSF). "The militant youth groups were at
first united by overlapping membership. For example, one prominent leader,
Uma Maheswaran, was at first both chairman of the LTTE and the Colombo
secretary of the TYF."[30] In addition Adele Balasingham, the wife of the
LTTE press secretary Bala Balasingham, refers to two prominent members in
the LTTE as "originally youth wing leaders of the Tamil United Liberation
Front (TULF) who were inducted into the LTTE by Mr. Pirabakaran [Prab-

hakaran]."[31] Although TULF refused culpability in the violence, they were pressuring Tamil youth to commit acts of violence.

In addition, Prabhakaran was behind the scenes harnessing the TUF men he could recruit. He had respect for Amirthalingam (although the LTTE later assassinated him) and quietly developed a relationship with him and other TULF members. He would meet with them periodically. "Although his interest in political work was minimal, Prabhakaran used to quietly meet Amirthalingam and other TULF members at their homes."[32] Later the relationship became more complicated when "the boys," or LTTE, got more violent.

> The TULF boss [Amirthalingam] was not averse to a bit of violence, and thought it was the only way to send a message or two to Colombo. Overtly, he would never admit his links with the "boys", and merely chose to heap lavish praises for their more daring exploits. He even told Uma that the LTTE should operate underground parallel to the TULF's mainstream politics, but that arrangement should remain a secret. But as violence by the militants continued even after general elections, the TULF got worried. After the party's second rung leadership complained that the "boys" seemed to be running out of control, Amirthalingam called a meeting of the LTTE leadership at his residence at Moolai village in November 1977. Seven LTTE men, including Prabhakaran, Uma and Baby, attended. Amirthalingam spoke slowly but firmly. The TULF, he reminded the Tigers, had won the elections and should be given a chance. The killings, he added, had gone up and should be put on hold at least for the time being. "I am not asking you to give up violence, but you should cool down," he said.[33]

It is evident that there was a relationship between the LTTE and the TULF.

The radicalization of the Tamil Federal Party, S. J. V. Chelvanayagam's party and the main representative of the Tamil people since 1949, serves as part of an explanation as to why the LTTE was eventually created. It took almost thirty years for the Tamil Federal Party to radicalize and to call for violence. When the FP joined the Tamil United Front, which later became the Tamil United Liberation Front, it joined an organization that not only advocated violence but also created a military wing. This unification of the FP to a movement that used violence created a precedent for the Tamils. If violence was acceptable to the Tamil Federal Party, the original representative Tamil political party, then it was acceptable for Tamils to use violence to accomplish their goals. Not only this, but the TULF pushed the young Tamils toward violence and influenced them. In addition, the violent members of the TULF and members of the TSF joined to create the LTTE, the premier Tamil terrorist organization. Prabhakaran himself was once part of the TSF and TYF.[34]

In addition, the radicalization of S. J. V. Chelvanayagam, the founder of the Tamil social movement and party, helped to create the LTTE, which still advocates that they are the legacy of Chelvanayagam. Chelvanayagam began early in his career advocating for a Tamil province with more autonomy. As time progressed and legislation failed to be passed or was not implemented, Chelvanayagam began calling for a separate Tamil nation that would be accomplished through nonviolence and the acquiescence of the Sinhalese people and government. Eventually, Chelvanayagam realized that the only way to achieve the Tamil state was through the use of violence. Through his radicalization, S. J. V. Chelvanayagam created a goal for the LTTE and a path to follow. Swamy states:

> Sri Lankans need to look back and ponder if they want to look beyond. If the Federal Party had been treated with some respect and its minimum demands accepted, there would have been no TULF. If the government had at least come to minimum terms with the TULF, in 1977 or even later, there would have been no raison d'etre for LTTE and other groups.[35]

On July 29, 1979, the Sri Lankan government passed the Prevention of Terrorism Act, which had the opposite effect of its intentions. Instead of scaring the Tamil youth into submission, it further called them to action. The act denied trial by jury, enabled the detention of people for up to eighteen months, and allowed confession procured under torture to be admissible in court. The war was in full swing at this point and it continued until the assassination of the LTTE's leader Prabhakaran in 2009.

FRUSTRATION AND AGGRESSION WITHIN THE LTTE

The frustration-aggression theory is helpful in explaining why the LTTE turned toward terrorism. After repeated frustrations, whether caused by the Sri Lankan government or some other entity, the LTTE began to use violence. After the Official Language Act was passed in 1956, the FP threatened nonviolent protests if the government did not commit to a federalist system, the prohibition of Sinhalese settlements in Tamil areas, and the expungement of the Official Language Act by August 20, 1957. The Language Act caused incredible amounts of frustration for the Tamil people. It literally crippled their livelihood and left them as a suppressed minority in their own country. Chelvanayagam stated, "The threat to communal amity, or rather the killing of communal amity, was carried out by the government by its language policy."[36]

Chelvanayagam created the B-C Pact, which would allow Tamil regions to be administered in Tamil, to give a minority language status to Tamil, and give greater autonomy to Tamil regions. This pact was not passed by parliament. In addition, the Tamil Language (Special Provisions) Act was passed in 1958 but was not implemented. The Tamil Language Act allowed Tamil to be spoken for administrative purposes and judicial purposes in the Tamil provinces. Then the D-C Pact, which was an attempt to revive the B-C Pact in 1965, was not passed either. In fact, Prime Minister Dudley Senanayake (UNP) almost resigned over the pact because of the tension it created within his own party and the SLFP. Balasingham, the public representative of the LTTE, stated, "The collaborationist strategy of the Federal Party, suffered the inevitable fate of betrayal and in humiliation, the Party withdrew its support to the Government in 1968."[37] No matter what they did, the Tamils could not accomplish anything. In addition, no matter how hard the Tamils tried, the Sinhalese would not recognize their rights or give their protests any attention.

Problematically, language acts such as the B-C Pact, the Tamil Language (Special Provisions) Act, and the D-C Pact were only created to pacify the Tamil population. The Sinhalese were not interested in giving up any of their power as the majority race. One actually wonders why the Sinhalese did not institute the Official Language Act directly after independence because they could have done this. They were not interested in allowing Tamils access to good jobs, resources, or a higher standard of living. In fact, racism was quite apparent even in the public political forum. The truth is that the Sinhalese were worried about a civil war occurring if the Tamil situation was not bandaged. So they would try a little bandage to pacify the Tamils but would never pass any legislation or implement passed legislation.

At first Chelvanayagam's peaceful protests were respected by the Sinhalese. Tamils stood and peaceably assembled outside parliament. The SLFP and the UNP did not want a Tamil situation on their hands so a little leeway was given. However, the Tamils soon found out that *satyagraha*, or Gandhi's method of peaceful protest, did not work.

> The FP's policy demanding a federal state and their methods of ahimsa and satyagraha [peaceful protest] have brought horror on the Tamils. Wherever the Tamils exercised their elementary right to protect their person and property by force if necessary, they were safe. Wherever they were shackled down by satyagraha, they were slaughtered.[38]

It was becoming evident to the Tamils that nonviolent methods were not successful.

In 1972, the new constitution was created in Sri Lanka. The Tamils considered this new constitution to be degrading and threatening to the Tamils. Standardization was implemented and this meant that Tamils had to have higher entrance scores than other ethnicities. One school employee stated, "We advised the boys not to protest and to keep studying. But I couldn't convince even one person after standardization."[39] Tambiah states, "Indeed their resistance became militant in 1972, when the government introduced its so-called standardization policy with regard to university admissions, which was realistically seen by Tamil youth as serious discrimination against them."[40] Because the Sinhalese-dominated parliament refused to listen to any of the Tamil requests, this resulted in the "Most of the Tamil members walking out in utter frustration and hopelessness."[41] The new constitution was passed on May 22, 1972. Later in May 1972, the moderate Tamil parties formed a coalition called the Tamil United Front (TUF). "The belated unity of this Tamil United Front (TUF) appears to have been dictated more out of frustration and as a way to appease the increasingly disgruntled Tamil youth than by any strategic design."[42] Balasingham states:

> The most crucial factor that propelled the Tamil United Front to move rapidly towards the secessionist path was the increasing impatience, militancy, and rebelliousness of the revolutionary Tamil youth. Disillusioned with the political strategy of non-violence which the bourgeois nationalist leadership advocated for the last thirty years and produced no political fruits, the Tamil youth demanded drastic and radical action for a swift resolution to the Tamil national question. Caught up in a revolutionary situation generated by the contradiction of national oppression and constantly victimized by police brutality, the youth were forced to abandon the Gandhian doctrine of "ahimsa" (non-violence) which they realized was irreconcilable with revolutionary political practice and inapplicable to the concrete conditions in which they were situated.[43]

The TUF developed a six-point program. The first goal was a place for the Tamil language. The second goal was the secularization of Sri Lanka. The third goal TUF strove for was to improve the rights of ethnic minorities. The fourth goal was citizenship for everyone. The fifth goal was the decentralization of the Sri Lankan administration, and the sixth goal was to eliminate the caste system. Some of these goals lacked specificity.[44]

In 1974, district quotas were introduced and Tamils were even further disadvantaged. Universities had to comply with government mandated university admission requirements. Although the Federal Party had been peacefully trying to accomplish changes for several years, it was apparent that their strategies were not working. Anton Balasingham, the top adviser and negotiator for the LTTE, states:

> The leaders of the Federation were capable of verbal inspiration only; they were not prepared to offer leadership and guidance to carry out an effective programme of action. They lacked the knowledge and the courage to organize and spearhead an armed campaign against the repressive state apparatus. Frustrated with the impotency of the leadership of the Student Federation the disenchanted young militants resolved to launch violent campaigns, individually and as groups.[45]

Even Chelvanayagam was frustrated and advocated for a more radical policy. In October 1972, Chelvanayagam stated, "In view of the events that have taken place, the Tamil people of Ceylon should have the right to determine their future, whether they are to be a subject race in Ceylon or they are to be a free people."[46] As time passed, the Tamil youth were becoming radical and at one point actually stormed an All Ceylon Tamil Conference, refusing to leave until the members promised to boycott parliament.

In 1973, standardization was introduced forcing Tamils to have higher grades to enter a university. Shortly after, the Tamils began asking the TUF for an independent Tamil state. On January 10, 1975, at the fourth international Tamil Conference Sinhalese police broke up a professor's speech on Tamil literature. They began running at Tamils with tear gas and batons. However, this time the Tamils retaliated, throwing slippers and rocks. One Tamil who had helped to organize the conference stated, "It left a deep scar in all of us."[47]

In addition, the anti-Tamil riots that occurred in response to both violent and peaceful Tamil protesting caused a lot frustration and anger. Balasingham states:

> Violent anti-Tamil riots exploded in the island in 1956, 1958, 1961, 1974, 1977, 1979, 1981, and in July 1983. In these racial holocausts, thousands of Tamils, including women and children were massacred in the most gruesome manner, billions of rupees worth of Tamil property and hundreds of thousands made refugees. The state's armed forces colluded with Sinhalese hooligans and vandals in the violent rampage of arson, rape and mass murder. The cumulative effect of this multi-dimensional oppression had far reaching consequences. It threatened the very survival of the Tamil people. It aggravated the ethnic conflict and made reconciliation and co-existence between the two nations extremely difficult. It stiffened the Tamil militancy and created conditions for the emergence of the Tamil armed resistance movement.[48]

Sathasivam Krishnakumar (Kittu), an original LTTE member, had personal experiences that stemmed from the riot of 1977 because he worked to rehabilitate these people. Kittu confided in Bose. She writes, "He recalled to me how their horror stories of atrocities cemented his conviction that there was no safety, leave alone any future, for Tamils within a unitary, Sinhaleses-dominated state of Sri Lanka."[49]

This constant accumulation of the frustration within the Tamil population led to the creation of the LTTE, a terrorist organization. The Tamils began peacefully protesting every piece of legislation that the Sinhalese passed that deprived them of their rights. However, as time passed, peaceful protests did nothing as the Sinhalese just kept passing legislation that further disadvantaged the Tamils. The accumulation of this frustration and powerlessness to do anything, not to mention the bad effects of the Sinhalese legislation on the Tamil standard of living led ,to aggression.

The goals of the LTTE as defined by Bose are relatively simple and precise: 1) The Sri Lankan Tamils want to be recognized as a distinct nationality; 2) The northern and eastern provinces of Sri Lanka need to be recognized as the historical and traditional homeland of the Sri Lankan Tamil people; 3) The right of the Sri Lankan Tamils to self-determination needs to be acknowledged; 4) The plantation Tamils, though outside the Eelam formation, should be restored to full rights of citizenship and franchise. [50]

Prabhakaran sums up this section perfectly in his Heroes Day message on November 27, 2008. He states:

> Pooling together all its military resources and arsenal, and with all its national wealth to buttress it, the racist Sinhala state has waged a fierce war on our land. Our freedom fighters, have dedicated themselves to unbending resistance against this war of aggression launched by the racist Sinhala state. With various countries of the world buttressing the genocidal war on the people of Tamil Eelam, we are waging a defensive war for the freedom of our people. [51]

THE CHARISMATIC LEADERSHIP OF VELUPPILLAI PRABHAKARAN

People like you are afraid of blood. You have to kill. —Prabhakaran

Table 4.1 illustrates Weber's criteria of charismatic leadership. These criteria will be used to evaluate the leadership of Veluppillai Prabhakaran, the founder and leader of the LTTE. As a side note, it is difficult to find primary sources on Prabhakaran because he was a private individual and spent most of his time in hiding or on the run. There are several speeches and a few biographies concerning Prabhakaran, but an autobiography has never been written.

On November 26, 1954, Veluppillai Prabhakaran was born in Valvettiturai, a northern town on the coast of the Jaffna peninsula. He was the youngest of Vallippuram Parvathy and Thiruvenkadam Veluppillai's four children. Thiruvenkadam Veluppillai was a government civil servant and was affectionate toward his children, often buying them presents. Prabhakaran was his favorite and Veluppillai would often snuggle with his young son at night. The nickname "master" was soon given to Prabhakaran by his family to demonstrate the favoritism he received from his father.

In school, Prabhakaran was an average student. This worried his father tremendously because Tamils were adamant about educating their children. In an effort to help his son, a tutor was hired. This tutor may have influenced Prabhakaran tremendously in his revolutionary goals stating "It is he [the tutor] who impressed on me the need for armed struggle and persuaded me to put my trust in it." [52] Prabhakaran would often sit and listen to his father and

Table 4.1.   Weber's Assessment of Veluppillai Prabhakaran's Charismatic Leadership

Max Weber's Criteria for Charismatic Leadership	Characteristic of Veluppillai Prabhakaran ?
Authority of Higher Being for Mission?	Yes
Complete Obedience of Followers?	Yes
Brings Followers Material and Social Rewards?	Yes
Charismatic Leader Directs and Organizes Organization?	Yes
Delegates Power to Followers?	Yes
Seeks to Defray Costs from His Own Pocket?	Yes
Develops an Army Trained and Equipped by Leader?	Yes
Rejects Personal Profit from Organization and Has No Rational Economic Behavior?	Yes
Followers Do Not Elect Him?	Yes
Leadership Is Not Stable?	Yes
Charismatic Leader Selects His Successor?	Yes

his father's friends talking about the current political situation. It is certain that Prabhakaran would have heard about the worsening ethnic relations between the Tamils and the Sinhalese. He also attended speeches that lamented Sinhalese abuses of the Tamils. This was most likely his political education often spoken in both English and Tamil.

Prabhakaran's heroes were peculiar for a child. When most Tamils were admiring the peaceful protest methods of Gandhi and cheering for India's independence from Britain, Prabhakaran was fascinated by Subash Chandra Bose. Bose was a warrior who had taken on Gandhi and used violence to fight for Indian independence. Prabhakaran loved Bose's slogans such as, "I shall fight for the freedom of my land until I shed the last drop of blood."[53] His other heroes were military leaders such as Napoleon and Bhagat Singh.

Prabhakaran was interested in military techniques and strategies as a child. Prabhakaran's favorite weapon was the catapult and he became an excellent marksman from his early age shooting stones at squirrels, chameleons, or birds. Later he advanced to the air gun. He was also interested in judo and karate and learned these fighting techniques. He would also tie himself up in a bag and lie in the hot sun all day, preparing himself for the physical and mental rigor of torture. Prabhakaran would also stick pins into bugs until they died, preparing himself for the rigors of using torture against the enemy. He would make bombs from empty soda bottles with his friends and explode them, one time in a toilet at school. [54]

In approximately 1970, Prabhakaran quit school and formed a group with seven others to fight the Sinhalese army. In 1972, after Satyaseelan was arrested, the police began cracking down on the TYL. Prabhakaran roamed from town to town because the Sri Lankan Army was constantly raiding his house since he was known as a fugitive. He would also attend meetings at both the Tamil Students' League and the Tamil Youth League.

He joined the TIP in 1972. He was soon elected leader because the former leader had been arrested and tortured, thus giving all the names of his compatriot leadership. [55] Prabhakaran left shortly after his nomination to Madras, India, and when he came back, he formed the Tamil New Tigers (TNT) with Chetti in 1972. He had met Chetti in Madras and the two formed a fast friendship considering they were both looking to actively fight the Sinhalese. Unfortunately, when Prabhakaran returned to Jaffna, Chetti was arrested for robbing a store.

The first action that brought attention to the TNT was the assassination of the former mayor of Jaffna. In July 1975, Prabhakaran walked into a friend's house with a rusty revolver and began making bullets. Prabhakaran assassinated the mayor of Jaffna, Alfred Duraiappah, the next day because he was known as an unabashed loyalist to the Bandaranaike government. Although Prabhakaran had three accomplices, he stayed away from them and told them nothing about his whereabouts.

In 1976, S. Subramanian joined forces with Prabhakaran and on May 5, 1976, the TNT was changed to the Liberation Tigers of Tamil Eelam, or LTTE. Prabhakaran had recently robbed the People's Bank in Jaffna and used that money to create LTTE training camps in the forest of Killinochchi and Vavuniya. Shortly thereafter, the LTTE assassinated N. Nadarajah, who was suspected of being a police informer, on July 2, 1976.

Although Weber states that the charismatic leader needs to have the authority of a higher being for his mission, this component of charismatic leadership can be widely interpreted. Some leaders like Prabhakaran replace religion with the will of the people that he represents. In a sense, to Prabhakaran, the higher being is the Tamil people.

Prabhakaran was a member of relatively lower Karaiyar caste in the Caste system in Sri Lanka although his grandfather was the builder/owner of a local Hindu Siva temple. Religion is not a major factor in his philosophy or ideology. The LTTE is also an organization that does not cite any material from religion or religious texts in any of its ideological documents and propaganda but are driven only by the idea of Sri Lankan Tamil nationalism and considers it as the only single-minded approach and inspiration towards the attainment of an independent Tamil Eelam.[56]

In addition, Balasingham, one of Prabhakaran's closest advisers, states that Prabhakaran "made a resolute determination to dedicate his life to the liberation of his people."[57] Tamil nationalism and the independence of Tamil Eelam are the higher beings that give Prabhakaran authority for his mission.

It is quite easy to find examples in the literature that illustrate the complete obedience that Veluppillai Prabhakaran demands from members of the LTTE. Foremost, all members swear absolute loyalty to Prabhakaran.[58] When one journalist visits the LTTE camp, he asks one LTTE member why he is fighting. The man looks at him suspiciously and states, "We do what the leadership says."[59] Margaret Trawick describes that absolute loyalty to Prabhakaran as disturbing when she visits the LTTE camps. "The unquestioning devotion of LTTE members to their leader, Vellupillai Prabhakaran, is troubling to me as a liberal Westerner. It seems inconsistent with the secular socialism that Tamil Eelams envision for the independent state they are fighting for."[60] Chris Smith describes Veluppillai Prabhakaran's leadership as based on a "cult of personality."

He appears in public infrequently, and his thoughts are rarely committed to print. Moreover, contacts between him and LTTE members are rare; only suicide bombers and the most senior officers are ever permitted access. In addition, Prabhakaran demands the maximum possible allegiance to his leadership and therefore to the cause of the organization. . . . Prabhakaran has overcome any problems related to legitimacy by operating the LTTE on a strict, authoritarian basis.[61]

If this larger-than-life impression of Veluppillai Prabhakaran is not enough, the new members are required to swear loyalty after being inducted to the movement to Prabhakaran, whose nickname means "little brother."[62] In addition, Prabhakaran requires his men and women to not have premarital or extramarital affairs in addition to abstaining from alcohol, drugs, and tobacco.[63]

As an interesting side note, several scholars mention the importance of cyanide capsules and suicide bombing to the LTTE. Members are required to wear cyanide vials around their neck at all times. This requirement begins immediately after a person joins the LTTE. The purpose of this is to escape capture and to die for the Tamil cause if necessary. Prabhakaran stated, "You won't find people from our movement in jail. . . . It is this cyanide which has helped us develop our movement very rapidly. . . . In reality this gives our fighters an extra measure of belief in the cause, a special edge; it has instilled in us a determination to sacrifice our lives and our everything for the cause."[64]

Martyrdom also is one of the highest honors for a Tamil Tiger. Bose believes that the recruiting abilities, longevity of the organization, and establishment of a Tamil nation have been built on the extreme commitment and obedient nature of dying for the cause. She states:

> I strongly believe that the cult of the cyanide capsule and the suicide bomber cannot be dismissed out of hand as some kind of bizarre, fanatical quirk of a nationalist movement that has gone out of control. On the contrary, the cult of violence and martyrdom is of *absolutely central significance* to the forging of a Tamil national identity.[65]

The martyrs serve a recruiting purpose. The egalitarian society of Tamil in the LTTE has no class differences. Indeed, anyone can die for the cause. Lastly, the death of martyrs provides a sense of solidarity and national pride to the Tamil people, ensuring loyalty and obedience.

When joining the LTTE shortly after the organization was created, members would receive material and social rewards from Prabhakaran. New members were driven to self-supporting farms where recruits helped grow vegetables, chilis, and peanuts. Meat came from hunting wild animals in the nearby forests. Once a recruit was baptized, he would begin training in the use of revolvers.[66] LTTE members also receive free haircuts, fruit, a salary, clothing, and could watch movies or listen to the radio. Often, the only meals a member would have would come from the LTTE.[67]

In addition, the LTTE members receive recognition and a type of community martyrdom for their service in the LTTE. Heroes Week occurs every November to remember slain Tiger soldiers. Large displays of flowers stand next to a tribute to the first female tiger to be killed, Lieutenant Malathy. Euphemisms such as, "Eternally, your remembrance is deep in our heart" grace entrances to buildings, and yellow and orange ribbons are displayed. Huge tents are erected with ribbons and banners. It is one of the highest honors to be killed in action in the LTTE and the LTTE and community pay special attention to those who have been lost.[68] Balasingham describes Heroes Day, November 27:

> Ecstatic crowds flagged down our convoy of vehicles and garlanded the LTTE cadres and our journey ended up taking twice as long as we had planned. As we traveled through the area, people rushed out of their houses congratulating us and expressing their appreciation that the negotiations had finally succeeded in getting the Indian troops out of their homeland. Throughout Amparai, from one town to the next, were dotted memorial shrines and the red and yellow of the LTTE flag fluttered, and groups of people gathered to celebrate Heroes' Day. . . . People queued at the meeting places hoping for an opportunity to express their appreciation by garlanding the LTTE cadres with jasmine flowers.[69]

Prabhakaran also directed and organized the LTTE. He decided to "form an armed organization [LTTE] under his leadership."[70] After approving the LTTE logo, "he went on to form a five-member central committee of the LTTE, putting himself as a member of the leadership council. He charted a constitution, which all members were expected to sign and accept."[71] "Demonstrating extraordinary talent in planning military strategy and tactics and executing them to the amazement of the enemy, Prabhakaran soon became a symbol of Tamil resistance."[72] Prabhakaran created the LTTE and managed the organization both militarily and politically. Prabhakaran once stated, "Those who bear arms acquire and wield an extreme measure of power. We believe that if this power is abused it will inevitably lead to dictatorship. That is why we keep our military organization in such a strict state of discipline."[73]

Prabhakaran delegated his power. The following statement outlines Prabhakaran's strategy for the LTTE:

> The LTTE machinery was much like the human body. Prabhakaran was the brain who controlled all the organs with ruthless efficiency. His word was final on any issue of contention. His authority was unchallenged and cadres took a personal oath of loyalty to Prabhakaran when they were admitted into the LTTE. Prabhakaran coordinated the day-to-day military struggle with the help of Mahattaya, while Anton Balasingham—the high-profile propaganda face of the LTTE—was in-charge of liaisoning with the media, LTTE offices abroad and diplomats. Kittu headed the Indian operations . . . while the low-key Shankar, a trusted lieutenant controlled the crucial logistics division . . . Shanmuganathan Sivasankaran alias Pottu Amman was the chief of the intelligence wing . . . K. Pathmanabha alias KP alias T.S. Kumaran, another Prabhakaran confident headed the shadowy financial wing. All of them reported directly to Prabhakaran.[74]

Everything was controlled by Prabhakaran and all the top leaders reported directly to him.

In addition, a leader like Velluppillai Prabhakaran sought to defray costs from his own pockets to support the LTTE or an earlier version of the group. One example of this occurred in Prabhakaran's early years. His group, the Tamil New Tigers (TNT), needed a revolver, so each member would give Prabhakaran 25 cents a month to purchase the gun. When the time came to buy the revolver, the TNT still did not have enough money to purchase the gun, so Prabhakaran "quietly sold off a gold ring, gifted to him during his sister's marriage for 30 rupees."[75]

Also, Prabhakaran had developed and trained his own army. Balasingham states that Prabhakaran "committed a lengthy period of time to train his cadres and organize underground cells"[76] when the LTTE was first created. Later, the suicide bombing sector of the LTTE was developed and trained by

Prabhakaran and called The Black Tiger Squad. "Prabhakaran is said to go over the written applications personally before inducting members into the Black Tiger Squad, after which they are put through rigorous physical and psychological training."[77] The day before the mission, the selected suicide bomber eats dinner with Prabhakaran. The LTTE has even developed a navy called the Sea Tigers, which uses suicide bombings to destroy Sri Lankan ships.

Prabhakaran rejected personal profit from the LTTE and had no rational economic behavior. Prabhakaran quit school at age sixteen to fight for the Tamil movement. He lived as a hobo, sleeping where he could, and eating what he could find. After he created the LTTE, Prabhakaran did not develop any permanent residence and still lived like a hobo when the police were after him, which was constantly. "Prabhakaran and the others led a low-key life, spending the least amount of money on food."[78] Prabhakaran did not make any money from the LTTE and even when he robbed banks, the rupees went to fund something for the LTTE. The *Wall Street Journal* states:

> His [Prabhakaran] arch foes in the Sri Lanka military, meanwhile, portrayed the Tamil Tiger chief as a well-fed armchair commander who lived in luxury as he sent others to fight and die. But for the past year, as Sri Lanka's 26-year civil war wound down to a bloody end, Mr. Prabhakaran fit neither of those images. Instead, he beat a desperate retreat, trying to stay one step ahead of the brutal offensive the Sri Lankan army launched to capture him and his senior leadership.[79]

Although this previous sentence only refers to one year, it is true that Prabhakaran spent his life dedicated to cause, not living in luxury. After he created the LTTE, he spent most of his life shuffling from place to place, eluding the Sri Lankan military. In addition, at one point the LTTE was forced to think about eliminating its tax policies in Jaffna. This would cost the LTTE a lot of income. Prabhakaran stated, "'I don't want the money to be given to me.' It was for the Tigers."[80]

In addition, Prabhakaran was not elected, nor did he even believe in democracy. Prabhakaran created the LTTE in 1975 and remained the leader of the LTTE until his death in 2009. No one else was ever elected leader, nor did any elections occur.

In addition, Prabhakaran's leadership was not stable. An early incident occurred with Uma Maheshwaran around 1980. Uma was the chairman of the leadership council while Prabhakaran was the military commander of the LTTE. The incident began when Uma started having sex with an LTTE woman; it was illegal to have premarital sex in the LTTE. Prabhakaran reported him to the council, but to little avail. Prabhakaran and Maheshwaran also shared ideological differences regarding the LTTE that could not be resolved. Other minor issues surrounded the dispute and because it could not be settled, Balasingham was called to provide ideological classes for the Tigers and help them overcome their differences. Although Prabhakaran and Uma went to these classes together, the rift grew larger. At one point, a shootout began between the two men.[81] Prabhakaran thought that Uma was an academic without any real-world experience who was afraid to kill, and Uma maintained that their differences arose over the TULF. Uma eventually flew back to London although he still maintained that he was the leader of the LTTE from London, infuriating Prabhakaran who had had Uma expelled from the LTTE.[82]

In addition, after the incident with Uma, two LTTE members were murdered and Prabhakaran was rumored to be responsible. A new leadership council was elected although Prabhakaran demanded to have authority over any decisions. One group even left the LTTE to form the Tamil Protection League. At one point, Prabhakaran even quit the LTTE and went to join TELO although they did not want him to join the group. He threatened suicide if they did not let him join. Eventually, Prabhakaran called his old friends in the LTTE and repaired the rift, joining forces with the TELO. One man whose father was a moderate gunned down by the LTTE remarked, "Nobody knows this, but Prabhakaran left the LTTE for awhile. When he came back to the LTTE, that's when the killing started."[83] These minor incidents support the fact that leadership of the LTTE was not always stable and that there were some challenges to Prabhakaran's leadership.

It is widely accepted that Prabhakaran chose his successor, T. S. Pamanathan, or KP as he is called. KP was immediately promoted after Prabhakaran's death.

> The Liberation Tigers of Tamil Eelam (LTTE) have a new chief. Its former head of arms procurement, Selvarasa Pathmanathan, has been named as successor to the slain Velupillai Prabhakaran, according to a statement issued by its Executive Committee. Fifty-four-year old Pathmanathan, aka Kumaran Pathmanathan or "KP," was serving as the LTTE's chief of international relations before rising to the top post.[84]

According to Max Weber, Prabhakaran fulfills all the criteria for charismatic leadership. Prabhakaran was a unique individual who grew out of Tamil resistance to Sinhalese domination in Sri Lanka. He developed the Tamil Tigers and trained his own military to fight the Sri Lankan government. It was Prabhakaran who planned and developed the terrorist attacks for the LTTE and it was Prabhakaran that transformed the LTTE into a terrorist organization. Prabhakaran's soldiers swore complete obedience to him even to the point of becoming suicide bombers. Prabhakaran once stated, "I must do what my followers do and I must do it first."[85] Prabhakaran had complete control of his entire organization. He used terrorism to attack both Tamils and Sinhalese to accomplish his political objectives.

To his people, Prabhakaran is a hero. Adele Balasingham, the wife of Bala Balasingham (Press Secretary), wrote of her friendship with Prabhakaran:

> In his personal life Mr. Pirabakaran [Prabhakaran] is disciplined in all dimensions. There has never been, from the outset of his days in struggle, a whisper of impropriety or scandal surrounding him. He has never smoked or taken alcohol and prefers if other people don't. . . . Courage is inextricably linked to a positive and certainly inspiring feature of his character, which is that of not being subdued or deterred by anything in life, no matter how formidable and powerful it may be. He has an indomitable will and confidence that anything can be achieved if the mind is applied and focused on the project. [86]

Lastly, Prabhakaran made sure to destroy rival Tamil groups. The LTTE has destroyed or overtaken other guerrilla groups since 1975 so it could become the dominant Tamil group. [87] These groups include the Tamil Eelam Liberation Organization (TELO), which was destroyed by the LTTE, and the Eelam Revolutionary Organization of Students (EROS), which allied itself with the LTTE. In addition, the LTTE has killed Tamil moderates on a continuous basis to ensure its control over Tamil society. [88] A list includes:

> V. Dharmalingham, representative for Manipay, in September 1985; K. Alalasunderam, representative for Kopay, in September 1985; A. Amirthalingam, TULF and opposition leader, in July 1989; Sam Tambimuttu, representative for Batticacola, in May 1990; V. Yogasnadari, representative for Batticola, in June 1990; K. Kanagaratnam, representative for Pottuvil, in July 1990; Sarojini Yogeshwaran, mayor of Jaffna, in May 1998; P. Sivapalan, mayor of Jaffna in September 1998; and Neelan Tiruchelvam, TULF parliamentarian, in July 1999. [89]

The list goes on. This strategy has consistently worked in the LTTE's favor.

CONCLUSION

Three factors provide an alternative explanation for the rise of the LTTE. The first of these factors was the radicalization of the Tamil Federal Party and its founder Chelvanayagam. Had the founding party of Tamil nationalism and its founder not radicalized, it is likely that the LTTE would not have been created or tolerated by the Tamil people. Second, tremendous frustration within Tamil political parties and the Tamil population due to government exclusion and repression rationalized the use of violent tactics. Eventually the accumulation of this frustration led to the creation of the LTTE and the ascendancy of a violent personality like Prabhakaran. Lastly, Prabhakaran's charismatic leadership harnessed the frustration of the Tamils from the TULF and created the terrorist organization LTTE.

In order to definitively conclude the effect of charismatic leadership, more case study research is necessary. It seems, however, that when the charismatic leader commands his or her subordinates to use violence, his or her command is typically obeyed. Their role in the radicalization is paramount.

Naturally, more research needs to be completed that would provide some conclusive evidence as to what occurs after a charismatic leader is removed from the organization either by assassination or incarceration. Is the removal of leadership an effective way to destroy terrorist organizations or does it lead to the re-creation of a vindictive, vengeful terrorist organization that is even more violent than its precursor?

In May 2009, Prabhakaran was killed by Sri Lankan troops. At first, there appeared to be some inconsistency in this report, although DNA evidence later found that Prabhakaran was actually assassinated.[90] Prabhakaran's chosen successor, T. S. Pathmanathan, or KP as he is called, has since done little with the LTTE since Prabhakaran died. In fact, the LTTE's numbers have drastically dwindled. Like most terrorist organizations such as the Red Army Faction, FARC, or Muslim Brotherhood, once the charismatic leader is killed or taken captive, the organization experiences a quiet period wherein it may be determined that the organization has died. There is often a period of uncertainty of whether the organization will be able to rebuild. In the case of the Muslim Brotherhood, after the death of Hasan al-Banna, the Brotherhood regrouped and became even more violent with the rise of Sayyid Qutb. Conversely, after the death of Manuel Marulanda and Jacobo Arenas, the FARC has not recovered, but time will tell. After the death of Andreas Baader and several other Red Army Faction leaders, the RAF eventually recovered but never reclaimed the same level of violence that the original leadership had pursued.

Time will be the final arbitrator ascertaining whether the LTTE will rise again. The cost of the conflict has been astronomical for the Sri Lankan people and the devastation is massive from a political, social, and economic standpoint.[91] It is up to the Tamil people to demonstrate when they have had enough of the LTTE and to choose whether peace or separatism is the final goal.

NOTES

1. Jimme Briggs, *Innocents Lost, When Child Soldiers Go to War* (New York: Basic Books, 2005), 85.

2. Neil DeVotta, *Blowback Linguistic Nationalism, Institutional Decay, and Ethnic Conflict in Sri Lanka* (Stanford, CA: Stanford University Press, 2004), 166.

3. Central Intelligence Agency, "Sri Lanka" *World Factbook*, June 24, 2010, accessed August 3, 2010, www.cia.gov/library/publications/the-world-factbook/geos/ce.html.

4. D. Hellmann-Rajanayagam, *The Tamil Tigers, Armed Struggle for Identity* (Stuttgart, Germany: Franzsteiner Verlag, 1994), 9.

5. Bryan Pfaffenberger, "Introduction: The Sri Lankan Tamils," in Chelvadurai Manogaran and Bryan Pfaffenberger (eds.), *The Sri Lankan Tamils, Ethnicity and Identity* (Boulder, CO: Westview Press, 1994), 1–27, 3.

6. Marl Stephen Meadows, *Tea Time with Terrorists, A Motorcycle Journey into the Heart of Sri Lanka's Civil War* (Berkeley, CA: Soft Skull Press, 2010), 94.

7. Neil DeVotta, *Blowback Linguistic Nationalism, Institutional Decay, and Ethnic Conflict in Sri Lanka* (Stanford, CA: Stanford University Press, 2004), 67.

8. Yasmine Gooneratne, *Relative Merits A Personal Memoir of the Bandaranaike Family of Sri Lanka* (New York: St. Martin's Press, 1986), 155.

9. Neil DeVotta, *Blowback Linguistic Nationalism, Institutional Decay, and Ethnic Conflict in Sri Lanka* (Stanford, CA: Stanford University Press, 2004), 48.

10. Neil DeVotta, *Blowback Linguistic Nationalism, Institutional Decay, and Ethnic Conflict in Sri Lanka* (Stanford, CA: Stanford University Press, 2004).

11. Asoka Bandarage, *The Separatist Conflict in Sri Lanka, Terrorism, Ethnicity, Political Economy* (New York: Routledge, 2009).

12. A. S. Balasingham, *Liberation Tigers and Tamil Eelam Freedom Struggle* (Sri Lanka: Liberation Tigers of Tamil Eelam, 1983).

13. S. Sinvanayagam, "The Phenomenon of Tamil Militancy," in V. Suryanarayam (ed.), *Sri Lankan Crisis and Indian Response* (New Delhi: Patriot Publishers, 1991), 30–47.

14. Asoka Bandarage, *The Separatist Conflict in Sri Lanka, Terrorism, Ethnicity, Political Economy* (New York: Routledge, 2009), 61.

15. S. Sinvanayagam, "The Phenomenon of Tamil Militancy," in V. Suryanarayam (ed.), *Sri Lankan Crisis and Indian Response* (New Delhi: Patriot Publishers, 1991), 30–47.

16. A. Jeyaratnam Wilson, *S. J. V. Chelvanayakam and the Crisis of Sri Lankan Tamil Nationalism 1947–1977, A Political Biography* (Honolulu: University of Hawaii Press, 1994), vii.

17. A. Jeyaratnam Wilson, *Sri Lankan Tamil Nationalism, Its Origins and Development in the Nineteenth and Twentieth Centuries* (Vancouver: UBC Press, 2000), 82.

18. A. Jeyaratnam Wilson, *S. J. V. Chelvanayakam and the Crisis of Sri Lankan Tamil Nationalism 1947–1977, A Political Biography* (Honolulu: University of Hawaii Press, 1994), 20.

19. A. Jeyaratnam Wilson, *Sri Lankan Tamil Nationalism, Its Origins and Development in the Nineteenth and Twentieth Centuries* (Vancouver: UBC Press, 2000), 89.

20. A. Jeyaratnam Wilson, *Sri Lankan Tamil Nationalism, Its Origins and Development in the Nineteenth and Twentieth Centuries* (Vancouver: UBC Press, 2000), 90.

21. A. Jeyaratnam Wilson, *S. J. V. Chelvanayakam and the Crisis of Sri Lankan Tamil Nationalism 1947–1977, A Political Biography* (Honolulu: University of Hawaii Press, 1994), 84.

22. A. Jeyaratnam Wilson, *Sri Lankan Tamil Nationalism, Its Origins and Development in the Nineteenth and Twentieth Centuries* (Vancouver: UBC Press, 2000), 99.

23. Neil DeVotta, *Blowback Linguistic Nationalism, Institutional Decay, and Ethnic Conflict in Sri Lanka* (Stanford, CA: Stanford University Press, 2004), 167.

24. Edgar O'Ballance, *The Cyanide War, Tamil Insurrection in Sri Lanka, 1973–1988* (London: Brassey's, 1989).

25. M. R. Narayan Swamy, *Tigers of Lanka, From Boys to Guerrillas* (Delhi: Konark Publishers PVT Ltd, 1994), 21.

26. A. Jeyaratnam Wilson, *Sri Lankan Tamil Nationalism, Its Origins and Development in the Nineteenth and Twentieth Centuries* (Vancouver: UBC Press, 2000), 108.

27. A. Jeyaratnam Wilson, *Sri Lankan Tamil Nationalism, Its Origins and Development in the Nineteenth and Twentieth Centuries* (Vancouver: UBC Press, 2000), 108.

28. A. Jeyaratnam Wilson, *Sri Lankan Tamil Nationalism, Its Origins and Development in the Nineteenth and Twentieth Centuries* (Vancouver: UBC Press, 2000), 110.

29. A. Jeyaratnam Wilson, *S. J. V. Chelvanayakam and the Crisis of Sri Lankan Tamil Nationalism 1947–1977, A Political Biography* (Honolulu: University of Hawaii Press, 1994), 135.

30. A. Jeyaratnam Wilson, *Sri Lankan Tamil Nationalism, Its Origins and Development in the Nineteenth and Twentieth Centuries* (Vancouver: UBC Press, 2000), 125.

31. Adele Balasingham, *The Will to Freedom, An Inside View of Tamil Resistance* (England: Fairmax Publishing Ltd), 51.

32. M. R. Narayan Swamy, *Tigers of Lanka, From Boys to Guerrillas* (Delhi: Konark Publishers PVT Ltd, 1994), 58.

33. M. R. Narayan Swamy, *Tigers of Lanka, From Boys to Guerrillas* (Delhi: Konark Publishers PVT Ltd, 1994), 62.

34. Narayan Swamy, *Inside an Elusive Mind, Prabhakaran, The First Profile of the World's Most Ruthless Guerrilla Leader* (Dehli: Konark Publishers PVT LTD, 2003), 25.

35. M. R. Narayan Swamy, *Tigers of Lanka, From Boys to Guerrillas* (Delhi: Konark Publishers PVT Ltd, 1994), 336.

36. Neil DeVotta, *Blowback Linguistic Nationalism, Institutional Decay, and Ethnic Conflict in Sri Lanka* (Stanford, CA: Stanford University Press, 2004), 160.

37. A. S. Balasingham, *Liberation Tigers and Tamil Eelam Freedom Struggle* (Sri Lanka: Liberation Tigers of Tamil Eelam, 1983), 20.

38. As cited in Neil DeVotta, *Blowback Linguistic Nationalism, Institutional Decay, and Ethnic Conflict in Sri Lanka* (Stanford, CA: Stanford University Press, 2004), 140.

39. M. R. Narayan Swamy, *Tigers of Lanka, From Boys to Guerrillas* (Delhi: Konark Publishers PVT Ltd, 1994), 53.

40. S. J. Tambiah, *Sri Lanka, Ethnic Fratricide and the Dismantling of Democracy* (Chicago: University of Chicago Press, 1986), 17.

41. Anton Balasingham, *War and Peace Armed Struggle and Peace Efforts of Liberation Tigers* (England: Fairmax Publishing Ltd, 2004), 17.

42. Neil DeVotta, *Blowback Linguistic Nationalism, Institutional Decay, and Ethnic Conflict in Sri Lanka* (Stanford, CA: Stanford University Press, 2004), 140.

43. A. S. Balasingham, *Liberation Tigers and Tamil Eelam Freedom Struggle* (Sri Lanka: Liberation Tigers of Tamil Eelam, 1983), 23.

44. Satchi Ponnambalam, *Sri Lanka, the National Question and the Tamil Liberation Struggle* (London: Zed Books), 178.

45. Anton Balasingham, *War and Peace Armed Struggle and Peace Efforts of Liberation Tigers* (England: Fairmax Publishing Ltd, 2004), 22–23.

46. Neil DeVotta, *Blowback, Linguistic Nationalism, Institutional Decay, and Ethnic Conflict in Sri Lanka* (Stanford, CA: Stanford University Press, 2004), 140.

47. M. R. Narayan Swamy, *Tigers of Lanka, From Boys to Guerrillas* (Delhi: Konark Publishers PVT Ltd, 1994), 20.

48. Anton Balasingham, *War and Peace Armed Struggle and Peace Efforts of Liberation Tigers* (England: Fairmax Publishing Ltd, 2004), 9.

49. Sumantra Bose, *States, Nations, and Sovereignty Sri Lanka, India, and the Tamil Eelam Movement* (Thousand Oaks, CA: Sage Publications, 1994), 94.

50. Sumantra Bose, *States, Nations, and Sovereignty Sri Lanka, India, and the Tamil Eelam Movement* (Thousand Oaks, CA: Sage Publications, 1994), 138.

51. V. Prabhakaran, "Full text of the Speech of V. Prabhakaran, leader, Liberation Tigers of Tamil Eelam on annual Heroes' Day on 27 November 2008," *The Hindu* November 27, 2008, accessed August 30, 2010, www.hindu.com/nic/prabhakaranspeech.htm.

52. Narayan Swamy, *Inside an Elusive Mind, Prabhakaran, The First Profile of the World's Most Ruthless Guerrilla Leader* (Dehli: Konark Publishers PVT LTD, 2003), 23.

53. M. R. Narayan Swamy, *Tigers of Lanka, From Boys to Guerrillas* (Delhi: Konark Publishers PVT Ltd, 1994), 51.

54. M. R. Narayan Swamy, *Tigers of Lanka, From Boys to Guerrillas* (Delhi: Konark Publishers PVT Ltd, 1994).

55. Sumantra Bose, *States, Nations, and Sovereignty Sri Lanka, India, and the Tamil Eelam Movement* (Thousand Oaks, CA: Sage Publications, 1994).

56. Lankan Newspapers, "Veluppillai Prabharakan," *Lankan Newspapers*, May 19, 2007, accessed August 19, 2010, www.lankanewspapers.com/news/2007/5/15036_space.html.

57. Anton Balasingham, *War and Peace Armed Struggle and Peace Efforts of Liberation Tigers* (England: Fairmax Publishing, 2004), 24.

58. Neil DeVotta, *Blowback, Linguistic Nationalism, Institutional Decay, and Ethnic Conflict in Sri Lanka* (Stanford, CA: Stanford University Press, 2004), 170.

59. Narayan Swamy, *Inside an Elusive Mind, Prabhakaran, The First Profile of the World's Most Ruthless Guerrilla Leader* (Dehli: Konark Publishers PVT LTD, 2003), xv.

60. Margaret Trawick, *Enemy Lines Childhood, Warfare, and Play in Batticola* (Berkeley: University of California Press, 2007), 81.

61. Chris Smith, "Sri Lanka: The Continued Armed Struggle of the LTTE," in Jeroen de Zeeuw (ed.), *From Soldiers to Politicians, Transforming Rebel Movements After Civil War*, 205–224, (Boulder, CO: Lynne Rienner Publishers, 2007), 214–215.

62. Sumantra Bose, *States, Nations, and Sovereignty Sri Lanka, India, and the Tamil Eelam Movement* (Thousand Oaks, CA: Sage Publications, 1994), 127.

63. Dagmar-Hellmann Rajanayagam, "The 'Groups' and the Rise of Militant Secessionism," in Chelvadurai Manogaran and Bryan Pfaffenberger (eds.), *The Sri Lankan Tamils, Ethnicity and Identity*, 169–207 (Boulder, CO: Westview Press, 1994).

64. N. Ram, "Understanding Prabakaran's LTTE," in V. Suryanarayan (ed.), *Sri Lankan Crisis and India's Response*, 24–29, (New Delhi: Patriot Publishers, 1991), 28.

65. Sumantra Bose, *States, Nations, and Sovereignty Sri Lanka, India, and the Tamil Eelam Movement* (Thousand Oaks, CA: Sage Publications, 1994), 119–120.

66. M. R. Narayan Swamy, *Tigers of Lanka, From Boys to Guerrillas* (Delhi: Konark Publishers PVT Ltd, 1994).

67. Narayan Swamy, *Inside an Elusive Mind, Prabhakaran, The First Profile of the World's Most Ruthless Guerrilla Leader* (Dehli: Konark Publishers PVT LTD, 2003), 97.

68. Jimme Briggs, *Innocents Lost, When Child Soldiers Go to War* (New York: Basic Books, 2005), 100.

69. Anton Balasingham, *War and Peace Armed Struggle and Peace Efforts of Liberation Tigers* (England: Fairmax Publishing, 2004), 181–182.

70. Anton Balasingham, *War and Peace Armed Struggle and Peace Efforts of Liberation Tigers* (England: Fairmax Publishing Ltd, 2004), 25.

71. M. R. Narayan Swamy, *Tigers of Lanka, From Boys to Guerrillas* (Delhi: Konark Publishers PVT, 1994), 59.

72. Anton Balasingham, *War and Peace Armed Struggle and Peace Efforts of Liberation Tigers* (England: Fairmax Publishing, 2004), 27.

73. N. Ram, "Understanding Prabakaran's LTTE," in V. Suryanarayan (ed.), *Sri Lankan Crisis and India's Response*, 24–29, (New Delhi: Patriot Publishers, 1991), 28.

74. Neil DeVotta, *Blowback Linguistic Nationalism, Institutional Decay, and Ethnic Conflict in Sri Lanka* (Stanford, CA: Stanford University Press, 2004).

75. Narayan Swamy, *Inside an Elusive Mind, Prabhakaran, The First Profile of the World's Most Ruthless Guerrilla Leader* (Dehli: Konark Publishers PVT, 2003), 27.

76. Anton Balasingham, *War and Peace Armed Struggle and Peace Efforts of Liberation Tigers* (England: Fairmax Publishing, 2004), 26.

77. Neil DeVotta, *Blowback, Linguistic Nationalism, Institutional Decay, and Ethnic Conflict in Sri Lanka* (Stanford, CA: Stanford University Press, 2004), 175.

78. M. R. Narayan Swamy, *Tigers of Lanka, From Boys to Guerrillas* (Delhi: Konark Publishers PVT Ltd, 1994), 74.

79. Peter Wonacott, "A Notorious Terrorist Who Refused to Compromise to the End," *The Wall Street Journal*, May 19, 2009, accessed August 30, 2010 http://online.wsj.com/article/NA_WSJ_PUB:SB124269099109232581.html.

80. Narayan Swamy, *Inside an Elusive Mind, Prabhakaran, The First Profile of the World's Most Ruthless Guerrilla Leader* (Dehli: Konark Publishers PVT LTD, 2003), 163.

81. Narayan Swamy, *Inside an Elusive Mind, Prabhakaran, The First Profile of the World's Most Ruthless Guerrilla Leader* (Dehli: Konark Publishers PVT LTD, 2003), 62.

82. A similar story is also recited by Adele Balasingham, *The Will to Freedom, An Inside View of Tamil Resistance* (England: Fairmax Publishing Ltd), 51–53.

83. Marl Stephen Meadows, *Tea Time with Terrorists, A Motorcycle Journey into the Heart of Sri Lanka's Civil War* (Berkeley, CA: Soft Skull Press, 2010), 121.

84. Sudha Ramachandran, "Tamil Tigers Name New Chief," *Morung Express*, no date. Accessed August 30, 2010, www.morungexpress.com/analysis/29666.html. Shamindra Ferdinando, "Reconciliation Not Possible with Foreign Mediated Efforts: LTTE Leader," *The Island* July 30, 2010, accessed August 30, 2010, www.asianewsnet.net/home/news.php?id=13370

85. Narayan Swamy, *Inside an Elusive Mind, Prabhakaran, The First Profile of the World's Most Ruthless Guerrilla Leader* (Dehli: Konark Publishers PVT LTD, 2003), 32.

86. Adele Balasingham, *The Will to Freedom, An Inside View of Tamil Resistance* (England: Fairmax Publishing Ltd), 337–338.

87. Chris Smith, "Sri Lanka: The Continued Armed Struggle of the LTTE," in Jeroen de Zeeuw (ed.), *From Soldiers to Politicians, Transforming Rebel Movements After Civil War*, 205–224 (Boulder, CO: Lynne Rienner Publishers).

88. Rajan Hoole, *Sri Lanka The Arrogance of Power, Myths, Decadence, and Murder* (Colombo, Sri Lanka: University Teachers for Human Rights, 2001).

89. Chris Smith, "Sri Lanka: The Continued Armed Struggle of the LTTE," in Jeroen de Zeeuw (Ed) *From Soldiers to Politicians, Transforming Rebel Movements After Civil War*, 205–224 (Boulder, CO: Lynne Rienner Publishers).

90. For the most recent work on Sri Lanka and the LTTE, see G. H. Peris, *Twilight of the Tigers, Peace Efforts and Power Struggles in Sri Lanka* (New York: Oxford University Press, 2009).

91. See Siri Gamage and I. B. Watson (eds.), *Conflict and Community in Sri Lanka, "Pearl of the East" or the "Island of Tears"?* (New Delhi: Sage Publications, 1999).

Chapter Five

Conclusion and Analysis

The principal purpose of this book is to explain why social movements sometimes radicalize and form terrorist organizations. One of the primary motivations for the completion of this volume was to look at the internal dynamics of social movements as an alternate explanation for the formation of terrorist organizations. The state is often blamed for the creation of these groups whether it is attributed to the style of government, inability to use the state institutions, or industrialization, in addition to many other external causes. In addition, the leadership of these groups has either been ignored or understudied.

The secondary motivation for writing this book was to help policy makers comprehend why and how terrorist groups are created and in addition, to perhaps find a way to prevent a terrorist group from forming. If the causes of terrorism are better understood, then policies to combat terrorism might be more effective. In addition, how should governments implement these policies to protect citizens against terrorist attacks? These counterterrorist policies should not only be suggested, but the best way to implement the policies also needs to be determined. These questions are extremely important in a current world where states have ceased to fight nations and instead have begun to fight nonstate actors such as terrorist organizations and drug cartels. The process of the formation of the terrorist group is complicated, yet there are some similarities amongst the case studies presented within this book.

The first similarity found amongst all four case studies in the book is that the groups all emerged from larger social movements. In addition, all of these groups, which were part of large social movements, took several years to radicalize. In the case of the Muslim Brotherhood, it took approximately seventeen years for the group to radicalize, from 1928 to 1945. In the case of the ETA, it took nine years to use terrorism, from 1952 to 1961. Likewise, the FARC took eighteen years to use terrorism, from 1947 to 1965. Also, the Federal Party was formed in 1949 and the LTTE began using terrorism in 1976, which amounts to twenty-seven years. The amount of time it takes to create a terrorist organization varies, yet one can see that there is a process and that terrorist groups do not appear out of thin air. Terrorists groups take time to form. Often, the leaders of these social movements try peaceful methods first before they choose violence. It is important for governments to deal with these movements before they turn to violence. Excluding these social movements should not be a part of the government's strategy.

However, different elements within these groups radicalized. In the case of the Muslim Brotherhood, the founder, Hasan al-Banna, was radicalized. In the case of ETA, the group was hijacked by violent extremists. The FARC, to an extent, radicalized over time because it was created to defend the peasants and eventually started attacking noncombatants. The LTTE was radicalized because many people in the group that belonged to the Tamil United Liberation Front were encouraged to use violence. The LTTE then grew out of this group. Although different components of these groups radicalized, it is important to see that some process of radicalization took place in every social movement.

The second similarity among three of the case studies is the presence of the charismatic leader. Hasan al-Banna, Manuel Marulanda, and Veluppillai Prabhakaran were all charismatic leaders as seen through evaluation with Weber's criteria. The importance of charismatic leadership is the ability of leaders to not only recruit participants to their movement but also to command those participants to use terrorism. In all three of these case studies, members swore absolute loyalty to their leader and terrorism was eventually used when the charismatic leader chose to use terrorism. As a side note, the leaders of the FARC and the LTTE have recently been killed and it will be interesting to see if the groups reappear. In addition, the future of the Egypt is dependent on the actions of the Egyptian Muslim Brotherhood and what it does with its recently earned political power.

However, the anomaly to the charismatic leadership argument is ETA. ETA is different from the other groups because it was created by as many as thirteen men as opposed to one leader. ETA was eventually hijacked by Zabilde, who was not a founder, and under his watch ETA became a much more violent organization. Perhaps, it is also possible that Zabilde is the charismatic leader responsible for the radicalization of ETA. If Zabilde truly was the charismatic leader responsible for later radicalizing ETA, it can be ascertained that the ETA actually went through at least three radicalization stages, becoming more violent each time. The question remains as to why ETA presents a different picture than the Muslim Brotherhood, the FARC, and the LTTE. Possibly, it may be because the ETA was created by so many people as opposed to the other groups, which had clear leaders in their founders. This style of leadership is known as a horizontal style of leadership and it is possible that this horizontal leadership is why ETA was able to cast out all of the original members of the group.

The third similarity among the case studies is the frustration present in each group that led to aggression. It is evident that each of these groups tried to accomplish their various missions through peaceful attempts over many years. Each of these peaceful attempts was rejected in some way, and so eventually each of the groups chose violence. It is noteworthy that events and statements exemplifying frustration can be connected with the group and its actions.

A fourth similarity can be found between the FARC and the LTTE. Both of these groups came from political parties, even though each had their roots in a social movement. Both of these parties radicalized, choosing to use violence after many events occurred. The Egyptian Muslim Brotherhood and the ETA later had connections with large political parties after they were formed. Weinberg[1] and Weinberg and Pedahzur[2] argue that political parties turn to terrorism because they have grandiose goals to achieve and because they view the current government as illegitimate. Circumstances that lead political parties to become terrorist organizations include recent national integration, recent national disintegration, coup d'états and military interventions, a crisis of political legitimacy, elections, and polarized multiparty systems.[3] In the case of the FARC, the Colombian Communist Party created defense groups to protect the people after a massive civil war broke out. In the case of the LTTE, the Federal Party just stopped trying to work with the Sinhalese parties because nothing was getting accomplished for the Tamils. None of the reasons that Weinberg and Pedahzur give provide an explanation to the violent paths that these parties chose. More research needs to be completed as to why political parties turn to terrorism.

PRODUCTION OF THEORY

Although only four case studies were included within this volume, there are some possible theoretical contributions. The conditions that cause social movements to resort to terrorist tactics may be attributed to three factors. The first of these factors is leadership. Leadership is important in a social movement because it establishes the future path that the movement will pursue. If key leaders of a social movement are prone to violence, there is a good chance that the social movement will resort to terrorism or violence down the road. Moderates who do not agree with the use of violence will most likely be forced out of the organization or killed. Likewise, if the leaders of an organization are not prone to commit violence, the social movement could well remain on a peaceful path. In the case of the Muslim Brotherhood, members swore complete obedience to Hasan al-Banna and did as he wished when they were commanded. The same is true for the FARC and the LTTE.

The second condition that may lead to the use of terrorist tactics by a social movement can be summarized using frustration-aggression theory. As frustration builds from the lack of success of the social movement to accomplish its goals, so does the propensity to commit violence. Frustration builds and builds, thus accumulating in an explosion of anger and wrath that could come to fruition in the form of a terrorist attack. The number of frustrating incidents it takes to cause violence is unknown, but certainly its accumulation over time does lead to violence. What causes frustration appears to be the inability to accomplish political goals.

The third condition that may lead to the use of terrorist tactics by a social movement is the ascendance of violent personalities to leadership positions. These people frequently hijack social movements. In some cases, this may include the radicalization of the leader of the social movement, which is the ascendance of a violent personality through different channels. The violent personalities in the ETA were able to usurp these positions of leadership because moderate leaders were not present to control the organization. In addition, the radical ETA members made sure to vote the founders out of the organization so that the founders of the movement could not challenge their leadership. In the case of the Muslim Brotherhood, the FARC, and the LTTE, violent personalities eventually took over the groups and led them to the use of terrorism.

FUTURE RESEARCH VENUES

There are some interesting avenues for future research pertaining to points made within this book. For example, why is it that social movements that form in liberal atmospheres in universities or colleges often eventually become terrorist organizations? Terrorist organizations such as the Black Panthers, the ETA, the Weathermen, the Red Army Faction (RAF), and Red Brigades all have roots within universities. What is it about university atmospheres that breed terrorist organizations?

Following from the above research idea, why is it that most terrorist organizations are Marxist in ideology? Most of these terrorist organizations that were created by students in the 1970s and 1980s are Marxist. The ETA, the FARC, and the LTTE were all Marxist groups. Since communism has lost to capitalism, why is it that the violent dissenters within society turn to failed economic systems to provide a better way of the life for the people they purport to fight for? What is it about Marxism that is so attractive to terrorist organizations? Currently, most terrorist groups are religious; the cause of this is another worthwhile research project. Perhaps Marxist terrorist organizations are a product of their time period.

Lastly, scholars need to study why terrorist organizations disaffiliate or die. Several organizations, such as the Black Panthers, the Weathermen, the Red Brigades, and the Red Army Factions, have all expired as terrorist organizations. Why does this happen? In several situations, it may be that governmental repression does actually destroy terrorist organizations. However, several governments have violently suppressed terrorist organizations and have gotten no results. It may also be that the terrorists have accomplished their agenda and there are no more reasons to use terrorism. It would be interesting to examine what methods might be useful in killing off terrorist organizations. Although a few scholars, such as Cronin and Weinberg, have completed some research on this question, more work needs to be done. Finding the answer to the preceding questions would help to bring peace and resolution to many areas of the world that suffer daily from terrorist attacks.

NOTES

1. Leonard Weinberg, "Turning to Terror: The Conditions Under Which Political Parties Turn to Terrorist Activities," *Comparative Politics* 23 (4) (July 1991), 423–438.
2. Leonard Weinberg and Ami Pedahzur, *Political Parties and Terrorist Groups* (New York: Routledge, 2003).
3. Weinberg and Pedahzur, *Political Parties and Terrorist Groups,* 17.

Bibliography

Abdalla, Ahmed. *The Student Movement and National Politics in Egypt, 1923–1973*. London: Al Saqi Books, 1985.

Aclimandos, Tewfik. "Revisiting the History of the Egyptian Army." in *Re-Envisioning Egypt, 1919–1952*, edited by Arthur Goldschmidt, Amy Johnson, and Barak Salmoni, 68–93. Cairo: The American University Press in Cairo, 2005.

Alape, Arturo. *Las Vidas de Pedro Antonio Marin Manuel Marulanda Velez Tirofijo*. Bogotá, Colombia: Planeta Colombia Editorial S.A., 1989.

———. *Tirofijo: Los Sueños y Las Montañas*. Bogotá, Colombia: Planeta Colombiana Editorial S.A., 1994.

Aldana, Luis Alberto Matta. *Colombia y las Farc-EP Origen de la lucha guerrillera. Testimonio del Comandante Jaime Guaraca*. Naffaroa, Colombia: Txalaparta, 1999.

Alonso, Rogelio. *The IRA and the Armed Struggle*. New York: Routledge, 2007.

Appelbaum, Nancy P. *Muddied Waters, Race, Region, and History in Colombia, 1846–1948*. Durham, NC: Duke University Press, 2003.

Arenas, Jacobo. *Cese el Fuego, Una Historia Politica de las FARC*. Bogotá, Colombia: Editorial Oveja Negro, 1985.

———. *Diario de la Resistancia de Marquetalia*. Colombia: Ediciones Abejón Mono, 1972.

Armstrong, Karen. *The Battle for God*. New York: Ballantine Books, 2000.

Ayyad, Abdelaziz A. *The Politics of Reformist Islam Muhummad Abduh and Hasan al-Banna*. Unpublished doctoral dissertation, Georgetown University, Washington, DC, 1987.

Balasingham, Adele. *The Will to Freedom: An Inside View of Tamil Resistance*. England: Fairmax Publishing Ltd, 2003.

Balasingham, Anton. *War and Peace Armed Struggle and Peace Efforts of Liberation Tigers*. England: Fairmax Publishing Ltd, 2004.

Balasingham, A. S. *Liberation Tigers and Tamil Eelam Freedom Struggle*. Sri Lanka: Liberation Tigers of Tamil Eelam, 1983.

Bandarage, Asoka. *The Separatist Conflict in Sri Lanka, Terrorism, Ethnicity, Political Economy*. New York: Routledge, 2009.

al-Banna, Hassan. *Basic Teachings* (S. A. Qureshi, Trans.). Karachi, Pakistan: International Islamic Publishers, 1983.

———. *Between Yesterday and Today* (Charles Wendell, Trans.). Berkeley, CA: University of California Press, 1978.

———. *The Concept of Allah in the Islamic Creed* (Sharif Ahmad Khan, Trans.). Dehli, India: Adam Publishers and Distributors, 2000.

———. *Fifth Conference in (10 Years—1347–1357 Hijra)* (S.A. Qureshi, Trans.). Karachi, Pakistan: International Islamic Publishers, 1983.

————. *Memoirs of Hasan al-Banna Shaheed* (M. N. Shaikh, Trans.). Karachi, Pakistan: International Islamic Publishers, 1981.

————. *On Jihad* (Charles Wendell, Trans.). Berkeley, CA: University of California Press, 1978.

————. *What is Our Message?* Lahore, Pakistan: Islamic Publications, 1995.

Beach, Steven W. "Social Movement Radicalization: The Case of the People's Democracy in Northern Ireland." *The Sociological Quarterly* 18 (3) (Summer 1977): 305–318.

Beltza (pseudonym of Emilio López). *El Nacionalismo Vasco En El Exilio 1937–1960*. San Sebastián: Editorial Thertoa Plaza de Las Armerias, 1977.

Ben-Ami, Shlomo. "Basque Nationalism between Archaism and Modernity." *Journal of Contemporary History* 26 (3/4) (September 1991): 493–521.

Berreciartu, Gurutz Jáuregui. *Ideologia y Estrategia Politica de ETA, Análisis de su evolución entre 1959–1968*. Madrid: Siglo Veintiuno Editores, 1981.

Berkowitz, Leonard. *Roots of Aggression, A Re-examination of Frustration-Aggression Hypothesis*. New York: Atherton Press, 1969.

Bose, Sumantra. *States, Nations, and Sovereignty Sri Lanka, India, and the Tamil Eelam Movement*. Thousand Oaks, CA: Sage Publications, 1994.

Braun, Herbert. *The Assassination of Gaitán, Public Life and Urban Violence in Colombia*. Madison: University of Wisconsin Press, 1985.

————. *Our Guerrillas Our Sidewalks, A Journey Into the Violence of Colombia*. Niwot, CO: University Press of Colorado, 1994.

Briggs, Jimme. *Innocents Lost, When Child Soldiers Go to War*. New York: Basic Books, 2005.

Broderick, Walter J. *Camilo Torres, A Biography of the Priest-Guerillero*. Garden City, New York: Doubleday and Company, Inc, 1975.

Bushnell, David. *The Making of Modern Colombia A Nation in Spite of Itself*. Berkeley: University of California Press, 1993.

Central Intelligence Agency. "Sri Lanka." *World Factbook*, June 24, 2010. Accessed August 3, 2010, www.cia.gov/library/publications/the-world-factbook/geos/ce.html

Chenoweth, Erica. "Terrorism and Instability: A Structural Study of the Origins of Terror," Paper presented at the International Studies Association, Honolulu, Hawaii, March 2005.

Clark, Robert P. *The Basques: The Franco Years and Beyond*. Reno, NV: University of Nevada Press, 1979.

————. *The Basque Insurgents ETA, 1952–1980*. Madison, WI: University of Wisconsin Press, 1984.

————. "Euzkadi: Basque Nationalism in Spain since the Civil War." In *Nations without a State, Ethnic Minorities in Western Europe,* edited by Charles R. Foster, 75–100. New York: Praeger Publishers, 1980.

————. *Negotiating with ETA, Obstacles to Peace in the Basque Country, 1975–1988*. Reno, NV: University of Nevada Press, 1990.

Conversi, Daniele. *The Basque, the Catalans, and Spain, Alternative Routes to Mobilisation*. Reno: University of Nevada Press, 1997.

Crenshaw, Martha. "The Causes of Terrorism." *Comparative Politics* 13 (4) (July 1981): 370–399.

————. "The Causes of Terrorism, Past and Present." In *The New Global Terrorism*, edited by Charles W. Kegley, 92–105. Upper Saddle River, NJ: Pearson Education, Inc, 2003.

————. "The Logic of Terrorism: Terrorist Behavior as a Product of Strategic Choice." In *Origins of Terrorism, Psychologies, Ideologies, Theologies, and States of Mind,* edited by Walter Reich, 7–24. Washington, DC: Woodrow Wilson Center Press, 1998.

————. "Theories of Terrorism: Instrumental and Organizational Approaches." In *Inside Terrorist Organizations*, edited by David C. Rapoport, 13–31. Portland, OR: Frank Cass Publishers, 2001.

Cronin, Audrey Kurth. *How Terrorism Ends, Understanding the Decline and Demise of Terrorist Campaigns*. Princeton: Princeton University Press, 2009.

Da Silva, Milton, M. "Modernization and Ethnic Conflict." *Comparative Politics*, 7 (2) (January 1975): 227–251.

Dawson, Lorne L. "Crises of Charismatic Legitimacy and Violent Behavior in New Religious Movements." In *Cults, Religion, and Violence*, edited by David G. Bromley and J. Gordon Melton, 80–101. Cambridge, UK: Cambridge University Press, 2002.

De Aguirre, José Antonio. *Escape Via Berlin.* Reno: University of Nevada Press, 1991.

Della Porta, Donatella and Mario Diani. *Social Movements, An Introduction.* Oxford, UK: Blackwell Publishers, Ltd, 1999.

DeVotta, Neil. *Blowback, Linguistic Nationalism, Institutional Decay, and Ethnic Conflict in Sri Lanka.* Stanford, CA: Stanford University Press, 2004.

Dollard, John, Neal E. Miller, Leonard W. Doob, O. H. Mowrer, and Robert R. Sears. *Frustration and Aggression.* New Haven, CT: Yale University Press, 1939.

Domínguez, Florencio. *Dentro de ETA, La Vida Diaria de Los Terroristas.* Madrid: Santillana Ediciones Generales, S. L., 2002.

Dreyfuss, Robert. *Devil's Game, How the United States Helped Unleash Fundamentalist Islam.* New York: Metropolitan Books, 2005.

Dudley, Steven. *Walking Ghosts, Murder and Guerrilla Politics in Colombia.* New York: Routledge, 2004.

Echandía, Camilo. "Expansión Territorial de las Guerrillas Colombianas," In *Reconocer la Guerra para Construir la Paz,* edited by Malcolm Deas and María Victoria Llorente. Bogotá, Colombia: Cerec, 1999.

Edelen, Annamarie. *The Muslim Brotherhood's Quiet Revolution.* Unpublished doctoral dissertation, University of Wisconsin–Madison, 1999.

Eickelman, Dale. *The Middle East and Central Asia,* 4th ed. Upper Saddle River, NJ: Pearson Education Inc, 2002.

Eickelman, Dale F., and James Piscatori. *Muslim Politics.* Princeton, NJ: Princeton University Press, 1996.

El-Awaisi, Abd Al-Fattah Muhummad. *The Muslim Brothers and the Palestine Question 1928–1947.* London: Tarris Academic Studies, 1998.

Ferdinando, Shamindra. "Reconciliation Not Possible with Foreign Mediated Efforts: LTTE Leader." *The Island,* July 30, 2010. Accessed August 30, 2010, www.asianewsnet.net/home/news.php?id=13370

Fluharty, Vernon Lee. *Dance of the Millions.* Pittsburgh: University of Pittsburgh Press, 1957.

Gallego, Carlos Medina. *Autodefenses, Paramilitaries and Narcotrafficking in Colombia.* Bogotá, Colombia: Editorial Documentos Periodisticos, 1990.

Gamage, Siri, and I. B. Watson (eds.). *Conflict and Community in Sri Lanka, "Pearl of the East" or the "Island of Tears"?* New Delhi: Sage Publications, 1999.

Garmendia, José María. *Historia de ETA,* 2 vols. San Sebastián: L. Haranburu, 1978 and 1979.

Garmendia, José María, Gurutz Jáuregui, and Florencio Domínguez Iribarren. *La Historia de ETA.* Madrid: Temas' de Hoy, 2000.

al-Ghazali, Zainab. *Return of the Pharaoh, Memoir in Nasir's Prison* (Mokrane Guezzou, Trans.). Leicester, UK: The Islamic Foundation, 1994.

Goldberg, Ellis. "Bases of Traditional Reaction: A Look at the Muslim Brothers." *Mediterranean Peoples* 14 (1981): 79–96.

Gooneratne, Yasmine. *Relative Merits A Personal Memoir of the Bandaranaike Family of Sri Lanka.* New York: St. Martin's Press, 1986.

Granada, Camilo. "La evolución del gasto en seguridad y defensa en Colombia, 1950–1954." In *Reconocer la Guerra para Construir la Paz,* edited by Malcolm Deas and María Victoria Llorente. Bogotá, Colombia: Cerec, 1999.

Green, John W. *Gaitanismo, Left Liberalism, and Popular Mobilization in Colombia.* Gainesville: University Press of Florida, 2003.

Grimmet, Richard F., and Mark P. Sullivan. "United States Army School of the Americas: Background and Congressional Concerns." 2005. Accessed December 23, 2009, from www.globalsecurity.org/intell/library/reports/crs/soa.htm

Gupta, Dipak K. *Understanding Terrorism and Political Violence.* New York: Routledge, 2008.

Gurr, Ted Robert. "Terrorism in Democracies: Its Social and Political Bases." In *Origins of Terrorism, Psychologies, Ideologies, Theologies, and States of Mind*, edited by Walter Reich, 86–102. Washington, DC: Woodrow Wilson Center Press, 1998.

———. *Why Men Rebel*. Princeton: Princeton University Press, 1970.

Haag, Michael. *The Timeline History of Egypt*. New York: Barnes and Noble, 2005.

Halpern, Manfred. *The Politics of Social Change in the Middle East and North Africa*. Princeton: Princeton University Press, 1963.

Hedges, Chris. *War Is a Force That Gives Us Meaning*. New York: Anchor Books, 2002.

Heyworth-Dunne, John. *Religious and Political Trends in Modern Egypt*. Washington: privately printed, 1950.

Hislop, Macdougall J. *Spanish State Policy, Basque Nationalism and ETA Terrorism*. Unpublished master's thesis, University of Alberta, Edmonton, Alberta, Canada, 1995.

Hoffer, Eric. *The True Believer*. New York: Harper and Row Publishers, 1951.

Hoole, Rajan. *Sri Lanka The Arrogance of Power, Myths, Decadence, and Murder*. Colombo, Sri Lanka: University Teachers for Human Rights, 2001.

Hoskin, Gary. "The State and Political Parties in Colombia." In *Colombia, The Politics of Reforming the State*, edited by Eduardo Posada-Carbó, 45–70. New York: St. Martin's Press, 2000.

Human Rights Watch. *You'll Learn Not To Cry, Child Combatants in Colombia*. New York: Human Rights Watch, 2003.

al-Husaini, Ishak Musa. *The Moslem Brethren, The Greatest of Modern Islamic Movements*. Westport, CT: Hyperion Press, Inc, 1981.

Iribarren, Florencio Domínguez. *ETA: Estrategia Organizativa y Actuaciones 1978–1992*. Bilbao, Spain: Universidad del País Vasco, 1998.

Janke, Peter. "Spanish Separatism: ETA's Threat to Basque Democracy." *Conflict Studies* 123 (October 1980): 1–20.

Jankowski, James. "Egyptian Responses to the Palestinian Problem in the Interwar Period." *International Journal of Middle Eastern Studies* 12 (1980): 1–38.

———. *Nasser's Egypt, Arab Nationalism, and the United Arab Republic*. Boulder, CO: Lynne Rienner Publishers, 2002.

Jonsson, David J. *Islamic Economics and the Final Jihad: The Muslim Brotherhood to the Leftist/Marxist-Islamic Alliance*. Maitland, FL: Xulon Press, 2006.

Kaplinsky, Zvi. "The Muslim Brotherhood." *Middle Eastern Affairs* (December 1954): 377–385.

Kellen, Konrad. "Terrorists: What Are They Like? How Some Terrorists Describe Their World and Actions." A Rand Note prepared for the Sandia Laboratories, November 1979.

Khatab, Sayed. *The Power of Sovereignty, The Political and Ideological Philosophy of Sayyid Qutb*. New York: Routledge, 2006.

Kirk, Robin. *More Terrible Than Death, Violence, Drugs, and America's War in Colombia*. Cambridge, MA: Public Affairs, 2004.

Kline, Harvey F. *Showing Teeth to Dragons, State Building by Colombian President Álvaro Uribe Vélez, 2002–2006*. Tuscaloosa: The University of Alabama Press, 2009.

Krutwig, Federico. *Vasconia*. Buenos Aires: Ediciones Norbait, 1962.

Lankan Newspapers. "Veluppillai Prabharakan." *Lankan Newspapers*, May 19, 2007. Accessed August 19, 2010, www.lankanewspapers.com/news/2007/5/15036_space.html.

Larson, Eric John. *Islamist Opposition and Political Opportunity: The Muslim Brotherhood in Egypt, 1928–1942*. Unpublished master's thesis, University of South Carolina, Columbia, SC, 2004.

Lawrence, Bruce B. *Shattering the Myth*. Princeton, NJ: Princeton University Press, 1998.

Leech, Gary M. *Killing Peace, Colombia's Conflict and the Failure of US Intervention*. New York: Information Network of the Americas (INOTA), 2002.

León, Juanita. *Country of Bullets Chronicles of War*. Albuquerque, NM: University of New Mexico Press, 2009.

Levine, Daniel H. *Religion and Politics in Latin America, The Catholic Church in Venezuela and Colombia*. Princeton, NJ: Princeton University Press, 1981.

Li, Quan. "Does Democracy Promote or Reduce Transnational Terrorist Incidents?" *Journal of Conflict Resolution* 49 (2005): 278–297.

Lia, Brynjar. *The Society of the Muslim Brothers in Egypt, The Rise of an Islamic Mass Movement, 1928–1942.* Reading, UK: Ithaca Press, 1998.

Llera, Francisco J. "ETA: Ejercito Secreto Y Movimiento Social." *Revista de Estudios Politicos* 78 (October–December 1992): 161–193.

Lutz, James M. and Brenda J. Lutz. *Terrorism: Origins and Evolution.* New York: Palgrave Macmillan, 2005.

MacClancy, Jeremy. "The Culture of Radical Basque Nationalism." *Anthropology Today* 4 (5) (October 1988): 17–19.

Malik, Hafeez. "Islamic Political Parties and Mass Politicization." *Islam and the Modern Age* 3 (1972): 26–64.

McCauley, Clark R. and Mary E. Segal. "Social Psychology of Terrorist Groups." In *Group Processes and Intergroup Relations,* edited by Clyde Hendrick, 231–256. Newbury Park, CA: Sage Publications, 1987.

Meadows, Mark Stephen. *Tea Time with Terrorists, A Motorcycle Journey into the Heart of Sri Lanka's Civil War.* Berkeley, CA: Soft Skull Press, 2010.

Meertens, Donny. *Ensayos Sobre Tierra, Violencia, y Género.* Colombia: Universidad Nacional de Colombia, 2000.

Mees, Ludger. *Nationalism, Violence, and Democracy, The Basque Clash of Identities.* New York: Palgrave Macmillan, 2003.

Merari, Ariel. "Social, Organizational, and Psychological Factors in Suicide Terrorism." In *Root Causes of Terrorism,* edited by Tore Bjørgo, 70–86. New York: Routledge, 2005.

Mitchell, Richard P. *The Society of the Muslim Brothers.* New York: Oxford University Press, 1969.

Molano, Alfred. "Violence and Land Colonization," In *Violence in Colombia, The Contemporary Crisis in Historical Perspective,* edited by Charles Bergquist, Ricardo Peñaranda, Gonzalo Sánchez, 195–216. Wilmington, DE: SR Books, 1992.

Navarro, Joe. *Hunting Terrorists, A Look at the Psychopathology of Terror.* Springfield, IL: Charles C. Thomas, 2005.

Nicolas, J. N. and Paxto Unzueta. *Documentos Y* (Vols. 1–3, and 5). Itxaropena, Spain: Hordago S. A, 1979.

O'Ballance, Edgar. *The Cyanide War, Tamil Insurrection in Sri Lanka, 1973–1988.* London: Brassey's, 1989.

Ortzi (pseudonym of Francisco Letamendia). *Historia de Euzkadi.* Aleconnaise: Ruedo Ibérico, 1975.

———. *Los Vascos, Sítesis de Su Historia.* Donostia: Hordago Publicaciones, 1978.

Osterling, Jorge P. *Democracy in Colombia, Clientelist Policies and Guerrilla Warfare.* New Brunswick: Transaction Publishers, 1989.

Pape, Robert A. *Dying to Win, The Strategic Logic of Suicide Terrorism.* New York: Random House, 2005.

Payne, James L. *Patterns of Conflict in Colombia.* New Haven, CT: Yale University Press, 1968.

Pearce, Jenny. *Colombia: Inside the Labyrinth.* London: Latin American Bureau, 1990.

Pearlstein, Richard M. *The Mind of the Political Terrorist.* Wilmington, DE: SR Books, 1991.

Perdomo, María Eugenia Vásquez. *My Life as a Colombian Revolutionary, Reflections of a Former Guerrillera.* Philadelphia: Temple University Press, 2005.

Peris, G. H. *Twilight of the Tigers, Peace Efforts and Power Struggles in Sri Lanka.* New York: Oxford University Press, 2009.

Pfaffenberger, Bryan. "Introduction: The Sri Lankan Tamils." In *The Sri Lankan Tamils, Ethnicity and Identity,* edited by Chelvadurai Manogaran and Bryan Pfaffenberger, 1–27. Boulder, CO: Westview Press, 1994.

Pizarro, Eduardo. "Revolutionary Guerrilla Groups in Colombia." In *Violence in Colombia, The Contemporary Crisis in Historical Perspective,* edited by Charles Bergquist, Ricardo Peñaranda, and Gonzalo Sánchez. Wilmington, DE: SR Books, 1992.

Ponnambalam, Satchi. *Sri Lanka, the National Question, and the Tamil Liberation Struggle.* London: Zed Books, 1983.

Portell, José María. *Los Hombres de ETA.* Barcelona: Dopesa, 1974.

Post, Jerrold M. "Terrorist Psycho-logic: Terrorist Behavior as a Product of Psychological Forces." In *Origins of Terrorism, Psychologies, Ideologies, Theologies, and States of Mind,* edited by Walter Reich, 25–40. Washington, DC: Woodrow Wilson Center Press, 1998.

Prabhakaran, V. "Full text of the Speech of V. Prabhakaran, leader, Liberation Tigers of Tamil Eelam on Annual Heroes' Day on 27 November 2008." *The Hindu,* November 27, 2008. Accessed August 30, 2010, www.hindu.com/nic/prabhakaranspeech.htm.

Qutb, Sayyid. *Milestones* (revised translation). Indianapolis, IN: American Trust Publications, 1993. (Original work published 1964).

Rajanayagam, Dagmar-Hellmann. "The 'Groups' and the Rise of Militant Secessionism." In *The Sri Lankan Tamils, Ethnicity and Identity,* edited by Chelvadurai Manogaran and Bryan Pfaffenberger, 169–207. Boulder, CO: Westview Press, 1994.

Ram, N. "Understanding Prabakaran's LTTE." In *Sri Lankan Crisis and India's Response,* edited by V. Suryanarayan, 24–29. New Delhi: Patriot Publishers, 1991.

Ramachandran, Sudha. "Tamil Tigers Name New Chief." *Morung Express,* no date. Accessed August 30, 2010, www.morungexpress.com/analysis/29666.html.

Rapoport, Anatol. *The Origins of Violence: Approaches to the Study of Conflict.* New Brunswick: Transaction Publishers, 2005.

Reid, Donald M. "Political Assassination in Egypt, 1910–1954." *The International Journal of African Historical Studies* 15 (4) (1982): 625–651.

Reinares, Fernando. *Patriotas de la Muerte, Quiénes Han Militado en ETA y Por Qué?* Madrid: Grupo Santillana de Ediciones S. A., 2001.

———. "Who Are the Terrorists? Analyzing Changes in Sociological Profile among Members of ETA." *Studies in Conflict and Terrorism* 27 (2004): 465–488.

Rezazadeh, Reza, and Joseph Mac McKenzie. *Political Parties in Colombia, Continuity in Political Style.* Ann Arbor, MI: University Microfilms International, 1978.

Richani, Nazih. *Systems of Violence, The Political Economy of War and Peace in Colombia.* New York: State University of New York Press, 2002.

Richardson, Louise. *What Terrorists Want, Understanding the Enemy, Containing the Threat.* New York: Random House, 2006.

Rippy, J. Fred. *The Capitalists and Colombia.* New York: The Vanguard Press, 1931.

Robbins, Thomas. "Sources of Volatility in Religious Movements." In *Cults, Religions, and Violence,* edited by David G. Bromley and J. Gordon Melton, 57–79. Cambridge, UK: Cambridge University Press, 2002.

Robins, Robert S., and Jerrold M. Post. *Political Paranoia, The Psychopolitics of Hatred.* New Haven: Yale University Press, 1997.

Rochlin, James. *Social Forces and the Revolution in Military Affairs, The Cases of Colombia and Mexico.* New York: Palgrave Macmillan, 2007.

———. *Vanguard Revolutionaries in Latin America.* Boulder, CO: Lynne Rienner Publishers, 2003.

Rojas, Cristina. "Elusive Peace, Elusive Violence: Identity and Conflict in Colombia." In *Elusive Peace: International, National, and Local Dimensions of Conflict in Colombia,* edited by Cristina Rojas and Judy Meltzer, 209–237. New York: Palgrave Macmillan, 2005.

Rosenthal, Franz. "The 'Muslim Brethren' in Egypt." *The Moslem World* 37 (1947): 278–291.

Rucht, Dieter. "The Impact of National Contexts on Social Movement Structures: A Cross-Movement and Cross-National Comparison." In *Comparative Perspectives on Social Movements,* edited by Doug McAdam, John D. McCarthy and Mayer N. Zald, 185–204. Cambridge, UK: Cambridge University Press, 1996.

Ruiz, Bert. *The Colombian Civil War.* Jefferson, NC: McFarland and Company, Inc., Publishers, 2001.

Sabit, Adel M. *A King Betrayed, The Ill-Fated Reign of Farouk of Egypt.* New York: Quartet Books, 1989.

al-Sayyid-Marsot, Afaf Lutfi. *Egypt's Liberal Experiment: 1922–1936.* Berkeley, CA: University of California Press, 1977.

Silke, Andrew. "Cheshire-Cat Logic: The Recurring Theme of Terrorist Abnormality in Psychological Research." *Psychology, Crime and Law* 4(1) (1998): 51–69.

Simons, Geoff. *Colombia, A Brutal History*. London: SAQI, 2004.

Sinvanayagam, S. "The Phenomenon of Tamil Militancy." In *Sri Lankan Crisis and Indian Response,* edited by V. Suryanarayam, 30–47. New Delhi: Patriot Publishers, 1991.

Sixta, Christine M. "The Illusive Third Wave: Are Female Terrorists the New "New Women" In Developing Societies?" *The Journal of Women, Politics, and Policy* 29 (2) (2008).

Smith, Chris. "Sri Lanka: The Continued Armed Struggle of the LTTE." In *From Soldiers to Politicians, Transforming Rebel Movements After Civil War,* edited by Jeroen de Zeeuw, 205–224. Boulder, CO: Lynne Rienner Publishers.

Sorenson David S. *An Introduction to the Modern Middle East*. Boulder, CO: Westview Press, 2008.

Stern, Jessica. *Terror in the Name of God*. New York: Ecco, 2003.

Stokes, Doug. *America's Other War, Terrorizing Colombia*. New York: Zed Books, 2004.

Sullivan, John. *ETA and Basque Nationalism, The Fight for Euskadi, 1890–1986*. New York: Routledge, 1988.

Swamy, Narayan. *Inside an Elusive Mind, Prabhakaran, The First Profile of the World's Most Ruthless Guerrilla Leader*. Dehli: Konark Publishers, 2003.

————. *Tigers of Lanka, From Boys to Guerrillas*. Delhi: Konark Publishers PVT Ltd, 1994.

Tal, Nachman. *Radical Islam in Egypt and Jordan*. Brighton: Sussex Academic Press, 2005.

Tambiah, S. J. *Sri Lanka, Ethnic Fratricide and the Dismantling of Democracy*. Chicago: University of Chicago Press, 1986.

Tilly, Charles. "Terror as Strategy and Relational Process." Paper presented at the American Sociological Association Conference, August 14–17, 2004.

Trawick, Magaret. *Enemy Lines Childhood, Warfare, and Play in Batticola*. Berkeley: University of California Press, 2007.

Turk, Austin T. "Social Dynamics of Terrorism." *Annals of the American Academy of Political Science, International Terrorism*, 463 (September 1982): 119–128.

Unzueta, Patxo. *Los Nietos de la IRA, Nacionalismo y Violencia en el País Vasco*. Madrid: Ediciones El País, S. A, 1988.

Urla, Jacqueline. "Cultural Politics in an Age of Statistics: Numbers, Nations, and the Making of Basque Identity." *American Ethnologist*, 20(4) (November 1993): 818–843.

————. "Ethnic Protest and Social Planning: A Look at Basque Language Revival." *Cultural Anthropology* 3 (4) (November 1988): 379–394.

U.S. Agency for International Development (USAID). "U.S. Overseas Loans and Grants: Obligations and Loan Authorizations, July 1, 1945–September 30, 2007 (1945–2007)." Accessed December 23, 2009 from http://gbk.eads.usaidallnet.gov/.

Vatikiotis, P.J. *Nasser and His Generation*. London: Croom Helm, 1978.

Vertigans, Stephen. *Militant Islam, A Sociology of Characteristics, Causes, and Consequences*. New York: Routledge, 2009.

Von Tangen Page. *Prisons, Peace, and Terrorism*. Chippenham, Wiltshire: Antony Rowe, Ltd, 1998.

Waldmann, Peter. *Radicalismo Étnico*. Madrid: Ediciones Akal, S.A., 1997.

Watson, Cameron J. *Basque Nationalism and Political Violence: The Ideological and Intellectual Origins of ETA*. Reno: University of Nevada Press, 2007.

Weber, Max. *Religionssoziologie* [The Sociology of Religion (4th ed.)]. Translated by Ephraim Fischoff. Boston: Beacon Press, 1963 (original work published 1922).

Weinberg, Leonard. *The End of Terrorism?* New York: Routledge, 2012.

————. "Turning to Terror: The Conditions Under Which Political Parties Turn to Terrorist Activities." *Comparative Politics* 23 (4) (July 1991): 423–438.

Weinberg, Leonard and Ami Pedahzur. *Political Parties and Terrorist Groups*. New York: Routledge, 2003.

Whitaker, Leighton C. *Understanding and Preventing Violence, The Psychology of Human Destructiveness*. Boca Raton, FL: CRC Press, 2000.

Whittaker, David (ed.). *The Terrorism Reader*, 2nd ed. New York: Routledge, 2001.

Wickham-Crowley, Timothy P. *Guerrillas and Revolution in Latin America*. Princeton: Princeton University Press, 1992.

Wieviorka, Michel. *The Making of Terrorism*. Chicago: University of Chicago Press, 1993.

Wiktorowicz, Quintan. *The Management of Islamic Activism*. Albany: State University of New York Press, 2001.

———. *Radical Islam Rising, Muslim Extremism in the West*. Lanham, MD: Rowman and Littlefield Publishers, 2005.

Wilson, A. Jeyaratnam. *S. J. V. Chelvanayakam and the Crisis of Sri Lankan Tamil Nationalism 1947–1977, A Political Biography*. Honolulu: University of Hawaii Press, 1994.

———. *Sri Lankan Tamil Nationalism, Its Origins and Development in the Nineteenth and Twentieth Centuries*. Vancouver: UBC Press, 2000.

Wonacott, Peter. "A Notorious Terrorist Who Refused to Compromise to the End." *The Wall Street Journal*, May 19, 2009. Accessed August 30, 2010, http://online.wsj.com/article/NA_WSJ_PUB:SB124269099109232581.html.

Zirakzadeh, Cyrus Ernesto. *A Rebellious People, Basques, Protests, and Politics*. Reno: University of Nevada Press, 1991.

Zollner, Barbara H. E. *The Muslim Brotherhood, Hasan al-Hudaybi and Ideology*. New York: Routledge, 2009.

Zulaika, Joseba. *Basque Violence Metaphor and Sacrament*. Reno: University of Nevada Press, 1988.

Zulaika, Joseba, and William A. Douglass. *Terror and Taboo, The Follies, Fables, and Faces of Terrorism*. New York City: Routledge, 1996.

Zumalde, Xabier. *Mi Lucha Clandestina en ETA*. Spain: Status Ediciones, S. L., 2004.

Index

About the Author

Dr. Christine Sixta Rinehart is an assistant adjunct professor of women's and gender studies at the University of South Carolina. She earned her PhD in political science from the University of South Carolina in 2008. Her research focuses on the origins of terrorism and female terrorists. She married Brian Todd Rinehart, her college sweetheart, in 2008. Dr. Sixta Rinehart currently resides in Newberry, South Carolina, where she enjoys gardening, oil painting, and spending time with her family.